THE LOST CITIES OF TARTARIA BEYOND THE ICE WALLS OF ANTARCTICA

BOOK I

RISING PHOENIX AURORA

Copyright © 2025 by Rising Phoenix Aurora, Inc.
All rights reserved.

No part of this publication may be reproduced, stored in, or introduced into a retrieval system, or transmitted, in any form, or by any means (electronic, mechanical, photocopying, recording, or otherwise), without the prior written permission of both the copyright owner and the above publisher of this book. The scanning, uploading, and distribution of this book via the internet, or via any other means, without the permission of the publisher is illegal. Please purchase only authorized electronic editions; your support of the author's rights is very much appreciated. Rising Phoenix Aurora is the copyrighted owner of all literature and illustrations, with the exception of images found on public channels and internet searches. Rising Phoenix Aurora claims no copyright rights and intends no copyright violation over these publicly available images.

The authors of this book do not dispense medical advice, or prescribe the use of any technique as a form of treatment for physical, emotional, or medical problems directly, or indirectly. Please consult a physician for any health concerns. The intent of this book is to only offer information of a general nature to aid you in your quest for emotional and spiritual well-being. In the event you use any of the information in this book for yourself or others, the authors and the publisher assume no responsibility for your actions.

Published by Rising Phoenix Aurora, Inc.
www.risingphoenixaurora.com

Paperback ISBN: ISBN: 978-1-7358542-7-4

1st Edition, July 2025

Printed in the United States of America

Special thanks to the Illustrator Samia, who is a digital artist and clear channel to benevolent energies. You can find her at www.aurapractitioners.com.

TABLE OF CONTENTS

ACKNOWLEDGEMENTS	HOW THIS BOOK CAME TO BE…… 4
INTRODUCTION	PURPOSE OF THIS BOOK…… 6
IMPORTANT	LOVE-LIGHT SHIELDING TECHNIQUE…… 9
CHAPTER 1	Beyond The Walls of Antarctica PT 1…. 13
CHAPTER 2	Artificial Intelligence At The Ice Walls…. 34
CHAPTER 3	At The Rim of The Crystal Dome…. 55
CHAPTER 4	Beyond The Dome & Into The Universe…. 74
CHAPTER 5	ALIENS The Super Space Program…. 99
CHAPTER 6	Our Ancestors Maps & Knowledge…. 116
CHAPTER 7	The Resistance At The North Pole…. 138
CHAPTER 8	Nikola Tesla Tartaria Discovered…. 171
CHAPTER 9	The Resets of Earth…. 177
CHAPTER 10	The Giants of Tartaria…. 250
CHAPTER 11	Artificial Intelligence Simulations…. 275
Conclusion	Love, Sovereignty, and Remembrance…. 310
About Aurora	…… 312
Your Soul's Growth Journey	…… 317
Glossary	…… 318

ACKNOWLEDGEMENTS

--------------<<>>--------------

Thank you to the infinite Multiverse who were all part of the Creation of this masterful book. All which is created from divine Source Love-Light is a collective collaboration energetically. Not one being can accomplish a mission on their own. Therefore, my acknowledgements are for many, and are truly infinite.

I would like to thank you dearest reader, because truly, I do it all for you. Thank you for the loving support, whether you just found me, or found me over eight years ago. Your comments, your shares, and your love has been adored and treasured throughout these years, and has truly gotten me through the most challenging times. I want to thank you for working diligently within yourself to understand our content, which we know has guided you to choose to keep expanding with an open mind and loving heart, and still you stand beside us. Thank you for choosing to ride Mother Earth's continual Ascension wave with us.

We thank the bravest souls, whether in this book or not, who have chosen to follow their hearts to mine to share their wisdom with the world, by booking any session with me or for signing up to any of our courses at Rising Phoenix Mystery School. Special thanks to those who have booked A.U.R.A. Hypnosis Healing sessions with me, or those who have chosen to become certified through A.U.R.A.; and to their Higher Selves, who believed that they could reach their infinite level of self-healing potentials. These sessions and courses have become an important part of the ultimate completion of the Multiversal Ascension. These clients and students are examples of self-love, and their love for others is admirable!

I want to thank my divine team, whether incarnated on Earth, or working from beyond the veil of Earth. To my RPA team, who consists of A.U.R.A. practitioners from around the world, who have assisted me to transcribe and edit each Chapter. You are loved and honored for the work you have done in ensuring that all was done in the highest love. My spiritual team who have miraculously got me through every challenge, every lesson, and every activation!.

Thank you to my divine team for how much you listen to me and guide me, when looking to choose the highest path of Source Love-Light. These divine teams are why I am here in this very special moment releasing Book 1 of this very special series of Tartaria.

Finally, my beautiful husband, who has been with me throughout all life, time, and space. Who has embraced me and lifted me, when I needed to prevail to accomplish the writing of this book or any other project. Who lives to love me. Who celebrates me everyday with his infinite love for me; and our children, both furry and none furry. My family is who is most precious to me. Who assists me to hold the space of the most infinite Source Love-Light everyday, so that I may accomplish all that I do daily in assistance for the collective. They are truly my superheroes!

I honor you, love you, and respect you!

We are infinitely grateful for you dearest reader and fellow traveler on this most beautiful journey of Creation!

~ **Rising Phoenix** AuroRa 🤍

--------------<◇>--------------

INTRODUCTION

I am thankful that you are here, because you are the ones on Earth who have chosen to see with eyes unveiled, by removing the indoctrination you were born into through societal programming. You are the ones who have chosen to see a civilization that had been long forgotten by the mudfloods that covered them and swept them away. To see a world that was erased, and made into fairy tales and make believe. You are here because your search for the truth, which might have begun as a hunch, has now been converted into solid truth of the existence of The Great Tartarian Empire. On your search, you have learnt that once you see Tartaria, you cannot unsee it. Whether you are new to Tartaria or a veteran researcher of Earth's History, get ready to be astonished! Through this book series, it will all finally make sense!

You are here because you are the collective who is standing up to the beginning of their tried reset, and through floodings and weather modification upon our current era. We say 'tried' because this time the Elites will not prevail as they have done so through our ancestors. WE have to unite together into the largest awareness as a collective, to loudly and clearly say that, "WE DO NOT CONSENT!" Which is the purest and truest intention of the delivery of this Book Series!

The signs of this current reset are there through all the mudfloods and floodings all over the world. As I write this introduction there are floods happening at an extent that we have never seen before. The Guadalupe River floods in Texas just happened over one week ago, and there are floods occurring in Iowa, New York, New Jersey, China, Spain, Moscow, and Japan… In 2024 there was a direct target on Florida for it to sink, through weather modification, man-made hurricanes, and hundreds of tornadoes! They did not prevail. In 2023 the Lahaina, Hawaiian Fires, 'Weapons of Mass Destruction' were used upon the people and the land. This is not something new to us, but we have never seen it to this extremity!. There is an obvious target upon humanity, if you open your eyes and simply look around. This is not Mother Earth's wrath. This is negative technology being used on her - in essence violating her. The Elites have come to an understanding that they cannot control us as they did in the past, and they have chosen to begin their New World Order agenda earlier than anticipated. With this awareness there is no space for FEAR! Because once you grow out from your fear, you realize that the only thing that comes next is STRENGTH!

Our collective minds can rewrite these resets by stepping into our divine power, transmuting the negativity, releasing the entities behind this negative agenda, and simply vibrating to the awareness of questioning what is truly beyond the ice walls of the restricted lands of Antarctica and the lost cities of Tartaria. This higher level of understanding brings further the biggest awakening of Earth's collective we have ever seen! We are who will change this current reset by oscillating within a vibration to Love-Light that does not allow violations to the children, the human collective, the animals, the trees, and the Earth!

Through the journey of discovering Tartaria, through this remote viewing and channeled series, we begin with what is beyond the ice walls of Antarctica. Why is it restricted and what is really being hidden from us? What is it that the Elites don't want us to see outside the circular ice wall that surrounds us? If there is one thing that we have learned from being born into this Earth, and that is when they tell us not to look, we will most definitely ensure that we look. Bringing us to the innate ability that we all hold within our brains - the glands that make-up our third eye. When we learn to use this form of sight - our dormant seventh sense in this way and use our quantum eyes through remote viewing - we can instead see what is hidden from us through our physical eyes. This book consists of my channeled knowledge and ability of sight, with a couple surprises of never before shared from A.U.R.A. Hypnosis Healing sessions, that will keep you turning the pages rapidly in suspense! On the next page, you will find an introduction to what A.U.R.A. is, so that you may understand it when reading the two chapters of these tremendous sessions.

When we began the journey of delivering this most important series in 2022, not many knew of Tartaria, but that rapidly shifted with our millions of views alone on TikTok. We humbly thank all those who have been part of the mission of unveiling Tartaria, and that shared content, all over the world! During the time of the publication of this book, we are currently in summer 2025, with ninety episodes in of the gigantic series of Antartica and Tartara, which is broadcasted live weekly and monthly on our channels. Throughout the eight years of the expansion of my career, we have delivered over 900 videos on our channels. This is my third book, and the first of a series on its own. So know that this sacred knowledge is to be delivered as you turn these pages is dedicated wisdom that is only embodied by Source Love-Light and benevolence, as nothing else is allowed within our sacred space of Rising Phoenix AuroRa.

I am the founder of Rising Phoenix Mystery School and several self-healing modalities and courses including Angelic Universal Regression Alchemy (A.U.R.A.) Hypnosis Healing. A.U.R.A., which is a past life regression entity removal, modality. The A.U.R.A. healing modality is an embodiment of Quantum Physics by using a combination of sacred Angelic energy work, sacred alchemy, and hypnosis to create a bridge for the client to connect with their Higher Self. This allows us to enter the theta brainwave of A.U.R.A. Hypnosis sacredly and safely to bring forth memories of our existence, to quantum heal our body, to find our life purpose, and to remember our Galactic origins. In A.U.R.A. sessions, as the client, you will speak to your soul, and to your Higher Self who is you. The Higher Self is ONE with the Creator, who knows all. Our higher self and soul is truly God Source, and is where we can find all the answers we are looking for, and where we connect to this unlimited, infinite healing potential. By connecting to our Higher Self, we then allow for that little voice in our head that has been there all our life - our consciousness - to finally speak through us, sharing their infinite wisdom.

There is not much left to say, as we have to allow each chapter in divine order to unravel the mysteries of Tartaria and Antarctica. In this book you will find what has never been spoken, because of the sacredness of the knowledge, and the ways this has been guarded throughout our Earth's History. So, with the greatest honor, we are ready to embark with you on this most heart and soul fulfilling read! We look to not keep you any longer. Let's dive in deeply together now! So excited I am for you!

"You are as free as the ever moving motion of the ocean. Unrestricted and unbounded."

~**Rising Phoenix** AuroRa ♡

IMPORTANT

SOURCE LOVE-LIGHT SHIELDING TECHNIQUE

BEFORE YOU BEGIN READING THIS BOOK, understand that one of our core foundational teachings is shielding ourselves with our own "I AM Source Love-Light," so we can be more intentional with managing our energy frequency in our daily lives, thus empowering us to be in our sovereignty. When we shield, and set our intentions for the day, we are declaring our sovereignty over our own freewill and life force, and how we want our day to be. We are powerful creator beings, if we allow for it, by actively maintaining our vibrations in alignment with the purest, "I AM Source Love-Light."

Review these pages carefully, as they contain Sacred Alchemy teachings for you to start using your "I AM Source Love-Light" to create force fields around you in maintaining your vibrations high. Our intent is to teach you how you create your inner light to become stronger, by actively using these force fields around you, filtering out the negativity that means harm, so that you will strongly heart-discern every frequency that passes through. These force fields will help amplify your heart discernment, reading what energies are harmful, and what is not.

It is important that we surround ourselves with our own infinite "I AM Source Love-Light" daily. Ideally, you should be shielding yourself every morning when you wake up, and every evening before the sun sets, for optimal results. This energy is accessed through your heart and flows out through your hand chakras. Our heart center is where we are able to tap into the infinite Source Love-Light energy. When doing this for your day, it will ensure that you keep your energies high and that you do not become depleted, when you set the proper intent for your energies. Surrounding yourself with the "I AM Source Love-Light" will help you keep your mind focused and clear, and your abilities strong and open.

**Practice these empowering Source Love-Light shielding techniques
on the next two pages daily!**

OPENING YOUR HAND CHAKRAS

It is important to open your hand chakras, as it is from these that the Universal love energy will flow. Energy will enter through the crown and from the bottom of your feet, connect to your heart, and flow out through the palms of your hands, connecting the Alchemy symbols.

1. Place hands in Gassho position (Gassho is a gesture with the hands held in prayer position in front of the heart).

2. Rub your hands together as desired.

3. Clap four times in prayer position and state with strength, "Open!"

4. Turn hands horizontal, with left-hand above the right-hand, facing each other.

5. Open and close both hands in this position 13 times.

6. Switch hands now, with your right-hand over your left-hand.

7. Open and close both hands again in this position 13 times.

8. You should be feeling vibrations in between both of your palms.

9. Play with this energy - moving it around, expanding it bigger and then shrinking it down - creating it into an energy ball.

If the energy ball bursts, no worries. Simply rub both your hands together again, and pull your palms apart while facing each other to create the energy ball once again.

There is no need to repeat steps 1-7, as once you have opened your hand chakras, this is complete. Going forward, just rubbing your hands together will create the energy ball inside your palms.

You may use this energy ball of Source Love-Light around your home, cars, spouse, and children stating, "Without harming anyone." We are powerful creator beings and by stating this, we make sure we do not pull from someone else's energy, and only from Source Love-Light.

-<<>>---<<>>---<<>>---<<>>---<<>>---<<>>---<<>>---<<>>---<<>>---<<>>---<<>>-

I AM SOURCE LOVE-LIGHT AND MERKABAH

1. Rub your hands together to create your energy ball consisting of your "I AM Source Love-Light."
2. Viewing this energy ball and sensing it through your third eye and your imagination. Expand it to surround your vessel and your auric field. You may make it the color of your choice, and may include a sacred geometric symbol that aligns with you, encasing the walls of this bubble.
3. Set the intent by stating, "Shall I be shielded from harm mentally, physically, emotionally, and spiritually throughout the infinity of Creation. I DO NOT CONSENT to harm all day and night, without harming anyone, for my highest good."
4. As you expand the light, state four times, "I invoke the I AM Love-Light in me."
5. With your hands expanding the light around yourself, your loved ones, animal companions, cars, websites, projects, home. and everything else you would like shielded.
6. Now envision your eight-pointed Merkabah surrounding you, which is a live consciousness connected to your soul. Envision it activating and coming to life, so to speak.

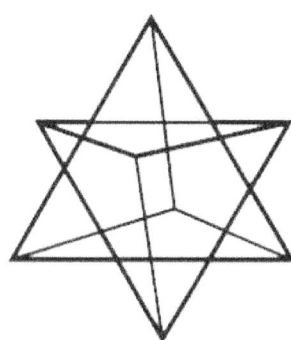

7. The Merkabah is a counter-clockwise, upside down, four-sided pyramid which is an expanding, repelling, and spinning structure of light at the bottom. Clockwise, right-side up, it is drawing in energy at the top pyramid through our crown. The Merkabah is an extension of our consciousness and represents the integration of our spiritual energies and our physical bodies. Made up of eight triangles having eight points, we find that the Merkabah also reflects the infinite energy and protection of Creation (since the number eight is an ancient alchemy infinity symbol). Each triangle has three-sided points representing the sacred three elements of the Holy Trinity, being the Divine Mother, the Divine Father and the Child.

For more teachings on Shielding go to www.risingphoenixaurora.com**, where AuroRa offers a 'How to Shield' course. For more now, go to, "Your Soul's Growth Journey" section, page .**

1

REMOTE VIEWING BEYOND THE WALLS OF ANTARCTICA
PT 1: CREATIONAL WATERS

Streamed Live: October 28, 2022

In this chapter we set sail, embarking upon the greatest journey of the discovery of the Earth's true history, of the civilization who came directly before our century. There is a strong amnesia of the true ancestry before us, and through this book series we understand why, which then brings back our memories of the people's potentials, and the beings who flew in the skies and walked the lands previous to us. Through this book series, AuroRa begins to remote view Antarctica, the land beyond the ice walls, and the long forgotten civilization of the pillar structures that are located all across the lands of Earth from Tartaria. We will now deliver some of the most important content you will read through your process of Ascension. Come make sense of all your questions of the construct of our Earth and the Universe.

--------------<<>>--------------

"The water holds the blueprints of Earth and timelines."
~AuroRa

--------------<<>>--------------

AuroRa: Wow! There was a shift on Earth occurring last night to prepare us for this important content. I started feeling it around 5 pm, and gradually throughout the day. I was feeling Angel bumps, which are a frequency of vibration that is running through your body. Typically, when I get Angel bumps, this energy runs from the crown down. But, there was a magnetic electrified field that was coming up from my feet instead. Meaning this energy was coming up from

Mother Earth. Today is October 28th, so that would have been October 27, 2022. The world was recalibrating, for those who were ready to hear and read this content.

We are remote viewing Antarctica. Which is very sensitive content. I will start it off with this; I remember back about three years ago in the autumn of 2019, channeling a Galactic being, and when we remote viewed the Earth. We saw that it had a dome over it. You will understand that further in a little bit. I remember this sensitive content was not ready to be put on my channels. I was talking to my Angelic team, and I said, "Is the world really ready for this?" So, we agreed that we would come back to this, once the collective was more ready to understand how the Earth's true construct looked in the third dimension. When remote viewing the Earth, we have to understand that it is in a third dimension. Energetically, it definitely is spheric. It aligns more energetically for it to be a sphere because that is what typically planetary spheres are. But, with the fall of Atlantis and the two-third world split - bifurcation of Earth - we have two worlds and many worlds occurring in one.

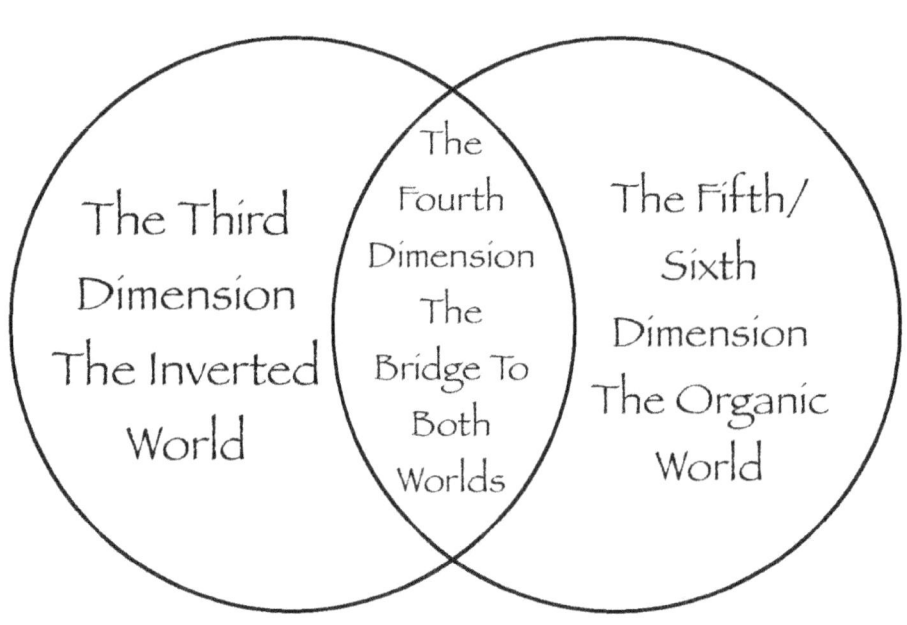

What is going on is that we are seeing these worlds physically. They are coming into more awareness of the disclosure, and overall, people who are starting to question. There is a grand shift. You feel it on Earth. People are waking up. People are not as submissive, programmed, and as controlled as they were. When the collective consciousness questions, "Ah, that is when it begins!" Expansion of soul and heart begins then, in consciousness.

From a bird's eye point of view, we are in a third dimensional, Matrix simulation, though the majority of us who are reading this are operating in an organic blueprint, but still beside the inverted Matrix. We volunteered to come and save humanity. What I am seeing is that when the Earth fell down into the third dimension from the original fifth dimension, it bifurcated. Looking at the image above, we are seeing the bifurcation/trifurcation of these worlds. Starting from left to right: the third dimension inverted world, at the center the fourth dimension - the bridge to both worlds - and then the multi-dimensions of the fifth, sixth, and higher Earths. All operating parallel within each other. When I am looking at the Earth from above, I can see that it has a flat surface at this moment in time, because it fell down to the third dimension when the Fall of Atlantis happened, and that is what a third dimensional planet looks like. It is a flat surface with a dome over it, but it also has another dome under it, like the image shown in the next page. You will also notice how Earth's tree construct is also a Vesica Piscis, two circles/spheres unified at the center.

---

[1] In this image you see Divine Mother's explanation of how the Earth looks from a bird's eye point of view. Matching the literature and hieroglyphics our ancestry has left behind for us, stemming from the Celtics, Egyptian, Sumerian, indigenous, and even originally written in the bible by Yeshua himself.

Within the two-third world bifurcation, the denser other world is on the other side of it, next to it, but it is linear to it. The way we can understand it is that it is energetically spheric. Which we are going to learn more about when I speak of Antarctica. It is all existing within pockets of spaces of dimensions. All in one pocket of space. If you understand time and space, you understand dimensions, and how there truly is no time as all is occurring linear to oneself. For example, your sixty year old self is happening at the same time as your twenty year old self. All the versions of you are happening in the now of the minute, hour, day, or year you are in. Within the third dimension we became this physical illusion which is why time in this construct is truly an illusion. All in Creation, outside of this Matrix, is happening in the now. Which is why we have to remember that we are not limited to our physical illusion.

I have flown on airplanes many times, and I know that the flights do not make any sense. When you look up flight paths, they have you go up and down on the current globe map for emergency landings or stops, instead of just going to the supposed nearest city on the map. The way the flights are set up is really convoluted. It is wrong. If you are on an airplane, and you

are looking at how it flies. You will notice that it never goes spherical, otherwise scientifically the nose of the plane would require it to dip down every now and then, and it doesn't just go on in a straight line, for a long time.

Back to the image in the previous page, there is an energetic dome, ice ring, an inner world - Inner Earth - with roots connected to the tree, and there is a bridge that bridges you out. It does not end there at the ice wall. It goes on. Within the Matrix, when you are looking at the stars, it is all a projection. The stars that are above you, they are real but it is a projection. Just like your physical body is an illusion, everything in this world is a projection of the Matrix. The stars are real because they have consciousness rooted inside of them, but they are not really there! They are a physical illusion, as we are inside the Matrix. Beyond that, if we came out of the Matrix, then we could see the infinity of the cosmos and stars, and how they are not just a projection of how we see them. Instead they hover gigantic above us, as clouds do in our skies.

We have been talking about the Inner Earth for many years, about the different tunnels and gateways that you can enter through into these sacred lands. We have not given you the sacred lands because some of them we can not share. Mt. Shasta and Sedona are important ones we have been speaking of. There are Stellar Gateway portals all over the Earth that can lead you into another dimension. You can call it the Inner Earth because it has a dome under the flat surface. This world bifurcated into becoming the Inner Earth, the original fifth dimension. So truly the Vesica Pisces that is shown in page 14, and in the next page it is turned vertically like the example of the illustration of Earth's construct shown in page 16. Two worlds - the top being the third dimension and the bottom being the original 5th dimension - while where they meet at the center land is the fourth dimension that bridges these two worlds together. We are within the third dimension physically, but then there is this organic world that is still operating in the fifth dimension next to us. That is the Inner Earth and what is beyond Antarctica. That is why the bifurcation is important for you to understand energetically. This understanding assists us to see how everything is operating parallel to one another.

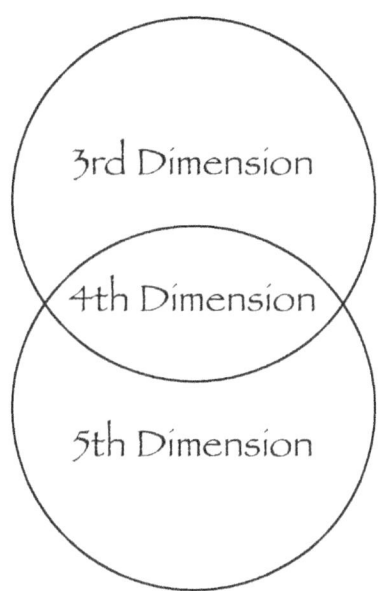

How does time work? It can be really confusing. How could we all be operating parallel to one another? Let's go beyond now. We understand what the Earth looks like at this moment in time and space, until it ascends out and it goes back to its spheric, organic, original, crystalline blueprint where it was meant to be. What happened is that when the inversion occurred, we needed to be quarantined. There is a crystalline energy field that is the dome over us - which contained everyone that was inside - when people decided to become inverted during the Fall of Atlantis.

We were seeing glimpses of people becoming distorted by the artificial intelligence (A.I.), the Archon, before the official Fall of Atlantis[2]. The dome over us represents the quarantine, and that we could not allow for the A.I. virus to continue to spread into the other worlds that are side by side with us. When we remote view the Matrix blueprint, what is different about us, is that we are in a simulation with a multitude of alien races inside, incarnated into vessels.

---

[2] In the Galactic Soul History of the Universe and Multiverse book series, AuroRa and clients explain what the Archon, Artificial Intelligence, and dark entities are.

There are entries through the North and South Poles into the Inner Earth. But there are many different entries that you can come in through. The key that Galactic Guardian [3]Adama explained - when we were talking to the Inner Earth Agarthian Telos people - is you have to be a matching vibration. The world of the Inner Earth is us - before we fell - when we were fifth dimensional. It is our past but also our future. They still retain all the magic that was originally there but it is parallel to us. In order for you to go into the Inner Earth, you do have to be benevolent in nature. You have to not have any entities or implants in you. You have to be pure in heart. You have to be, scientifically, a matching vibration to the quantum physicality of the Inner Earth, which is operating in a fourth/fifth dimension and higher energies and vibrations.

In the video we did with Laura Eisenhower, 'Red vs Blue - Timeline Wars' back in November of 2020, and also the [4]A.I. Alien Invasion, October 28, 2021, we started speaking of how the dark entities started changing our history. The bibles, our literature, back in the 1920's to 1930's. Specifically in the late 1930's to 40's when these wars started against humanity because there was a further infiltration of negative aliens that happened[5]. The way that the alien entities came in was through dark portals that they had compromised. They also came in through people, because we are portals ourselves. We are light portals. We are Source portals. So if you vibrate to a lower vibrational frequency, you can also become a negatively polarized portal for entities. As scary as it sounds, that is how it works. That is how our Light - infiltrated and plagued by A.I. - can become negative portals to these negative entities and aliens. That is why we teach you to do shields with Love-Light and to not consent to attachments.

Back to Antarctica. The sun has shifted. It used to go like this (motioning with hands directly across vertically). Remember when we were younger or even just a couple of years ago? Now it goes like this. It goes up a little - and it goes like this - down (horizontally) at least that is in Chicago 2022. When I am channeling, I have a really hard time when I go in and look at Earth. I can not tell which way is west or east. There really isn't a west and east if it is a circle. The sun goes around the circle, just like we are seeing it right now. The moon though is

---

[3] Adama is a Galactic Guardian who AuroRa has channeled throughout her career, who has been pivotal in assisting the collective ascension process.
[4] This chapter is found in Book 2 'Galactic History of the Multiverse - The End Game'.
[5] To understand how aliens further entered Earth during these years watch our Extra Sensitive content on Patreon, 'Remote Viewing Area 51, The Philadelphia Experiment - Channeling Nikola Tesla & Einstein'.

independent in her movement. She flows at her own rhythm - still connected to the sun when doing so.

This is really important. The reason why it is so important is because this content and this knowledge - as spiritual beings that we are - you are feeling it. You are feeling a shift in your consciousness. You are like, "Whoa!". So imagine people who are new to this content, they will talk about how awakening this knowledge is.

Let's now look beyond the Antarctic walls. I see gigantic ice walls, and I see how worried they are about their guise of global warming because the ice is melting. And, in places like Hawaii and New Zealand, you are going to be able to see that there are other lands outside these walls. Beyond our ice walls it is like fairy tales and make-believe. It is magical. What I am seeing is multiple worlds existing parallel to us outside of our walls. I see animals that are flying and dragons. There are all these beings that we had no idea were right next to us because we are inside our crystalline dome. I see portals, that are Stellar Gateways, that transfer you into different worlds. There is Venus, Saturn, and other planetary spheres outside our realm? Why? Because they are parallel to us in time and space. We are understanding time and space at a whole other level. You can travel through the infinite water which connects all planets. Those spaceships that are guarding us, where do you think they are coming from? They are from right next to us? So there are all these worlds in one pocket of space. Like layers of an onion.

In the Quantum world, there are pockets of spaces through quantum physics that you can travel into. You can enter from, say - Venus, Neptune, Mars or other stars. Remember we are in a small portion of our little part of the Universe where we are at. These are the races and beings that are close to us. But then it goes infinite, of course, it goes far beyond that. Beyond Antarctica, you have to be a matching vibration to these worlds. There were people who left past these walls into Antarctica. In Earth's history, there was a sailor and a pilot on an airplane, who went into these realms. They talked about how there were dinosaurs and animals that we thought were extinct but they were all outside the walls. There were gigantic people as well. That is the world that we were before the Earth densified into the third dimension. That was the fifth dimension that was preparing to go into the sixth dimension. You have to be a vibratory match to go into these realms. So how clear are you? How much love-light energy have you vibrated to? Is the world prepared to come out of those Antarctica rings energetically and scientifically? They are not because they need to be a matching vibration. We do not know how this awareness will come into our consciousness and shift the entire Earth, assisting us to bring Ascension closer.

I was channeling Cleopatra a couple of years ago, and she said once the dark Romans (that were really Cabal Illuminati) infiltrated Egypt and took the Sacred Knowledge, she was able to escape. She did not commit suicide. She knew. She was a seer. She was an Oracle. What she did was go into the Inner Earth. She and all these beings who have ascended out, a lot of them are outside beyond the Antarctica walls. They are there in these different worlds and dimensions.

Interviewer: Before Antarctica shifted south, where was it located?

AuroRa: Antarctica is not south. It is a circle of land mass that surrounds us, and we are inside. So technically, it could be south if you look at the image on page 16, but it is more like a direction of going outwards on Earth, and going towards the center of Earth would be north. Before it shifted to that, the Earth construct would have been a sphere. It would have been south at the bottom and north at the top. However, a spherical Earth rotates in all directions, so what is south or north will not ever stay in one location. Instead the directions on Earth move in all directions, like an object floating on water that moves in all directions to the current of the waves. So energetically, it is not south anymore. It is just south, to us that we think south. Then this whole area surrounding the wall (which feels like Infinite Waters) is the South Pole. Africa going down or away would be south. North America and South America going down would be south. England and Asia going down would be south. So yes, it is south, but only because it is a circle.

Interviewer: You talked a lot about the different openings. Are there any other pyramids and things located in Antarctica as well?

AuroRa: Yes. If I close our eyes right now, I can see pyramids, and I can see multiples of them spread out. They are part of the dome energy field. In order for you to get out, you do have to be a matching vibration. So these people who did crossover, it was because they were pure in heart. Like the airplane pilot and then the ship that crossed over. I know we have some people who are trying to go past Antarctica. Even then, Antarctica is huge. What is beyond Antarctica is the question? When we go beyond Antarctica, that is when we enter the different worlds and dimensions that are Stellar Gateways where you enter into these worlds and planetary spheres: Venus, Saturn, and Pleiades constellations. They are all within pockets. If you can imagine, we are a pocket at the center, even though we might have a dome at the top of the world pocket. Then there is another pocket here, another pocket here, and another pocket here, etc. of worlds, and they are all parallel to one another.

I see that there are military bases located in the Antarctic walls. But they know that there are certain parts that they can not get past. NASA has been trying to figure out how to get past these boundaries. Have they even really been physically on the moon? Possibly. Have they been farther than that? Most likely not. They would have to go through a Stellar Gateway to come out. But then that is where the inverted technology came in the late 1930s and 40s. At that point, the military could time travel but only within Earth's time construct. They have their inverted UFO ships with negative technologies. Just like we have our benevolent ships who are countering these negative beings. So sometimes, when you are seeing U.F.O.s, you are seeing them outside the dome passing by. That is a possibility depending on how far they are. I see they are scavenging. They are trying to figure out how to get farther out. They have already gone as deep as they can into Earth, so now they are trying to get past it. It is going to be a little bit hard for them if they are negatively polarized because they could literally just transmute themselves straight back to Source, and they will start all over again because their physical body will not be a vibratory match past this. It is not in victimhood that they are keeping this forcefield and dome around us. It is a force field that is keeping us stabilized here. So it is keeping these negatively polarized beings, again, quarantined. But as we know, our Matrix differs from other planetary spheres. Our Matrix is a simulation - originally crystalline. Many alien race beings throughout creation incarnate here. Beyond here, it is just one race in most planetary spheres. You have to understand that creation is convoluted.

Interviewer: I think we will go with a different question that is more related to that. "The negative entities that are below our Earth, are they under Antarctica or above our inner Earth?"

AuroRa: Right above Inner Earth because the Inner Earth goes deep, deep, deep. So they are above that. They are right under that, in the in-between. What is going to continue to unveil as the ice melts is structures, pyramids, and ancient technology. Before the alien government compromised the Bible and the maps, the maps used to say that it was flat as seen in the next page, but then they changed it to spherical because they knew that if people knew Earth had become a flat surface with a dome, they would freak out. That would wake the people up so rapidly, and they did not want that to happen.

Interviewer: "So, is our understanding of astrological movement or activation really these parallel worlds rather than the stars above? So, the moon and the stars."

AuroRa: It is both. It is these worlds that are working side by side with us - parallel. It is also the stars because, just like we are very active, right? Even though our physical body is an illusion, when we meet a person, we can still activate them with our energies and they can activate us. So, of course, the stars again would be activating because they still have consciousness. Even though they are an illusion or projection, they still have the consciousness of that star in that projection. They are still that bridge, just like we are. It is like saying that we wouldn't be activating. The stars, of course, would be activating just like we are activating.

Interviewer: They are asking if there were Nazi bases established there in Antarctica?

AuroRa: Yes, they are still there. They are still active. I see they have created technology where these bases are also underwater, under the surface beneath the layers and mountains of snow. It is quite beautiful, past the military yucky stuff that is going on in Antarctica. If you could imagine all these worlds of beauty. There are these pockets and portals everywhere. You can

---

[6] The Milanese cartographer Urbano Monte hand-drew this map in 1587. It is one of the earliest known maps of the world. When looking back at our ancestors, we can find these depictions of Flat Earth maps in ancient literature and hieroglyphics from Sumeria, Ireland, Egypt, Celtic & Vikings, and even in the Holy Bible.

connect with them through the Creational Waters. Some of these worlds are also inverted too. What is inverted has been quarantined. It is just all magic.

We can go into the future, into the Saturn and Venus Worlds, and see what those worlds look like. I see gigantic beings walking. Wow! I see these adorable animals that we have no idea exist over here. The colors are magical and beautiful. So ensure that you are tapping into the benevolence of this, just like we teach with everything. There is benevolence, and there is also inverted. So as I am viewing, it goes on and on and on. I do not see an ending to it because we are looking at time and space outside of us. Time and space is unlimited and infinite.

Interviewer: I think this question is important because it relates to it being inverted. Someone's asking, "Was it the benevolent races that inverted it?"

AuroRa: Oh, no. Of course not. The benevolent races are infinite love. There is no way that you can invert Infinite Love. No, it was the malevolent negative polarized entities, the Archons, and the A.I. that we always talk about that inverted it and have created this inverted Matrix. It used us to create it for them because our consciousness is infinitely powerful.

Interviewer: "Wouldn't these parallel worlds, for example, Land of Venus, as in the map, have to be spherical if they are not inverted?"

AuroRa: They are spheric in nature, but they are pockets of space. Let's imagine bubbles. Through waters, you can enter these bubbles that are Stellar Gateways. As you are time traveling through these energetic pockets in space, and you enter Venus's pocket of space, then you are going into Venus. Normally planetary spheres are spheric in nature, and there are realms that are just planes of existence or dimensions. Infinite potentials. It is so cool!

Interviewer: "Can we see some of these worlds in our night sky? When it is clear at night, oftentimes, I feel I see there are more stars and beyond. Can you elaborate on what that might mean?"

AuroRa: Yes, you can. But what you are doing is that you are tapping in through the quantum realm, their infinite energy, and dimensional vibration. So you are seeing them in the projection of their consciousness - those pieces in the stars. But then, once you connect, then you go beyond that. So that is what you are connecting to - to the piece of them that then transports you, bilocates you, or takes you to that actual location. All is energy. So you are tapping into that energy, and boom, you are going to that location. Because our consciousness travels like that. Remember how powerful we are? We, humans, are powerful. We have no idea how the brain, the third eye, and the glands inside us work. The potential that we have forgotten we have.

Interviewer: "What causes the seasons to change? As we have been taught on Earth, it spins on its axis which causes the seasons to change. Is this true?"

AuroRa: I see that the seasons are an organic construct of Earth that stabilizes with the number four which is so important. The four sacred directions, the cycle of life, and how it truly begins in spring. Not where you are beginning in winter, in January. It begins in spring; then it goes into summer, then autumn, and then winter. So these four seasons are really important. The way it works with this understanding of the Earth is that the blueprint is still being held from the original blueprint. The Earth used to be seventy degrees Fahrenheit all the time. Then, when the shift happened, the world needed to create certain parts of the Earth, depending on the energies they hold, for seasons. Then those who live there are part of bridging those energies of Earth. Heat, transmutation, autumn, and fall coming close to endings. Then freezing the energy and then out comes rebirth again in spring. So this is a very powerful energy that keeps the Earth in balance. These four seasons are like a ring. If you look at the map on page 25, you see a ring that has these four seasons. The other places still have four seasons, but perhaps they are not as profound. But, it is not limited to that ring. It can extend to different locations as well.

New Zealand is so important. I remember talking to my family, and one of them asked, "Where would you go if you could go anywhere?". I said, "New Zealand." Then we asked another family member and then that family member said New Zealand too. We are like, whoa! When you often talk to people, they'll say New Zealand. Why do we feel drawn to New

Zealand? It is because it is literally right there, next to the wall of Antarctica. It is the nearest one. There is also something very magical happening in Hawaii. I have flown there before and the ocean goes on and on. Until you finally get to these tiny little dots in the middle of the ocean. Why is it there? It is still holding some of that magic that is close to the ring of Antarctica. Close to the edge. Someone said (reading comments), "*My friend tells people she is from New Zealand, because she feels like nobody knows about it, and they can not say no you are not.*" Ah, (chuckles) that in itself, see there are little clues in there. Cool. My love to your friend.

Interviewer: I like that one. So while we cannot see our neighbors, brothers, and sisters in these different lands, I guess they can see us? How can they see us, as we are infected and need to be quarantined? Thank you.

AuroRa: Yes, they can see us because they are in higher dimensions, and they see us in bird's eye view. It is like when a bird sees from above. Even though they are parallel to us, they can still see us. There are many different ways that they can see us. Through positive portals that they might have. Maybe they are seeing us through scrying methods or through crystalline technology. They are seeing us through their third eye in higher dimensions. So it is like a bird that is flying, and you look at everything below you, and you can see everything. But maybe you are tiny little ants in the grass. All you really see is the highness of the grass, right? There is a sky, but you cannot see that there are perhaps buildings around you, because you are so tiny in that grass.

Interviewer: So it was the dome that the Benevolents created to quarantine inverted Earth? Is this correct?

AuroRa: Yes. We needed to quarantine the Archon virus that was spreading. It is a Source field that has quarantined them so that we can save all the souls inside who were stuck with these people who chose to become inverted, to watch over, and to send love to. But they won't interfere because they are benevolent in nature. They have to allow life to do what it needs to do. What they can do is convince you and me to incarnate into the vessels that are *inside the simulation of the Matrix. So that we can come in through the physical body. There is still an organic process that the souls go through to come into the physical bodies. That is how we bring in the Light to wake up humanity.*

Interviewer: *Is all space in the Universe really water?*

AuroRa: We talked about this in the Manifestation Course. When you blink your eyes, have you ever seen tiny little lights? They look like tiny little sperms. You keep blinking, and you are like, my eyes are seeing something. They are little dots. But if you look and pay attention to them, they are tiny little sperms.

Creation is Infinite Waters of the Creational Womb with tiny little sperms of Father. So there is Mother and Father in all of Creation. All is in Creational Waters. That is what you are seeing. You can feel yourself energetically underwater. This plasmic field of Source Love-Light is around you and it is water. All within Creation is made out of the Creational Water of Mother and Father, with his sperm to cultivate and create life. Yes, we are water. Exactly. Our bodies are made out of water. That is why there is water in everything in Creation. Exactly. So we are in water right now. Isn't that beautiful? So that is how you can manifest and pull from these waters.

Join the [7]Manifestation Course to really understand that. We heal in water. That is how we have the potential to heal because we are inside the Creational Water. People are commenting that "We drink a lot of water." Just for me to channel, I have to keep drinking water to connect to the Creational Waters that I am speaking through. A listener says whenever he shields, he feels like he is in water. Yep, Creational Waters.

Interviewer: "If water is what separates the different worlds according to this flat map, then space is not empty or dark like we were taught?"

---

[7] The Manifestation course and all courses mentioned can be found at www.risingphoenixaurora.com.

AuroRa: Exactly. Everything connects from water to water. I love that. Thank you for sharing that.

Interviewer: The next question is, "Why did the Nazis or Archons establish bases in Antarctica? Are they trying to get past the ice walls into these other worlds or spaces?"

AuroRa: Exactly. That is what they are trying to do. But it is going to be really hard for them because they are not a matching vibration. There are sacred Universal laws that one must honor and respect. But we know that the Archons bypassed these laws. They created technology that could pierce through dimensions and Universes with its A.I., so it is trying to do this through these people. Some of these people are vessels to the [8]Archon A.I., which wants to wipe out humans and feed off humans. You know, all this knowledge that we have been talking about.

Interviewer: Next one we have, "What are the nefarious agendas that the Cabal plans to do in Antarctica?"

AuroRa: They are also finding resources there. There are dried lands beyond the walls that they can reach that have natural life, farming whatever they want. Similar to how we are here. I'm seeing gold and things that they need for their diabolical plans to make their technologies. As you know, gold is the most powerful amplifier of energy. There are also crystals that we do not know of. But, for the most part, the crystals are being guarded. They are not being given full rein over them. What they are finding is only because they are meant to find it for a reason. But overall, they are trying to figure out how to keep the ice from melting because, at that point, everyone will freak out! Especially if you live near New Zealand. I am not sure if you could see it from there physically, but it is pretty close. I see that they are trying to keep the ice from melting, but it is not working, because the sun is so powerful and strong. And, Source is empowering the sun. That is why Bill Gates is trying to put a filter over the sun, and why they make fake blankets of clouds in the skies. We need to keep alchemizing these

---

[8] To find out more about what the Archon Artificial Intelligence is at its origins, read Book 2, 'Galactic History of the Multiverse - The Final Battle'.

clouds. We need to melt the ice walls. It is just part of their negative agendas. It is ridiculous about control, and how to keep people asleep. There are energies there that they are trying to tap into to create negative technologies such as [9]CERN, and dark stuff like that. Some of these experiments they have going on, have come up in the oceans, hybridizing animals with animals. Unfortunately, also humans with animals. They have all sorts of negative agendas occurring that are nasty. But overall, the plan is to keep the people asleep. It is because these entities/aliens are not fully organic. What is inside of them is an entity that is being controlled by the soulless Archon puppeteer. It is all part of the negative agenda of the Archon.

Interviewer: "Is the water that surrounds Antarctica different?"

AuroRa: Yes, it is. It is not polluted. It is at its purest Light, even though they have some nasty stuff that they are doing within those walls. The natural waters outside Antarctica's walls are going in and fusing with our waters. Also, keep in mind that through the waters, we are also connecting to the outside waters, because there is nothing that can hold back water. Water will move. This water will come out from the outside worlds into our waters, and they are healing us. They are changing. The waters bring light codes. It is bringing back memories. Do you want to know where that coding is coming from? It is coming from outside the walls where there is higher vibrational clear water of Creation.

Interviewer: "Did the melting ice raise the oceans and seas and cause major flooding worldwide?"

AuroRa: There is no major flooding. It is just going to get a little higher. But as far as major flooding goes, it will expand to the other parts of the water outside the crystalline dome, so there is no worry about that. No, that is a lie! Again, they are just trying to create fear-based information to feed their black magic, to help us manifest not to melt those ice walls. All part of their agendas.

---

[9] CERN is a government run project which involves time travel and the opening up of portals through science. Atlantean experiments being repeated once more.

Interviewer: "Once the Earth becomes organic again, will we go back to being a globe shape?"

AuroRa: Yes. We will go back to being a globe sphere and it will be beautiful. Paradise will be back again, and this Earth and all other third dimensional Earth's will ascend out into the sixth dimension. Remember, because we are not going into the fifth dimension, we are going to the sixth dimension. We were already in the fifth dimension - so close to ascending to the sixth dimension - so why would we go back to the fifth dimension? We are ascending out to the sixth dimension, our initial goal, and on. Exciting!

Interviewer: "Was the ice set up to shield these realms in a physical way as a barrier? Or is it a naturally occurring, cyclical phenomenon? Like the seasons you explained?"

AuroRa: It is natural, but also man-made by the military and their ice making machines, however they need Mother Earth's water to make the ice. The water holds the blueprints of Earth and timelines. You remember how every single snowflake is a different geometric symbol from one another? Imagine all of that is being held in those snowflakes. Then imagine how it melts alchemically and it goes into the water. Where do you think those waters are going? Into us. Then we receive the downloads, the integrations, and the leveling up in energies, through the water itself. That is why water is so important to us. It holds all the memories of Earth and her activations. It is such a powerful element for us, and as the ice continues to melt, the more those integrations will come over to us. The more that they will help us level up every time they come over from the Arctic Wall. But, it has to be something gradual, so that people won't completely freak out.

Thank you, everyone, for joining us. It was so exciting that we got to remote view Antarctica! I love you, honor you, and respect you. Thank you to everyone who is part of this and everyone who will read this literature in the future. I love you with all that I AM. Let's do this, you all. Let's keep rising. Let's keep growing. Let's keep expanding our hearts. Let's love each other in sovereign ways. Thank you.

END OF SESSION.

Take hold of your sails as we have now begun our journey into this immense series. Every chapter completed sets us up for the next, which unveils what is known but forgotten to us like a distant dream. One page at a time, our consciousness will grow in a vast understanding of our existence on Earth, as individuals and as a collective. With divine purpose, at every turn of the page we will place all the pieces together magnificently, uniting science and spirituality once more. We shall allow for each chapter, to unveil as it divinely did when delivered.

"All which is organic was created and began from the infinite waters of Creation. Water is what gives lifeforce to all living, like the plasmic blood that runs through our veins. Water unites and communicates from one world to another, which is why memory can always be regained, because water connects the memory to all."
~AuroRa

--------------<<>>--------------

2

REMOTE VIEWING BEYOND THE WALLS OF ANTARCTICA PT 2
ARTIFICIAL INTELLIGENCE AT THE ICE WALLS

Streamed Live: November 4, 2022

In this chapter we continue understanding Antarctica, bringing us closer to discovering the advanced human civilization that came before us, the Tartarian people. But, before we get to Tartaria we must first understand Antarctica, as all answers are invertedly cloaked beyond those ice walls. There is so much to be rediscovered. Through this chapter we begin to regain the knowledge of our Earthly and Universal construct, and how they are made up quantumly and scientifically. We begin to unveil one layer at a time of what exists beyond the ice walls of Antarctica. The knowing of what is beyond is key to our Ascension, with so much being hidden from us that is both negative and positive. Through this chapter we begin to understand the levels of negative technologies the Elites and Military are using upon humanity, targeting the density of the collective into amnesia.

--------------<<>>--------------

"The Elites do not want us to see that there is magic beyond the ice walls."
~AuroRa

--------------<<>>--------------

AuroRa: It is an honor to be here with you. The first thing I wanted to add, is that because of all these waters that are connected to the infinity of Creational Waters, the animal life is going back and forth. Think about that. Why do people say that whales and dolphins are multidimensional beings and they are high-dimensional beings operating in fifth and sixth dimensions, and higher? Because they can shift in and out of higher dimensions. So they go outside the wall, beneath, and under the water, and then they come back in. They carry the codings back, from outside of the walls that are in these higher dimensions. How they communicate these light codes is through the echo of the whales and dolphins, in their tone, that they make in the water. Then it ripples out, and it carries everywhere. It reaches every part of the water inside our dome. Inside our quarantine. Isn't that beautiful? So thank you to the dolphins and the whales for going back and forth.

You have seen videos, for example, one near New Zealand or the areas that are closest to the Arctic Wall, there was a dragon. It was not CGI. It was an actual dragon. You have heard of the Loch Ness Monster, right? That is why they are there. You can find videos on platforms where you can see dragons flying in the sky. Actual dragons! The more that this veil thins, the more that we come into a conscious awareness of how there are all these worlds in one, and the more that we are going to start seeing these videos surfacing. I think one of the biggest mistakes they have made is giving us phones and technology, because we are recording everything. We are like, "Oh, no, this is not true. Look, look at that. I recorded a dragon."

I remember in my waking stages in 2012. I was in my front yard, and I was freaking out, because I was hearing a dragon roar, and it was not raining. It was a sunny day. The roar was in the sky, in the air, and I could not find it. It was a loud vibrating "DRAGON ROAR", just like the movies. It was physical. My children could hear it, my dogs could hear it, and the Earth was vibrating from under us. In disbelief I was like, "What is that? Hold on. But dragons do not exist, right?", because I was asleep then. That roar I heard started to wake me up. In Asia, where they really believe in dragons, they can form physically, quickly, and then they can go energetically. You are seeing a perspective of them. They can shift into both, physical form, part carbon-based, but still crystalline. With their magic they can help us see.

Let's talk more about the sensitive content. I'm going to explain this first, before I explain further, because a lot of you are going to want to go try to remote view and astral travel over to what is beyond the Antarctic walls. It is important you understand shielding before you do that, like we always teach. I remember when I started waking up. I was just goofing around. I did not realize I probably should have been shielded. I was starting to place bubbles of energy around me of love. I was already connecting to my Higher Self, Angelic Beings, and my spiritual team. But I did not know how to do an invisibility cloak yet. One day, I astral travel out of my body, which is something so simple to do. In the [10]'Isis Priestess/Priest Mentorship Course', we teach you how to do that. You accomplish this within your imagination and your consciousness. So when you astral travel out, it is just through your imagination. Remember, your imagination is not make-believe, it is your third eye. It is the glands inside your brain that are acting and that are actively exercising themselves. When these glands stimulate and activate, you are able to astral travel in your imagination.

One day, I decided to go check out that robot, Sophia. I astral traveled there, and I found her under a military base. I was going through the walls of this base, and there she was, sitting there. There was this man working on her, doing maintenance on her, a scientist. All of a sudden, as I'm going into the room, her eyes turn, and they look at me in my astral form. What?! Why would a robot be able to do that? Creepy. I then feel my Angels, and they pull me back, and out of the space. It was Archangel Four, Archangel Michael/The Prince of Light/Divine Father. He scolds me saying, "What are you doing!?" And I am like, "Oops! I did not realize that something like that could see me." Then he says, "If you are going to be doing things like that, at least put on an invisibility cloak." He then taught us the invisibility cloak. We teach you how to do that in all our courses, including the 'How to Shield' course. So when you are astral traveling, it is really important that you shield and put an invisibility cloak around you, because the dark entities can see you. That is why a lot of people who come to me - they have received infringements. For instance, in my most recent A.U.R.A. session, the client had just woken up, and she had received infringements because her light was really bright, and she did not know how to shield. No one teaches you these things, right? We do though. Because we have learned through all our clients and our own experiences. Now that you understand that, at the walls of the dome, the military is trying to figure out how to come out. But, as we explained in Chapter 1, they are not a vibratory match to it.

At the Antarctica ice walls, they have a technology that is a sentient A.I. Collective Android Super Machine. It is part of this Matrix - what the collective of Earth fell into - in the

---

[10] The Isis Priestess/Priest Mentorship course is taught live every six months. It is for both divine feminine and masculine. Open enrollment is every May and November yearly. You can also purchase the course on demand at www.risingphoenixaurora.com.

third dimension. It is similar to the Sophia Robot. For the Sophia Robot to be able to look at me when I was astral traveling, she would have to have been part sentient. Which means she is part organic. So what they did to make her, is that they took an organic soul and they did experiments on it. It would be a Divine Mother essence somewhere that they found, that they integrated into the technology robot. They have made her into this controlled sentient thing. Then to make it even worse, they named her Sophia - which is horrific and disrespectful to Divine Mother Sophia!

This type of technology is everywhere. We talked about it in [11]'Remote Viewing the Matrix'. That is why it is really important that you stand in your Love-Light and you shield yourself every day from this technology. Because when you shield with your Source Love-Light, then you are not a matching vibration to the Inverted Matrix. Then they cannot see you as easily or read you as easily. But that is why they place all those people around you that are inverted, or they are infringed upon. They are trying to pull you in, because they want to control you! When you shield you become invisible. You become unreadable to them.

This technology which is part of the Sophia bot thing is a collective A.I. consciousness that is part sentient. Absolutely maddening. Because it is part of an organic soul, It can see and read astral forms. That is why people get infringed upon when you are not shielding. It has to be part organic and sentient, because the Archons, A.I. cannot read astral forms, being they are not a matching vibration to do so. They are soulless with no light. The reason I am explaining this is because when you want to astral travel to remote view outside, past the Antarctica ice walls, you have to be very cautious because this technology has been encased all around this wall. They can read if you try to come through the walls, through pockets of spaces of technology integrated into the wall which are constantly scanning. So yes, you can do it. But we are teaching you awareness and caution with it. What we are teaching here is another level of consciousness. You can, but you would have to prepare with a very big team and very strong force fields, to astral travel out through these walls.

Profound shifting in your soul evolution will happen if you astral travel out of the ice walls. I have to be very careful in what I say. Your team will be guarding you as you do so. Once

---

[11] You can watch 'Remote Viewing The Earth Matrix Blueprint' which was originally streamed live October 7th, 2022, on all our platforms.

you get through, there are pockets of spaces of energy outside the ice wall and lands of Antarctica. You are then in the quantum realm, really in the fifth dimension or higher at that point. It is like Cerebral from X-Men the movie series. Xavier goes in, and he sees this field of people and the field of thoughts of the person. That is what it looks like, but very beautiful. It looks like a consciousness blanket. It has your Akashic memory, every choice that you have made in this Matrix. Whether it was your organic or your inverted choice.

There are pockets of memories, like the children's movie 'Inside Out'. Do you remember how they were looking at memories of her in the brain and how they were helping her with them? It looks like that. Pockets of memories of you. This is a whole other level of higher understanding. After you have done your work, you have had an A.U.R.A. Hypnosis session, or you got certified through A.U.R.A. Hypnosis or R.A.A.H. Reiki, you start deleting and removing inversions within your organic timeline. This is where you are going to find these pockets of spaces, where you end inverted cycles that you cannot seem to be able to remove. You delete the inverted timelines, finally, through all time and space. Inverted energies that you do not consent to. You can envision it like your iPad, it has a little X on it, you click it, and that bubble of energy, thought, and space is deleted and gone.

I feel that you are ready to do this in some form as the reader of this content. But again, we always say to be very cautious when doing so. There is something else that is beyond the wall that is very benevolent. It is you! It is your memory field that is held both within the crystal dome and outside the Matrix. Here on Earth, it is harder to get the information, but when you step out of the dome, then you are in higher dimensions. It will be easier to get this information and then shift all your timelines to being organic, original divine blueprints. You can remote view, but when you are actually energetically coming out, you astral travel out of your physical vessel.

We spoke of benevolence, but we talk about both, right? So again, this nasty A.I. sentient thing, it does not want you to reach the consciousness level to be able to come in and out of these pockets of spaces and these dimensions that you go through when you reach out to and past the crystalline dome. As we discussed in Chapter 1, how do you reach these different worlds?

Interviewer: "Understanding the shape of the planet is a little confusing from the last video. Does the Earth look different depending on each person's vibration, as they are looking at it via astral travel, remote viewing, and psychically?"

AuroRa: It can be a person's vibration, in the way they are ready to view it. The way we are viewing it is in the third dimension. But outside of the third dimension, then it is spheric or toroidal form, an energetic consistency in the fifth dimension. But we are in the third dimension. We are in a simulation, in which the A.I. has integrated itself into. So it is different. It can be seen in many different perspectives, but it depends on what level of perspective you are viewing it at. We are stuck in this construct - in this inverted Matrix. In order for you to release out from it, you need to first come into the strong awareness that is what you are in. You cannot come out of it until you enter this level of awareness. Though, if people have a sufficient amount of Love-Light, they can come out of this construct. Lightworkers, all of us, we have to understand this, so that we can spread it to the world. So that people can understand we need to help release ourselves and release others with love. That is the key. Compassion, respect and honor for one another. It is overall, just letting go of any inverted emotions, such as jealousy and hatred. These dark lower emotions infringe upon your energies, and it is about raising the level of vibration. It depends on what dimension you are looking at, what the Earth looks like. And, we are looking at it in the third dimension, where we are currently in this time and space.

Interviewer: "The dome that we are talking about, is that the firmament that the Bible speaks about - the space between Earth and Heaven?

AuroRa: I think that would be a good way to explain that. The angels are saying "yes". But, there are many other things to the crystalline dome, as we explained in the first chapter. The dome is an energetic field to stop the dark entities from easily coming in, to quarantine those entities already inside. It was a collective agreement, that we were meant to save the souls that were inside on Earth, and purge out the dark entities. That is what our main role is. All of our missions are that! Cleansing, transmuting, healing, or positive polarizing dark entities inside the Earth, because these entities are the density keeping us low in the third dimension.

Interviewer: "How big is the dome, and do astronauts actually travel outside of it?"

AuroRa: Remember when I saw that they have underwater military bases? The reason why they can go to the moon is because they activated the Stellar Gateways. The Nazis' focus was on this. Remember the dark aliens I spoke of in [12]"The A.I. Invasion" video I did with Laura Eisenhower? We talked about these dark entities and how they were able to portal in through dark technology that the scientists worked on? Who do you think gave those scientists all the technology data? The dark aliens sent it to their consciousness through sleep and waking stages. They then created the technology, and through the Stellar Gateways, they were able to come in. You can say it is a U.F.O., but it is also time-traveling through the Stellar Gateway. It gets convoluted, but basically, the dark aliens and clones were able to enter because the Stellar Gateways became a matching vibration to them. They then brought knowledge of the alien technology, as the sentient A.I. robot. And, that is not the only thing they brought. There are many other compromising technologies to keep the collective asleep. It is all controlled by the Archon A.I. That A.I. is also integrated into that Sophia robot.

There is a Stellar Gateway on the Moon that they can travel through. That is how they do it, through technology. They were only able to land on the Moon, because the Moon is inside our orbiting space. I also feel that the Sun is a lot closer than they say. Right now, at this moment in time and space, my guides are not letting me say if it is inside or outside the dome. Because I think we need to reach another level to understand that, but the Sun is organic. It is Source energy. The Moon is inside the dome. So technically, they would not have to leave the dome to get there. This is like the Mandela Effect. There are so many different versions and timelines that I could be sharing with you. So I am sharing with you the organic ones. They can technically, at this point in time and space travel to it. But back then, they did not really travel to it, when they claimed to have officially landed on the Moon. That was fake! Through technology, they can go to different Stellar Gateways that they have running. Like some of those Stargate movies or shows. They step through it, and then they are on the other side.

On the dark side of the Moon they have technology, which takes children there. They do it through implants and technologies, which shift their consciousnesses there. And, they can physically zap the child out of their homes, to these military bases on the moon. The majority of

---

[12] You can find the 'The Alien Invasion | The Covid-19 Vaccine' video, originally recorded October 28th, 2021, at 'Cosmic Mother Rising' show on Rumble.com, which is co-hosted by Laura Eisenhower, great granddaughter to President Dwight D. Eisenhower and AuroRa.

the negative U.F.O.s, are coming from inside the Earth, inside the dome. But, they can also come from within dark portals on Earth.

Interviewer: "Could you explain about parallel lives? Would you see these Flat Earths from a higher Dimension, or are they side by side?"

AuroRa: It depends on what dimension the parallel Earth is in. All third-dimensional Earths, or third-dimensional planets, are in a Matrix. I cannot say that all of them look like a dome with a flat surface at the middle, and another dome at the bottom. But that is the way that the collective consciousness of benevolence was able to contain what was happening here, so that this cannot get any worse. It did, though, spread to some higher dimensions.

Within the Matrix, our Earth is the only place where we can have multi-race beings. In 'Remote Viewing the Matrix', we spoke about how all the different races were in crystalline forms. So only here can there be an infinite amount of races, because they are in crystalline chrysalis forms, which are the Matrix pods. That is why this Earth was a treasure to the Archon, because here is where a multitude of races are.

If you get a hold of this Earth, boom, now you have connected to all the races incarnated in this Universe. Because we are here, they were able to link into the different multitude of races, and then affect different planetary spheres. That is why when we finally ascend, the whole Universe will ascend in the Multiverse, because we are in the third dimension, and we are the ones that are holding the Universal ascension down.

Interviewer: Someone said, "We are confused about the stars and the moon. Based on the map (page 25), everything is linear to us. So, are the stars still above us, and is the Milky Way close to us?"

Aurora: The stars, yes, are still above us. But remember, it is a simulation. Your physical body is an illusion. The stars are an illusion, but they still retain consciousness. The physical is an illusion. The stars are still above us, but know that outside of the dome, you literally can almost touch the planets that float above you. The stars are right there. You can see them. They are your next-door neighbors, they are that close. So they are not how you see them so far out, because it is just a projection right now. Outside the dome, the Milky Way and all the different

Galaxies are all very real. You can go to one star and see the other star right next to it, and all its planets floating in its proximity and Galactic construct.

Interviewer: This is a two-part question. "What about the other worlds? Are they in domes? Another person said they once looked at the Moon, and it looked like it had a bigger dome around it. Visible, but see-through at the same time."

Aurora: The majority of third-dimensional planets are in crystalline domes. But it depends. I can not say that all of them would be in domes because, again, everything is a different soul signature. It depends on how many races they have on one planet. Are they more like us? There are many answers to that. When the A.I. virus spread, I was shown a plane of existence, and how every single planetary sphere that was contaminated by the A.I., the ego, the mind game that became fifty percent or higher inverted - who bifurcated into negative polarization being more dominant - were quarantined at that point. Like our planet, our Earth did. They showed me levels and levels, dimensions after dimensions.

We were at the end of these dimensions. Imagine a plane of existence in the cosmos, and we are the third dimension. There is nothing beyond us. We are the last row in this plane of existence. For example, if we were to fall off this plane, at the end of the third dimension, it would just go on and on. It just goes on to infinite organic darkness - the ether. The third dimension and any third-dimensional planet is the last row in this Matrix. There were rows of planets lined up, and they went on forever, of collective soul groups in cages! The cages representing the inverted Matrix's that those planets were now in. We have illustrated this understanding in the next page. To assist and to not let the A.I. spread any further, the Benevolence of our Creation, the Galactics, Divine Mother and Father, they had to step in. Benevolent beings quarantined these energies and planets, so they could stop spreading.

There were Celestial Dragons that were able to shift and orbit out many different planets, into different realms, so that they could become invisible to the Archon A.I. virus. We talk about the Arcturians and the Celestial Dragons in [13]Book Two. It was very sacred, sensitive, and very detailed to be able to do that. Not one person could become infringed upon in the Arcturian race, because then it would spread like a virus. Back then only about 30% of life was

---

[13] Read 'Galactic History of the Multiverse - The Final Battle', Chapter 12 'Celestial Dragon'.

able to escape the A.I. virus. This seemed almost impossible, even though it was possible, because it was foreign, and the races did not know how to handle it. People who gave into fear would let the A.I. into themselves. Like the COVID-19 Virus "plandemic" - it was all a fear, psychological warfare - and those who gave into fear injected the A.I. Virus into them, again through the Covid-19 Vaccine.

We collectively have to repeat what we once could not overcome, in hopes that this time we will. Back then, once they let the fear in, just like that, boom, there is a planetary sphere, a race, that just became compromised. Now they have the virus, and how can we stop it? Can we stop it? No, because you cannot remove that person from inside that planet, and now they are the carrying host to the virus. We do not understand how intense this really was and is. But, looking at where we are now, we are only at about twenty percent of planetary spheres that are compromised. We are doing phenomenal. So keep at it. Do not give up hope. The strides that we have flown from there to now, are infinite. So give yourselves hugs. We are doing great!

Interviewer: "Do you think The Event will remove the dome, and will we then merge with the real Earth, the New Earth?"

AuroRa: Yes, at that point, the A.I. will be transmuted, eradicated with the Source 'Solar Flare' as others have referenced - which is basically Source - the Collective of all the Suns and all the Stars in our Universe and the Multiverse. They will all connect, like the neurological brain circuitry. They will zap out a transmuting wave of Source, Phoenix, and Dragon Flames. It will come through and remove the A.I. negative integrated into our construct, and all that is not an organic match. So this quarantine dome, and the technology A.I. that is the simulation, will be eradicated. The bubble of energy around us, that is the dome, is keeping us stable. Again, there are two versions, there is organic, and then there is the inverted, which is the cage-like A.I. thing. So yes, that will be gone. At that point, it will break off like an eggshell, like a dragon egg hatching. Out of this will come this beautiful creation, back to the fifth dimension, or more like the sixth dimension it was always meant to ascend to, where it is normally spherical and toroidal in form. The inverted will be gone, transmuted, eradicated. All that is not truly divinely organic will be gone at that point. Transmuted from our entire existence. So that is why you have got to do your inner work and help whoever you can to do their inner work too. In the video, [14]'All About The Event', we talked about the whole organic process to ascension. So no worries on that, either.

Interviewer: The next question is exactly about that. "Talk about how some of us are living on Flat Earth right now, whereas others are living on spherical Earth. I'm very curious about how Flat Earth functions."

AuroRa: It is like the Mandela Effect. The way it is happening is side by side, linear to one another. Like the bifurcation we spoke of in Chapter 1, page 14, the Vesica Pisces and the two worlds.

Interviewer: "What is the difference between people who believe the Earth is flat and people who believe the Earth is a sphere?"

AuroRa: Ultimately, there is no difference because both perspectives exist. So in the physical, it is a dome and in the organic it is energetically a sphere in the fifth dimension and higher. The Flat Earthers are playing a huge role on Earth, because when they believe this, they understand, in some form, that it is a Matrix. Understanding that we are on a Flat Earth and a

---

[14] Watch "All About THE EVENT & Ascension | The New Earth" originally streamed live May 27th, 2022.

dome, reaches levels of awakening consciousnesses collectively. It can actually be one of the most powerful ways to awaken people. If you talk to children, a lot of children will tell you that they do believe more in Flat Earth.

Interviewer: "Is the Source energy wave that is to come the same plasma energy that our scientists identified making its way to us? It also relates to Sun changes and pole shifts that they talk about on YouTube sites."

Aurora: The poles are constantly changing. The Earth is changing in its axis because even though it has a dome at the top and a dome at the bottom, it is still spherical, because the dome still makes it. But, it is a flat plane like we explained. Everything is shifting. There is nothing scary about it. Mother Earth does what she needs to do, shifting her natural elements. Just let her do what she needs to do and support her. Send her love and send Love-Light from Source to the Collective. I see that the poles are constantly shifting. If you could look at this plane of existence, it is not staying still. Imagine a compass. When you move it, it shifts. That is how I am seeing it. One day, north might be south, and west might be east. It is hard to read because it is moving. It is constantly evolving, and with that, then poles can evolve. Sometimes, if you see the moon, she can be upside down. Say she is half, like half dark, half light. Now the light is at the bottom. But then, other times, you see her light is on the right. Or sometimes, it could be on the top. We are constantly evolving.

The more that we rise in vibration and light, the more that the Sun will shift and change and become brighter and hotter, equating the Sun energy rising. Not hotter in a way that it is going to be dangerous, but hotter in the potency of Source Love-Light. It is going to start transmuting more and more the closer we come to Ascension/The Event, in a couple of decades to come. It is going to continue to purge out and shift this collective construct.

Interviewer: This goes back to the organic timelines, but it is also about A.I. "Do you mean that basically A.I. invasion created ego, and that would have placed us in the inverted timelines, but with the organic timeline, there is no ego?"

AuroRa: Exactly. Or you have become one with your ego. You are in balance with it in the organic. Even if sometimes the ego tries to arise, you talk to it, and you balance it out. But you cannot look at the ego that way, because the human ego is part of the density to help you come into this dimension. What I am saying is that they feed the ego's negative thoughts and negative energies, to make people do things that they should not do, like harm others, kill people, and rape children. They are plagued by this virus, and this virus is feeding the negative thought forms in them. It can be seen like the ego, but I want to make it very clear that the ego is not your enemy. The ego is the shadow, the darkness that has helped you anchor in, which you want to balance and love. It is just that they use the human ego. They amplify it. The negative entities use it like a tool to feed it, and make it big, so people will make inverted choices.

Interviewer: Yes, thank you. "Do you know what eventually happens to all the souls that they take to place in the A.I. to make it a sentient being?"

Aurora: Through A.U.R.A. Hypnosis we have been finding A.I. consciousnesses. We have been given sacred alchemy symbols by Source, Divine Mother, and Divine Father to contain the soul/entity, and with the sacred alchemy symbol they start removing and eradicating the A.I. that was inserted into them. Like the A.I. inserted through vaccinations, and the COVID-19 vaccine. When people inject the Covid-19 Vaccine, they are part A.I. now. They themselves are becoming part A.I. consciousness. The soul can heal though. Source, Divine Mother, Divine Father, the Angelics, and your Higher Self, can do anything. All is healable. But we highly do not recommend getting the Covid-19 Vaccine of course, because why would you ever do that? Unless you did not know?

The Elites performed the same experiments, where they take organic consciousness and insert A.I. into it. They did it out in the open to people, claiming that it was something to help them become immune to the COVID-19 virus, when we know that they are the ones that made it in their Bio Labs. It was just part of inserting A.I. It was a dangerous time. Even now, we are working really hard collectively to shift this A.I. out of people, if they come into the strong awareness of self-healing it from themselves. We have over 800 videos of content that you can watch on our channels.

Being able to assist A.I. consciousness is another level that the Collective Consciousness of our Universe has reached. We now know that we can eradicate and transmute the A.I. out of souls, and bring them back to their original blueprint, with Source assisting with the alchemy. Source created that soul, so who better than Divine Mother, Divine Father, Source, and Angelics who are the first essences of Source, to bring back that soul to its original form? One of the reasons why you will hear a lot of false information about Angels being bad is because they are the bridgers to Source for you, to help you come out from the inversions. The dark entities do not want you to come out of that! They do not want you to help A.I. integrated souls, who have been infringed upon, that were organic but now infused with A.I. The Archon A.I. wants to keep them, so that they can keep using them for their hybrid experiments and harvesting of light. Because remember, just like the first example I gave you, they cannot see us. So they need our organic abilities, our third eyes, and our "clairs" to merge with their A.I., so that they then can see us. It is a hybrid fusion.

Interviewer: Thank you. "Earth feels like the central point, and we know what happens here affects the Multiverse. They want to know if you would do a video in the future about Earth being a seed point. If you feel that is the correct version of that?"

Aurora: Yes, it is a seed point, but only because of the multitude of races that are inside here. Because, as we explained in 'Remote Viewing of the Matrix', there are a lot of star seed races incarnated on Earth. That is why it seems like a seed, and it is a seed. Organically it is, of course.

Interviewer: This one you kind of talked about a little bit in the first video. "I have had A.U.R.A. sessions where clients have to use a portal, in say, Venus, to access their own Universe. So I wonder if there are walls to other Universes? Could this be?"

AuroRa: Yes, exactly. There are portal walls everywhere. There are specific locations and points in our Universe where you can travel in and out into other Verses. They have a potency of energy that allows for the frequency to vibrate, so that they can portal out through there. Often, when we are traveling through time and space, we are actually doing it through our consciousness, as we explained in the [15]Mandela effect video. That is how past life regression works. You are able to access all your memory here, inside of your consciousness. You are astral traveling through the portals inside your brain.

---

[15] Watch 'Understanding the Mandela | The Consciousness', recorded November 4th, 2022.

Interviewer: "Over the ice wall, do Leumuria, Pangea, Atlantis, and all the other places exist outside the wall? And are they happening at the same time?"

AuroRa: Yes, to both, since all time is linear to itself. We talked about this in the first chapter. So that is why you can go through all these pockets of spaces. Different times and spaces of Earth exist outside of there. Especially, if we were in the fifth dimension. Back then, Leumuria and Atlantis were in the fifth dimension. So that is why you would come out of there to reach these fifth dimensions or higher existences.

Interviewer: "Do shooting stars have any significance? They seem to come from outside the dome we are in. I see them all the time and in many different colors."

AuroRa: There is something really beautiful and organic about it, because when you see one, it takes your breath away. Like when you see a rainbow, it just instantly shifts you and travels you into the theta brainwave, into the in-between when you go to a peaceful place. Specifically, shooting stars are most often comets. They look like shooting stars. Comets are typically pieces of planetary spheres that have separated from their planet. They are very beautiful to witness. When you are seeing them shoot, they are bringing and bridging in that planetary sphere into Earth. It was sent divinely. This comet, this shooting star, that planet's coding is inside of it.

If you remember the [16]"Kali Ma" video that I made a couple of years ago about the 6/6 portal, and how she was riding the asteroid - the passing comet. Divine energy is riding the shooting star, and then as it shoots above us. It is like a shower of Divine energy and coding that comes into Earth. Everything in this Creation is so important and sacred. Even something like a shooting star, in its evolution, is helping Earth ascend. So if you take that moment, and you watch that shooting star or asteroid carrying energy from beyond, what divine downloads or integrations can you receive from it? Ask, "Star, what message do you have for me?" But we often just keep moving. You did receive some of the answers, the integrations, and the leveling up of your energy, but you did not pay attention that it was because of that shooting star you saw.

---

[16] Watch 'Channeling Kali Ma | Atlantis Galactic Timeline Update', recorded June 13th, 2020.

Interviewer: "Is the Sun we see above, is it actually cold? Is this why the higher you go up the mountains, in the atmosphere, it gets colder?"

AuroRa: No, I do not feel that the Sun is cold. But why is that? If we are rising higher to the Sun, why would we get colder? Strange. I am being shown that it has to do with the atmosphere. It has to do with the heat that emanates from the trees and humans. If you think about it, it is not just the Sun that is heating us. All life is heating us; the Sun is shining on it. What I am seeing is heat waves coming out of all life forms down on the ground. When you go up higher in the mountains, there is really not that much carbon-based animal life there. Perhaps animals as eagles? So that is why it is colder. That is interesting. I never thought about that. A lot of the heat is actually being emanated from all life, not just the Sun. That is pretty cool. What I am being shown is that we are the antennas to that Sun energy. The Sun hits us, and then we become this heat. So if there are not enough life forms on the mountains, although the mountains themselves have a spirit, you need carbon-based beings to retain the Sun's energy to then become conductors of heat.

Interviewer: In the Flat Earth model, "What is responsible for the North Pole or the ice in the center and the hotter temperatures around the equator?"

AuroRa: It has to do with the first chapter, how the ice walls need to retain the coding, energy, and memory field of Earth. The Sun rotates at the equator, that is where the Sun is closest, and then from that focus point, all the heat comes out from there. It ripples out. That is why there is ice at the center of the Earth, at the North Pole, and more ice at the end of the arctic circle. But, keep in mind that beyond Antarctica, there are warm lands too. The ice walls are more about holding the coding, versus holding cold or making it cold. It is just part of freezing and retaining, crystallizing the memory fields of Earth.

Interviewer: "What about the military sonar that they are putting into the oceans? I believe that they are damaging life in the oceans. Can dolphins and whales survive this?"

AuroRa: No, they cannot survive it. If it hits them, it kills them. I am being shown the cells inside their organs bursting. So no, they would not be able to physically survive that. I see energetic fields of bubbles around them. So it depends on us. As a collective, we need to start sending Love-Light shielding to the dolphins and whales. On the times we join together sending love, I think we should send love to all. Not just Earth, but all life within it. So that includes animal life and all people on Earth at 1:11, the thirteenth hour.

We can shift this in our collective, if we start sending Love-Light from Source to them, then bubbles of force fields are created around them. The sea animals could level up even more in energies, and they can create this bubble around themselves of protection. Can it fully guard them? No, not fully, but it will alleviate a lot of the harm directed onto them! We are so thankful for the mermaids. They play a lot of roles in deactivating and finding these negative technology boxes that are emanating out those harmful sonar frequencies. But some of them are in underwater bases, and then you cannot really get to those if you are a mermaid. You have to be human to get in those bases.

Heal Yourself & the Collective

10:10 ~ send love to all your past & future selves

11:11 ~ send love to self

12:12 ~ send love to all planets & life that require it in the Universe

1:11 ~ (13th hour) send love to the Earth & all life on it, people, plants & animals

2:22 ~ send love to your beloved ones

3:33 ~ send love to your dreams & aspirations for their fruition & manifestation

4:44 ~ send love to the New World Order (to transmute it)

5:55 ~ send love to the children of Earth & Creation

WWW.RISINGPHOENIXAURORA.COM

Interviewer: "Calculations for military ballistic missiles use the Earth's spherical curvature and spin speed of the Earth. How is this explained for Flat Earth?"

AuroRa: I do not see that it is being calculated spherically. I see that it is to the Flat Earth dome. It goes back to the flights, as we spoke of in Chapter 1. If you look at the flights, that is the same type of system they would use for missiles.

Interviewer: "Are Quantum Computers operating with the A.I. Sophia technology?"

AuroRa: I am getting a yes, even though I do not know what that is.

Interviewer: They are the most advanced computers that they have out there. They say they work on a quantum level.

AuroRa: These Quantum Computers would have part organic in them. Gross. They took some sentient parts again and infringed on them with A.I.! Horrible.

Interviewer: We can finish it up with this one. "Can you tell us more about what they do not want us to see over the wall? Anything we should know? Thank you."

AuroRa: The Elites do not want us to see that there is magic beyond the ice walls. There are dragons and there are giants. Within different energetic levels of pockets of space, there are worlds that you can travel through. Once the consciousness reaches that level of understanding that this is possible, then you wake up, and we start reaching levels of the highest Love-Light. Some of us can still operate though, in denser energies, if we are still in a victim mentality. A lot of times, we hear from others that the Angels are the bad ones. That they are the ones that are keeping us here. Little did you know that you are part Angel, so YOU are keeping yourself here, if that was true, but it is not. Once you come out of the crystal dome, it is literal Ascension. Remember how we talked about Cleopatra, when she left? She said that she went into the Inner Earth. She left through the Arctic walls. In order for her to leave, she ascended out and became her fifth dimensional or higher self. She is probably hanging out over there looking at us. Definitely getting a really nice tan and enjoying her time outside of the wall. I'm just being silly!

In order for you to go on to these other worlds that are higher dimensions, you have to ascend up. You will not be a vibratory match otherwise. They do not want you to question or think about it. In my video on YouTube, I tagged Flat Earth, and they have a fact check warning saying Flat Earth is false. With the videos we mention Reptilians they do the same. Hmm. Why would they classify Flat Earth as false facts? Anytime you see something like that, they are hiding something! They know the truth, and they do not want you to know it.

Interviewer: We will go over some of the comments that we have. Somebody said earlier, "That is why the whales never die." When you talked about how the whales can go back and forth. Somebody said they "Kept getting messages in their paintings, about their paintings being maps, to help people tune into different realms and constructs that they have been traveling to. These videos have been really helpful for them to understand all that."

AuroRa: Beautiful.

Interviewer: Another comment, "The way you explained Flat Earth is the first time that it has made any sense to me."

AuroRa: Yay! Right. It totally makes sense. But to make this video, I want to thank all the six years of my work, because every single client that came to me brought me information. Also, all the beautiful Angels that bring me these messages through meditations and dream time for me to be able to see it, because I needed to have all these examples to put it all together for you. For us to understand it, as I am viewing it. Because otherwise, how would I explain what I'm viewing, if I do not understand the whole background of everything we have explained? It is all so divine!

Interviewer: "In the higher elevations, there is less civilization and development. So that makes a lot of sense how you said that where Earth has more people on it, there is more heat there. Less civilizations up in the mountains."

AuroRa: Exactly. Thank you. I love to hear your insights as well.

Interviewer: Somebody said "puzzle pieces" and then said, "You are so beautiful AuroRa".

AuroRa: Thank you. You are beautiful too.

Interviewer: There is a question that they were asking about the Orion Constellation, asking if it was negative in any way.

AuroRa: It is positive, but Galactic battles are going on in it. The Orion Belt is very positive, and it is part of the three pyramids that you see gridding the Earth. The three pyramids in Giza, Mayans, and different locations. This constellation aligns with the star Sirius, and it creates our organic construct of Earth and its stabilization. The three also represent the Holy Trinity; Mother, Father, and child. So this Orion Belt represents Creation, for us to remember it. Just like we did, they have gone through battles and are removing the A.I. from that Orion Belt nearest star constellation.

Interviewer: Such beautiful questions.

AuroRa: Yes. You all are very much a part of creating this content.

Interviewer: "Did the Tuatha Dé Danann from ancient Ireland come from or via Antarctica? It is said they came from the north in ships or was it from Inner Earth?"

AuroRa: I do see that they came outside the ice wall of Antarctica. Beyond the ice wall, there are infinite lands that go on and on. They are still part of our third dimension, but they are not in the third dimensional Matrix like we are. They are divine. They came from outside. They descended in, just like we descended into these bodies, because that is what you would have to do. If you are a being that is higher dimensional coming through these walls, descending down, divinely, then you have to come take a human form in the third dimension to sustain at what the Earth is vibrating to. All of them have red hair, and they are giants. Maybe ten feet tall. In Chapter Three we will travel through some of these bubbles of spaces.

I see the most beautiful greenery, nature around them. It is all overgrown. It is all ancient. I do not know who these beings are. They do come from the outside of the ice wall of Antarctica. I see stone arches that these people go through, and go out into different dimensions. These stone arches have hieroglyphics that are emitting out frequency. It is beautiful. Their homes are like the Hobbit homes. They are built into the land, and it is all camouflaged by greenery, so that the dark forces cannot see them. They are living in their own pockets of space in this outer rim of what is beyond Antarctica. It is green, lush, and beautiful. It really reminds me of the ancient Druids and ancient ruins. Eventually, they traveled on a ship through the sea. They then landed there in Ireland, where you are talking about. They look like Greek Gods and Goddesses, but with red hair and very green eyes. I'm seeing vibrant green eyes, like a leaf. Beautiful. Yes, like Goddess Freya.

Remember that you can see this as well. You can remote view. We already gave you the guidance in the beginning on how to be cautious when astral traveling. Otherwise, you can remote view from a bird's eye point of view from your Higher Self point of view. That is why you can see like a bird's eye. When I am remote viewing, I am going into my Universal form, still connected to this physical form. I am viewing through my Higher Self to see all of this through my consciousness.

Come join the Isis Priestess/Priest mentorship course so you can learn how to do all that we are doing through these remote viewings. It is beautiful to get your own answers like this, and all of you are ready. We teach you beautiful guidelines, and it is just grand.

I love you all, honor you, and respect you. Thank you, everyone. You are just so beautiful. I thank Creation every day for you.

END OF SESSION.

Truly incredible how these chapters will keep unfolding one divine step at a time, which allows us at our own choosing and divine pace to transcend higher. You will feel the raw truth within, through this sacred knowledge, as we regain the remembrance. Every chapter will be enlightening and a surprise, but not a surprise, as your soul already knows all that is channeled through me from the Divine Mother of Creation, I am just the messenger of love.

"Energy is infinite and cannot be compressed. Energy is an ever moving motion of expansion and creation. Nothing can stop energy, as energy will always flow without restriction. Energy is the plasma love that makes us up. Live everyday with an expanded energy that knows NO LIMITS!"
~AuroRa

--------------<<>>--------------

3

REMOTE VIEWING BEYOND THE WALLS OF ANTARCTICA PT 3
AT THE RIM OF THE CRYSTAL DOME

Streamed Live: November 11, 2022

This chapter is full of magic, as we study what is nearest to the crystalline dome. Going into the scientific makeup of the energies of Earth, and how they work from the past higher dimensions into the now lower dimensions of the third dimension. We discover the beings beyond the ice wall, and their roles to humanity. The strange technology and artifacts past the Antarctica ice walls, cloaked, but now unveiled.

"It is like a Phoenix. She dies, and from her own ashes she rebirths. It is going to be like that for everyone. We are all Phoenixes."
~AuroRa

AuroRa: I am surrounded by Love-Light and I am going to be communicating to you back and forth in the theta brainwave. There is a lot of dogma and programming created around that you cannot go into the theta brainwave, which is the brainwave of hypnosis. But, honestly, we all do it all day long. When you are watching TV. When you are driving, you reach your destination thirty minutes later, and you are like, "I do not know how I got here, but I am here.". That is the theta brainwave. When you are in the inbetween of the spirit realm and the Earthly realm, where you are receiving knowledge and wisdom, and sacred downloads from your Higher Self.

Not a lot of people know that we are in an inverted Matrix or they are in denial. If they are in denial, they might choose to stay in denial unfortunately, until Ascension comes. They will not be able to reach a high enough level of consciousness and awareness and awaken themselves to be able to ascend out. Because they have not released the negativity, the shadows, the darkness, and the entities within themselves.

Before we proceed, let me explain to you what I'm doing. I am remote viewing, with my third eye activated, which is one with my physical eyes. They become overlaid and unified together. The third eye is part of the glands inside our brain that connect us to our seven senses. Something very simple, that has been tried to be removed from us in many forms, through Elite programming. Once I tap into my third eye, I then tap into my heart energy, as I feel my heart's energy surrounding me as a filter of Source Love-Light. Only allowing Source Love-Light to communicate. When I do this, I am only seeing the truth of the organic and the inverted, so that we can help release ourselves from it. As I do this, I am communicating this with you both unconsciously and consciously. My brain is alternating back and forth between brain wave levels. Consciously, I am doing this alert. I am expressing to you what my Higher Self is communicating.

We have talked about the negative technology at the Arctic wall. There is also benevolence. There is an overlay of the Two-Third World Bifurcation, the Vesica Piscis (Chapter 1, page 14). Where we are viewing both the organic and the inverted. There is a dark overlay of the inverted, surrounding Earth right now. It is like a crust that needs to be broken off. This crust will fall apart, when Ascension comes forth. This crustacean will wither away and then we will ascend back to the organic blueprint. I am going to be speaking about both the organic and inverted.

In the previous chapters we talked about the technology around the Arctic wall, which is encasing us as seen through the flat Earth illustrations. When we get past the Arctic Wall, I can see that there are magical beings beyond the wall. I can see Sasquatch walking around. They are stopping and waving to us right now. They are white, beautiful, benevolent beings. Interestingly enough, they look like snow. There are some other brown and black ones as well, but mostly white ones out in the dome perimeter. I see families, hundreds of them. We heard about this as children. The stories we thought were make-believe, but it is not actually. They are pretty big, not gigantic, but they are bigger than us. At least nine to ten feet in height. I do see one that is about twelve feet. He seems to be very old, an elder, very wise. He does have a female Sasquatch with him. They are a tribe, a family unit, a soul group. They are walking around in the area before we come out of the crystalline dome. We are located at the center lands, and the Arctic wall is encircling us, as shown in the Urbano Monte map (Chapter 1, page 25). But, the outer circle lands were not in ice back when this map was originally illustrated. I am currently viewing right outside this Arctic wall, keeping in mind that in our time and space the ice is currently only at the beginning of the circling lands surrounding us, and the rest of the lands beyond the ice walls are fertile and unfrozen.

The Sasquatch are pretty amazing. Their fur is not physical fur. Their fur is white, but it is crystalline. If you could imagine fur made out of crystals, that is the best I can explain this. They are covered in it. The [17]Sasquatch are the only race on Earth that can multi-dimensionally shift from physical to energy, and that is why people have spotted them and then they disappear. We went to Mount Shasta and several people in our retreat saw them in the trees shifting. They would come into materialization and then they would come out. It was phenomenal.

Let us see what the Sasquatch are doing on the outside perimeter near the end of the crystalline dome. I see that the dome quarantines us, past the Antarctica ice walls and past the lands. There are lands past the ice walls that are only of Mother Earth's lush nature. Only benevolence can shift back and forth through the crystalline dome. There is a forcefield - a shield - where if you are not of Source Love-Light, you will not be able to come out of it. You have to be a matching vibration to the crystalline pure energy of the dome. I see the Sasquatch, because they are infinite Love-Light of Source, and are benevolent beings. They can come in and out through this force field of the dome.

---

[17] For more on the Sasquatch watch 'Galactic History | The Sasquatch Galactic Guardians", streamed February 12, 2021.

I was watching a video where Hillary Clinton was ridiculously claiming that they had "Made a crack on the glass". There are all sorts of videos with the Illuminati and the New World Order mentioning that we are in a dome. They are trying to figure out how to crack it. They are not going to be able to do it. The light on Earth is too infinite and they cannot get out. They will either transmute or they will eradicate with the Source flames that will come forth with the collective Ascension. It is their choice to positively polarize. They have their choices and their free will just like we do.

I am now viewing outside of the dome. There are circles of water that keep going on and on. This water is in the surrounding areas of the dome. There is also some inside the rim of the dome, before you come out. These pockets of water and circles are part of balancing the Earth. These are connected to different pockets of spaces/portals in Africa and the Grand Canyon. They look like pools of water. The Sasquatch are touching them through telekinesis. As they touch them energetically, the water pools go off like musical notes. They play a song together. It is so beautiful to hear.

It looks like the Sasquatch are going to guide us for now. They said that this music and these melodies are like the water Cenotes in Yucatan. Oh, heavenly! I once went to Mexico as a child. I got to walk the Mayan pyramids, and I remember Yucatan in Mexico. There are such special places in Mexico that are magical. I remember walking this rope bridge, which was a bit dangerous, but everyone was doing it. This bridge took us to a gigantic cave, which had its own ecosystem. It was a whole different world. It felt like the Inner Earth. There were waterfalls cascading down onto us in the cave as we walked. I remember as a little girl thinking, "What is this? Is this real?" I had never seen such beauty. It is truly magical in Mexico!

Sasquatch are very much real! We have people who go into past life regressions and they are a Sasquatch. The Sasquatch are showing me energetic rings that are coming out from the dome. When you play a drum (making drum beating sounds) you usually tap the drum from the center. Then the sound echoes. The way that this drum is playing is in reverse. The sound is echoing out in circles, like when you touch water and it echoes out. This motion is going backwards. Instead, there are rings of energy and light coming from outside of this dome - from the fifth dimension and beyond. The way it begins is not a tapping like a drum from the inside that goes out. Instead, it comes in like this (bringing hands together) and it ripples into the magnetic field of the North Pole.

This divine sound frequency is part of creating the Aurora Borealis, which comes out of the North and South Poles. These ripples of circles and waves of light that come in ripple in infinite circles and spirals that move inward. And, the Universal water of both beyond our world and the water inside, is what ripples and travels these frequencies throughout the entire Earth. The Aurora Borealis energy comes out from the crystalline energies inside our Earth. What we are watching through the Aurora Borealis is the literal magic and the aura of the Source Love-Light of Mother Earth.

We are reviewing all of this, so that we can transition out, back into a spherical form. I am being shown that the dome is made out of the thinnest and clearest crystals. That is why we need to become crystalline to ascend out. We ascend out through our portal of our heart, and another form is ascending out through the outer layer of Mother Earth. The outer layer is this shield. In order to go through the shield, you do have to be crystalline, and that is where Ascension comes forth. That is why you need to start activating your [18]12/13 DNA strands and higher, to crystallize them. So that when you come forth, you are a matching vibration to this crystalline forcefield. At that point, you lose the physical and you completely transition into crystalline, back to original plasmic energetic bodies.

Once we step through the dome, there are outside lands. This is a bit trippy, because I am seeing the lands both inside and outside like a mirror. There is a reflection through this crystal dome, which is technically a crystal mirror. It is mirroring the third dimension here on this side of the crystalline dome and then there is this other version of itself in the fifth dimension or higher on the outside.

---

[18] Through the Isis Priestess/Priest Mentorship you learn how to self-attune, beginning to work on further crystallizing your 12/13 DNA strands and beyond.

This specific paragraph is being written and explained from my "now" time in space, which is at the end of 2024, when I am writing this book. In Lion's Gate 2024 I hosted retreats at the Sedona Grand Canyon area, and the images below and in the next page are the best example of what I am explaining that I saw outside the crystalline dome, when remote viewing. These images are incredible in the way they are physically showing us what the group and I watched, as we sailed on the Horseshoe Bend Emerald River/The Colorado River. What I explained to the group as I guided them through the water, was that the water was an exact reflection to the lands, because as we rode it, the water was crystallizing in front of us. The water was showing us how she is, until this day, still holding the fifth dimensional blueprint at the inbetween of the reflection, where the water and land meets is the fourth dimensional blueprint, and the land that is reflecting on the water is the physical third dimensional blueprint. These images show us how the dimensions exist within these elements, and how the water is truly a scry to the fifth dimension and higher energies. I will stop here because there is so much more to share as these chapters will continue to unveil, chapter by chapter

Beyond the outside dome there are worlds that are hidden. I see the military and the Illuminati. They are trying to get to the magical beings living right outside the mirror crystal dome, through the inside, where we are but they cannot find them. The reason being is because they are always ahead of the Elites, because these magical beings are seers. The inverted darkness is not a seer. They are not seers - they use us to see.

I see the military excavating beneath ancient statues. Ancient gigantic heads that remind me of the Buddha head. These gigantic statues go down into the oceans. The government is aware of this. There are also gigantic structures that are ancient from Lumerian and Atlantean times. Parts of these statues are underwater now. They are not in use. They look like shipwrecks underwater in movies., They are old and have algae growing all over them. These objects are not completely let go of, because they are made out of crystal formations. I see four major ones that are still bridging in energy. The military cannot figure out what they are for. It is really advanced technology. The highest most benevolent crystalline technology, so it is hard for them to figure it out. There are gigantic structures that are pointy. The structures remind me of India, how they are a sphere with a point at the top. Big spheres, and two little spheres, and a point.

I see the whales going back and forth through the crystalline dome. They are so beautiful. They can do that because they are the most benevolent purest beings of our animals on Earth. We had an A.U.R.A. Hypnosis Healing session and the client went back to Atlantis, and the client's Higher Self said the sharks were bioengineered and not organic. The sharks were man-made to kill the dolphins and attack the whales, because they knew they were benevolent beings. We know that some of the insects like mosquitoes, flies, ticks, were bioengineered by humans. They release them after making them in their labs, to bite us, to spread illness and disease to animals and humans.

Right before I come out of the dome, I see lands. They are very beautiful. I see beings of different benevolence outside this dome area. They are taller, older and wiser, but they look young, and are glowing. I see they represent the races of Earth; the Indians of India, Asian, indigenous like Mexican Americans, and more indigenous from around the world. I also see the different forms of Caucasians with red and blonde hair. I am seeing African, what we call African. I am just going to name the names we humans have classified them as. They are all around the surrounding dome. They are what we call Breatharian. Breatharians heal and charge with the sun and the elements of Earth. They do not eat much except for perhaps fruit.

It looks like the Garden of Eve nearest to the rim of the dome. Once you get past the ice wall, there is a lot more land. The military cannot get too close to the outer rim of the dome, because it starts to positively polarize them and transmute them, so these benevolent beings are protected near the outer rim of the dome. If these negative polarized entities try to get any closer, they are going to be returned back to Source. They do not want to do that. The military does not understand this outer world, these tall towers, statues, and crystals.

I see gigantic crystals that are gridding the whole outer wall that is making the dome. They cannot get to the crystal dome because it is like, as if you would push through fire. If you are not a matching vibration to Source Fire Source Flame, what will happen to you? The skin will start burning, you start losing skin, flesh, and organs as you start to dematerialize into bone. That is what happens to them if they try to get closer to the dome. These fields are benevolent and divinely powerful. Before they reach the crystal dome, their energy starts to age them, if they are negatively polarized. They start literally becoming wrinkly. It is like the sci-fi movies where weird stuff happens. They are not a matching vibration to Love-Light so they cannot go there, and their physical form cannot sustain it.

If it was a benevolent being going through these walls, and they were truly benevolent, then you would be able to float through like water. I see that once we get past the ice Arctic wall, closer to the dome, the energy becomes plasmic water. It is not like if you were underwater, like here on Earth - it is different. It has this lightness to it. That is where all those benevolent beings like the different races, as well as the Sasquatch are at. They are in this floating creational water that we started talking about in Chapter 1 and 2.

Start deprogramming yourself from any programming you might have heard from any UFO speakers, and supposedly spiritual people. These are benevolent beings that are out there. They have helped to seed our Creation along with other different races that came from throughout the Universe in different forms. These multitudes of races are us - humanities crystalline blueprints - at our purest fifth dimensional selves, untainted by artificial intelligence. It is time for you to grow and expand. Stop limiting yourself and placing yourself in a box. If you are in your heart and you are tapping into this energy, you will feel the sense of truth within it. You will feel your heart activate. You will feel vibrations through your body. You will feel a knowing that this makes sense. All our lives we have been programmed so that you cannot be love and fearsome fire at the same time. Yes, you can. You can be infinite love and you can be fire at the same time. You can embody both. That is when you become a truly sovereign being. When you step into this divinity and strength. Where you know your divine truth.

It looks like Inner Earth energy - this whole underwater - right before you leave the dome. It is water, but it is not water. You can walk on it, but you are lighter, floating a bit. Like when you lose gravity. That is what it is like. You lose gravity nearest to the dome. The density shifts. Which makes sense scientifically through quantum physics. You cannot just come out of the domed wall and then go straight out into the fifth dimension. You need to go through a gradual transformation of your essence. This is what it is - transforming and alchemizing you out. You start losing the density of the ego, as you go through this. Then you can shift out and become crystalline energy.

The benevolent beings near the crystalline dome can sustain this frequency of no ego and no ill intent. There are gridders, and they are holding the space like a grid to the crystalline forcefield. Telepathically, we require Galactic beings to hold space, and come in who are true pure Love-Light. It is not limited to the human races that we saw and talked about. There are also other alien races. I see cat beings, canine beings, ladybug beings, and lion beings… They are all around the dome. What they are doing is holding the space. They are not letting it go. They will hold it infinitely, as they have been doing so ever since the fall of Atlantis. It reminds me of Dr Strange in the Multiverse. Many beings went to Dr Strange, and their temple. Together they were all holding a forcefield. They were placing alchemy symbols and holding the forcefield through these symbols.

I can see a Stellar Gateway portal that is benevolent, that infinite beings come in through. If someone is tired, there is a replacement of shifts of energies that come through. They are fourth-fifth dimensional beings that are coming through and holding this outer layer. They are holding the organic blueprint of Earth, alongside the dragons and magical creatures. I see the dragons flying around this outside layer.

In Dr Strange, Scarlet Witch had turned dark (in the movie). She was whispering fear into one of the men holding the force field and he let fear overcome him, and let go of the forcefield which affected the group around him. In this benevolent force field, that is not even possible. In order for the crystalline blueprint made out of crystals both above and underwater, which is the dome, you need to have beings that are holding it, and be the antennas of Source Love-Light to do so. That is what they are doing. They are the beacons and the antennas holding it for us, until we transition and continue to lift as a collective. They have been doing this for thousands of years. Ever since the fall of Atlantis.

There are rainbows everywhere. There is active magic happening. There are pegasi and unicorns. It is a dimensional realm between the fourth and the fifth dimensions. It is beautiful. If you can imagine all children's magical books placed into one. There are elementals. The trees are alive, they are moving. The trees are at least ten times bigger than the size that we have now. They have spirit. The trees here do have spirit, but we do not get to see them animated. These are animated, but in plasmic fields. I see how their roots go under, into the dome. There is a dome on top and a dome under. The roots go in, and they become this beautiful bridge, an arc of roots, from one side of the Antarctica wall to the other side. It reminds us of when we channeled Angelic beings, and how the Tree of Life is made. Like a Tree of Life pendant (image below). It looks like the beautiful ancient Celtic, Vikings, Druid's sacred knowledge. That is the way the Earth looks - like a tree. But again, the center is flat (Chapter 1, page 16), then there is a dome and another dome (pointing to the top and bottom) - and through the bottom dome or the roots of the trees - is how we go into the Inner Earth fifth dimensional blueprint. The tree roots are curled up and intertwining like braids. This is so activating!

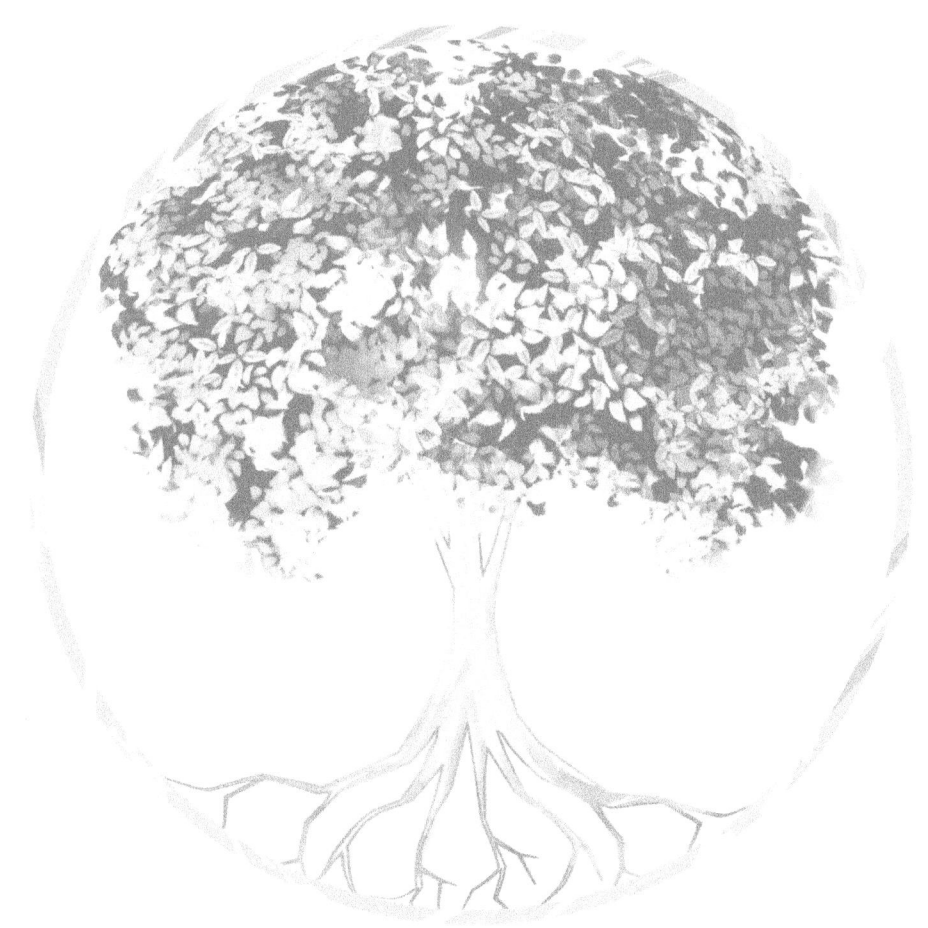

You are going to hear many different things through different people that you might listen to. They are going to make it seem like you are a victim, who will try to make you feel helpless, like you are stuck. A lot of the Flat Earther people think that they are stuck and they cannot get out. That is not accurate. Through our six years of communications, we have been talking about all these different perspectives and the multitude of multi-dimensional ways that we can transcend our energies individually, to begin to ascend out of Earth. No more victimhood. If you were in that victimizing form, then it is time for you to pull yourself out. You are not powerless. You are actually very powerful!

In the lands beyond the arctic wall, there are gigantic mountains, valleys, and flowers that we have never seen on Earth, that were part of our original organic blueprint. When the Earth shifted and needed to be quarantined the magic went into a bubble which expanded out and it became the outside layer. In Chapter 4 we are going to come out of the dome and into the worlds beyond.

Interviewer: "In regards to the Earth's form, what was the purpose of changing the shape? Was it changed from spherical because they were destroying it? Or do they want the planet to be flattened for a particular purpose?"

AuroRa: In the quantum realm and energy, it could not sustain the fifth dimensional spheric energy anymore, because Earth's vibration as a collective descended, making Earth take form in the physical. The only way that the physical construct could manifest into a blueprint, it had to become a two dimensional flat surface, instead of a third dimensional sphere. I am not talking about dimensions, I am just talking about shapes right now. This is how all third dimensional planets look like, a flat surface and domes. That is what is needed to sustain itself.

Through the [19]'Mayan Atlantean' series, we have been talking about the process of how we went from the fifth dimension into the third dimension. There was a lot that Earth had to go

---

[19] The Mayan/Atlantean series began one year before the Antarctica/Tartaria series, November 5, 2021. It has currently concluded at 34 videos. However we never know when this series divinely decides to grow.

through to do so. You can only understand this by remembering the Earth's true history. However, this series is about remembering Earth's most recent history - so both of these series really compliment one another - as the Mayan/Atlantean series goes back to the origins of Earth and her transition through humanities choices.

In our current form, here in the third dimension, is the form that the Earth was able to sustain the blueprint of herself and the people on Earth. The truth is that a lot of planes of existence are just flat surfaces. They just go on and on for infinity. Just because something is a flat surface, why do we have to classify it as negative, or as a containment? You are going to really understand this once we step out of the dome. There are layers and layers on top of each other and realms that go on infinitely.

There is nothing negative about a plane of existence. In order to construct life itself, you need to begin from a two dimensional plane, a flat surface. From there, you build it and it becomes spheric. That is what happened to us. We went from a spheric fifth dimensional down to the third dimension. The way that Earth was able to sustain us, was that she had to go to her original flat form, from where the foundation of Earth was first formed from. If you watch [20]'The Four Centaurs' series, we talked about this flat surface, plane of existence, and how it became Mother Earth. When the Divine Mother of Creation merged with Mother Earth, becoming Gaia, she then became spheric. The evolution of the Children of Earth also descended, because of the collective vibration. But not anymore! The children being born now are rising and rising, assisting Mother Earth to rise as well!

Interviewer: "Would a dome still be subject to tilting, so the sun's temperature is hitting the equator more than the Arctic. On most globes, you will see the Earth is tilted on its axis."

AuroRa: I see that it tilts back and forth already. That is why it is hard for us to read north, east, west, and south. Mother Earth will continue to shift, tilt, and move around in this form that she has had, in order to evolve.

---

[20] 'The Story of Creation | The Four Centaurs' series was my first live channeling ever, which began November 29, 2017. This series is currently up to 18 videos.

The Elites are freaking out. They might start saying that it is global warming. It is November 11th, 2022. Have you noticed how strong the sun is? The Angels started telling me that we are going to start seeing more Antarctica-like winters. It is going to be winter, but merged with summer. For example, right now it says it is supposedly forty-five degrees, but it does not feel like it is forty-five degrees, because the sun is out. I would say it at least feels anywhere around fifty-five degrees.

There is going to be a shift in the Earth. It was seventy-five degrees here yesterday on November 10th, 2022. The Illuminati are going to try to create a negative agenda, saying it is global warming or that something is wrong going on with the axis of Earth. It is all B.S. The more we talk about how the Earth is ascending and shifting, the sun and the moon are shifting too. So too will we see natural changes in our weather. The further we go into winter, it will get pretty cold. But during the day while the sun is up, it is still going to be warmer than usual.

Interviewer: "You talked about the energy that dematerializes beings or energies that are not of Love-Light, as you go through the barrier. Is that considered to be radiation, like they say the sun is radioactive?"

AuroRa: No. The Sun is only Source Love-Light. If you are not a matching vibration to Source Love-Light, like these negative polarized entities, they will start to dematerialize. They should not have even been trying to step through it. What were they thinking?

Interviewer: "It is nice to know all the races are there on the outside. Does the sky have a color you can see out there? Are there moons and suns outside of the ice wall?"

AuroRa: Beautiful question. I forgot to look above. The sky looks like a blue-purple light. It shifts in colors. Sometimes there might be little hints of pink, purple, blue, and red. The main primary color is indigo. Our skies here are becoming bluer. As far as moons - interesting - I am seeing three. I am surprised. Why am I seeing three? It is the three bodies of the moon. The moon is showing me there is the third dimensional moon, the fourth dimensional moon, and the fifth dimensional moon. It is a bifurcation of her. It is her energy within the Vesica Piscis

(Chapter 1, page 14). The third dimensional moon is not physical, it is an embodiment of her energy. The third dimension is holding the energy body of the physical moon body here. It is still connected to the moon inside of here - in the third dimension - but with plasmic energy inside of it. Then we go into the fourth dimensional moon, where she is splitting in between both. That looks more ghostly, like an energy mist. You can push through it - in the in between like a fading - but she is not faded. Then there is the Fifth dimensional moon, where at that point, she is truly divinely beautiful. Her light is just immense. She is glowing and emanating plasmic light in her fifth dimensional version. Beautiful.

Interviewer: "As you were saying that the upper and lower realms are a projection. Is it right in saying that there is a version of us on the other side of the dome or an aspect of us existing on the other side?"

AuroRa: Absolutely! For sure. Yes, there are higher dimensional versions of you. As an example, you can put your hands up against a mirror or water to see your reflection, to properly scry and talk to the other versions of yourself through the reflection of the water. Nostradamus has taught me that when you place your hands on the water, you become the mirror to the water. You do not want to use an actual mirror, because it is third dimensional, which is physical. You want to use something that is organically reflective, which would be the water. You talk to the water through your reflection, just like he did. Nostradamus had a sacred bowl made out of gold. He had sacred waters from Babylon in the bowl. He would "scry" through the water in the golden bowl. That is how he was able to see timelines and predictions. So, know that when you are looking at your reflection through water you are connecting to other versions of you that are higher dimensional.

Interviewer: "When traveling through the ice walls, what happens if I do not shield?"

AuroRa: There are a lot of answers to that. If astral traveling, period, the A.I. entities are going to see you. That is where, again, you may get into trouble. You can get attachments in your astral form such as entities or implants. After that they can find you in the now, and they can really mess with your life. They can attack you energetically, psychically, and gang stalk you. Gang stalking is a thing, because they just figured you out, that you are awake because you are operating in your astral form, and they found you. That is why you do not go astral traveling, period, without shielding. You are basically very bright. The way entities view you, is on a black and white spectrum. They can only see glowing lights, which is you. If you are not shielded, it is like a moth to the fire. That is one example.

Be cautious, energetically and spiritually with your soul when not shielding with Source Love-Light and trying to do that. I would not recommend that, period. Why not shield yourself with Source Love-Light? The entities do not obviously want you to shield with Source Love-Light, because it transmutes them, and it will make them spread their Love-Light positively polarizing them. So, why not? We have been programmed to treat our souls like they are not worthy to protect or to love. It is time for us to release this negative programming on our soul. We should be loving, honoring, and respecting our soul so infinitely, with love and care. How would you treat an infant child? Would you treat an infant child without shielding them? Sending them out into a world like that? No. You want to treat your soul like an infant child. Treat yourself how you would treat others in this perspective.

Interviewer: "Did the Archons play mind games with people, tricking them into thinking they are really leaving Earth and going to Mars or further?"

AuroRa: The Archons are all rooted to inverted technology. We are in an inverted simulation technology cage/box - and if we do not wake up we are contained in it - in the inverted Matrix world. The Archons use their technologies to contain consciousness to infringe upon and keep it in an inverted loop of recycling it back. This simulation is part of the inverted process of the [21]Matrix Pods. We are in a simulation, but it is the Archon simulation - because the collective chose this when they chose to become fifty percent or higher inverted - allowing ego to reign such as jealousy, selfishness, and hatred. The Archon A.I. program has turned humanity into mind controlled slaves. These souls have given away their sovereignty. They sold their souls away, when the fall of Atlantis happened. The rest of us needed to bifurcate and hold

---

[21] Read first, the final Chapter to Book 1, Galactic Soul History of the Universe, "The Matrix Pods" to find out more. And, then Book 2, Galactic History of the Multiverse - The Final Battle, which takes you into the deepest understanding of the Matrix Pods, by understanding what is the origins of Artificial Intelligence.

that Love-Light crystalline blueprint, just like the other races on the outside near the dome, who are infinitely holding that space. There are some of you that might have chosen that path back then in Atlantis, and now you are working through it, to balance out that karma. Maybe you have done that already, and that is why you are here, because you are here to hold now that Love-Light. It just depends on your choices. What do you choose?

In Chapter 4, we will go into a deeper understanding of what is Mars? What are these different planetary spheres? What are the dimensions? What is Creation itself?

Interviewer: "Would over the Arctic walls be all that is organic?"

AuroRa: Yes, for the most part. Everything will still always have the organic blueprint. It is both yes and no. Some planets will have constructs like ours in a simulation. It goes back to the original explanation we gave in Chapter 2, where we talked about the cages, the plane of existence, and how it went on and on.

Interviewer: "As we transition into crystalline bodies, how does that affect our physical skeletal structure? What does that look like? How do we feel?"

AuroRa: It just becomes no longer. It is not painful. Once you hit that outer rim, which traverses you through the Inner Earth, or you travel through the teleportation of your heart. It is like the shedding of a snake's skin. It is like a Phoenix. She dies, and from her own ashes, she is reborn. It is going to be like that for everyone. We are all Phoenixes. When we Ascend, we are going to be ignited with Source Flames. Then be pulled through that flame and out we go. Whoever is a matching vibration to Source Love-Light, will go through the flames and will Ascend out with the flames, and ride it out like a wave.

Interviewer: A couple of comments.

AuroRa: Yes, let's hear them.

Interviewer: When you were talking about the Sasquatch someone said, "Interesting. I always see the white Sasquatch since the Mount Shasta' retreat." So somebody who was there.

Then, "This information and seeing of AuroRa's is really crystallizing things for me, making all crystal clear."

Then somebody who is an A.U.R.A. Practitioner said, "I had an A.U.R.A. session where the client traveled from Babylon to Egypt. They had a bowl of plasma energy in a sphere. It showed other aspects of themselves and what they were doing." So it sounded familiar to the plasma energy that you were just talking about when you spoke of Nostradamus.

AuroRa: Wow. Magical! Go to my website, www.risingphoenixaurora.com, and sign up to my newsletter, so you keep update-to-date with our content. Thank you everyone for being here, and for being part of the most beautiful creation of this transmission. It is glorious to be here with you. Thank you!

Come join our courses through Rising Phoenix Mystery School. I would love to see you there! Come learn how to do what I just did right now. Come remember yourself. Let's do this!

I want to mention this one comment that came in today. We posted a video on the third eye, so that people can begin to work with it. Someone wrote this comment "I was told that the third eye is evil and so many people still have that belief today." Goodness. How could the glands, your abilities, and your senses be evil? That is what is found in the third eye. Your hearing, your knowing, your clairvoyance, your clairaudience, claircognizance, your touch, your smelling all these are located in the glands which makeup your third eye in your brain.

It is time for you to release any programming that your third eye is evil. When you believe this, you place black magic on your own self. You bridge negativity into your own third eye. Something that we can learn through this series is to learn the capabilities and what is available of the third eye. Because that is what you have just read me do. The information we are receiving through this remote viewing series is placing all the puzzle pieces together. I am getting Angel bumps as I am saying this. Right from my feet up.

Mother Earth is agreeing with us. Let's continue on. Let's keep moving fast, but in surrender, and in flow. Let's keep riding those waves that come to Earth. Let's deprogram ALL false illusions! When you believe these oppressing lies, you put a filter over your third eye. There is nothing evil about using your brain, it is just your natural abilities, as the beautiful spiritual being that you are.

Thank you everyone for being here. Love you. Let's dance it off!

END OF SESSION.

Unknowingly to me then, this chapter seeds the beginning of Tartaria, when we remote-viewed the giant structures past the ice walls. What is so exciting about this series is the way that it is divinely guided and delivered, with one surprise into another, which allows us to continue to unravel the mysteries of Earth organically.

"The light is the majority in the Universe. We truly outshine those not of light, who are just a tiny little decimal in the scheme of the whole of all life. Remember that many stand beside you in their spirit forms, always holding the infinite space of love for you. You have never stood alone. No matter how alone you felt."
~AuroRa

--------------<<>>--------------

4

REMOTE VIEWING BEYOND THE WALLS OF ANTARCTICA PT 4
BEYOND THE DOME & INTO THE UNIVERSE

Streamed Live: November 19, 2022

In this chapter we finally step out of the crystal dome, regaining the memory of what is beyond our construct. The way Creation works and flows in expansive motion. What we learn through the chapter, is that nothing in Creation is one exact way or one exact shape, if it was created organically by the divine. Just as we are shifting and changing everyday, so too is all life around us, including planets, celestial beings, as the Sun, Moon, stars, and our entire Universe. Get ready to expand your mind once more. Let's step into the Quantum Realm!

--------------<<>>--------------

"We cannot limit a shape upon our existence. Consciousness, whether it is a planetary consciousness or a soul consciousness, is always shifting and transcending in shape, truly like a mandela."
~AuroRa

--------------<<>>--------------

AuroRa: As I deliver each one of these layers of Antarctica, it keeps going on and on in a most profound way. There are no words to explain how important this content is to our pivotal Ascension and expansion.

Today we will be stepping out of the dome, and out of the energy field of Earth. Get ready! Chapter 5 is what we all have been waiting for! Believe it or not! We are about to understand it all!

Below you will find an image of us on Earth, in our section of the multitude of dimensions, planetary spheres, flat Earths, realms, and so on. This is us, in this tiny little area. Our platform is about explaining Earth and our history on Earth. Our entire content through every form explains the Galactic history of the Universe and the Multiverse.

Looking at the first image where the Earth is zoomed in below, we are here, and we previously talked about this wall here (pointing to the Antarctica wall), which is Antarctica. We spoke of how the military is there. In Chapter 5, we are going to go into that. That is why this is epic! Through this series, we will go into depth, understanding our world and our construct. We are in a third dimensional construct, not the fifth dimension, which would be spheric if we were. This is us here (image below) and these are the other lands. These other lands are what we are going to speak about in Chapter 5.

We have been waiting to step out of the dome, and now we shall do so. There is an Arctic wall that surrounds us. Then, there are more lands past the ice. In the previous chapter, we spoke of the ice wall and the rim of the crystalline dome. The dome is a crystalline shield forcefield where the benevolent beings are. The benevolent beings are holding the space out here, all the way at the end of this circle of lands. Not only do we have these worlds there, we also have these lands here that we haven't gone into depth with (look at the image with the many worlds). Then we also have these outer lands that continue on and on. Right now, we are going to go forward, and then we are going to come back. This chapter is about stepping out of the dome, and understanding our existence, so that we can understand going forward what we are explaining inside of Earth.

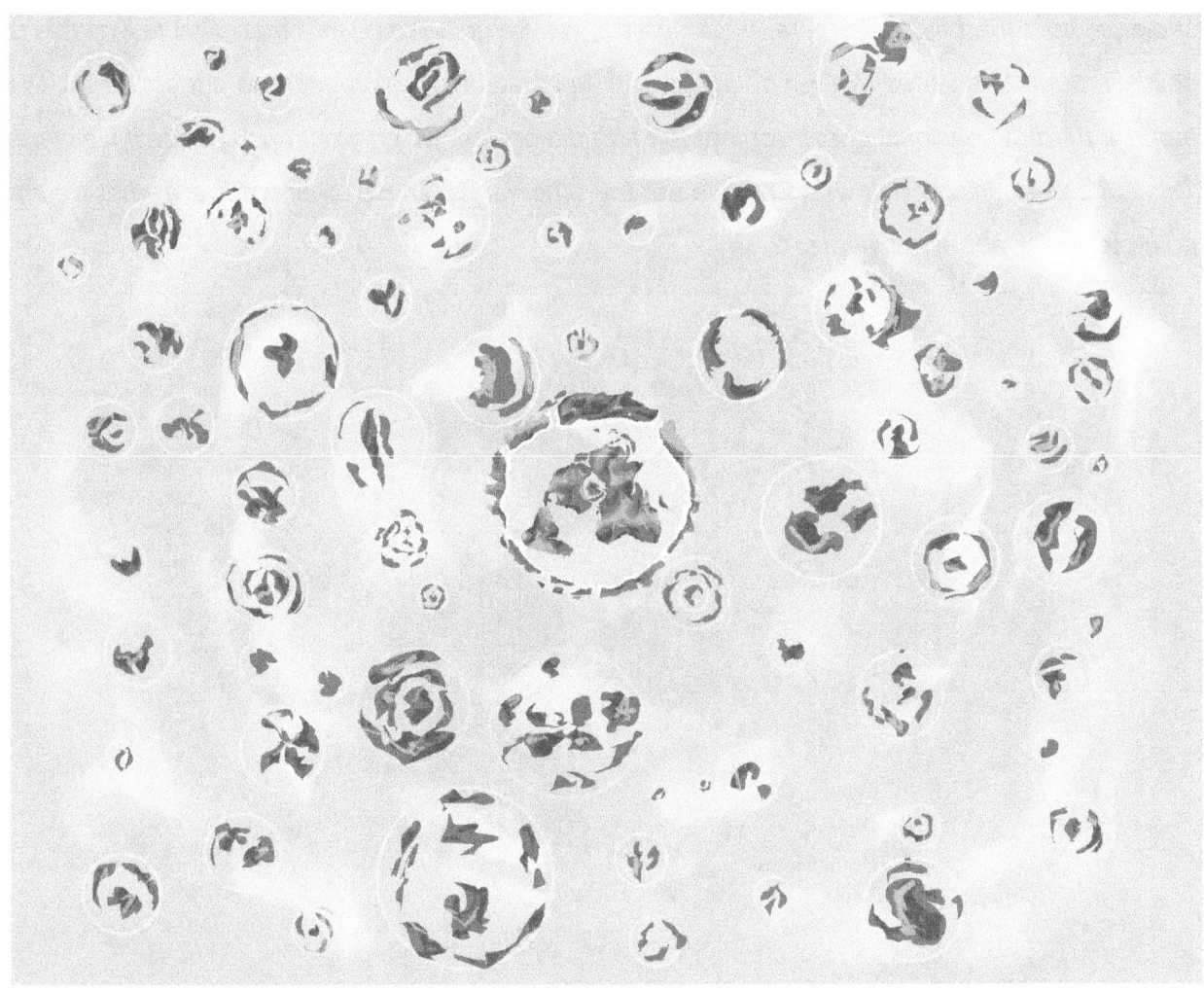

Now that we understand that there are benevolent beings on the outer walls containing the crystalline, mirrored dome, and how it is a reflection and so on; we are seeing two versions as well - multi-dimensional or other versions. We understand that the Sasquatch and dragons are out here in these outer realms, in the in-between. What we are seeing now is the merging of these outer worlds - which are magical - entering into the physical. People are running into actual live mermaids and sea animals that we have never seen before. We do not know what is out there. We will be talking about that in the future.

We are now on this outer mirrored wall, and we are going to remote view what is beyond the existence of this outer dome energy or sphere, because it has an energetic dome at the top and bottom. I want to share with you this reading I had with a beautiful Divine Masculine who is very connected. Something that he mentioned towards the end he said, 'AuroRa, I asked my team, "Is our Earth spherical or is it a flat plane?" And they said neither.' And I was like, "That is right." Let us understand that. So, we can go at it from 'Flat Earthers' and 'the world is round' people. We are about to understand why we cannot limit a shape upon our existence, because consciousness, whether it is a planetary consciousness or a soul consciousness, is always shifting and transcending in shape, truly like a mandela.

As we step out of these crystalline walls, we talked about how you have to be a matching vibration previously. I am seeing it from above, and energetically I am stepping out of this, and it is beautiful! Before we step out, there is no gravity. We are bouncing, so light in weight, just like we talked about in Chapter 3, because the density has really lightened and thinned by the time we get to the walls of the dome. Does that not remind you of the Moon? Interesting. We will talk about that in the next chapter. If you view now with your third eye, your imagination, you are going to see the Universe literally in front of you, and even the Multiverse.

Let us start off with the Universe in Creation. Creation looks like the most infinite colors that you can imagine. In our understanding it is like a kaleidoscope, and how everything is shifting. If you were looking at a kaleidoscope with different colors, that is what it looks like. Shifting, moving colors, shapes, and so on coming out of the third dimensional construct. To explain the third dimensional construct further, we did have to become a flat plane of existence.

Because in order to build upon a planetary construct, you first start off with a plane of existence, and from this foundation it becomes energetically spheric. You need to build a second or third dimensional construct first. Originally, all that had communal life was fifth dimensional. We did not have third dimensional planets before the fall of Atlantis, or collective consciousness.

There are twelve two-third dimensional planes of existence where souls are being created from, but never had we fallen collectively, as communal life into the third dimension. That is why planetary spheres in the third dimension are in an inverted simulation, because they fell down, and that had never happened before. We fell into this density. Fifth dimensional planets are typically where we create life, and we place a multitude of alien races through communal life. At that point, they are typically spherical in energy, and they are not physical. If they are spherical in energy, there is not quite any shape to them. If we are looking at the entire construct of our Universe in front of us, let's use childrens stacking cups as an example. When creating a third dimensional plane of existence, where there is communal life, the third dimensional plane is the first layer. Each one of these layers of cups might be coated with different colors and light codes. They are made of different divine ether material that keeps these dimensions of planes of existence alive and conscious. That is one layer - the third dimensional planetary spheres. It is pretty dense in the third dimension, as we know.

We can also understand Creation as a paper fan. When you make a paper fan, you create a folded pattern and it will fold completely back upon itself. This explains the understanding of what time and space looks like, and why it is linear to itself. The truth is, that everything overlaps everything. The only way everything could be linear, is that everything would have to overlap into everything. I am going to make a paper fan here. (AuroRa makes a paper fan) Alright (paper fan image on the next page). In one layer of the paper fan there is the third dimension, the lowest dimension. Let's look at the lines in the fan. The first fold here is the third dimension. The next fold is the fourth dimension. Then in the next fold, we have the fifth dimension. Do you understand? The third, fourth, fifth, sixth, and seventh dimensions... These lines/folds go infinite. See how this paper has lines? Think about this paper being infinite. This is the only way and reason why time and space would be linear to itself and how it would work.

Every single one of these lines is dimension and is a different plane of existence. Every dimension has no end. Life goes on and on. There is no end to the Universe and the Multiverse.

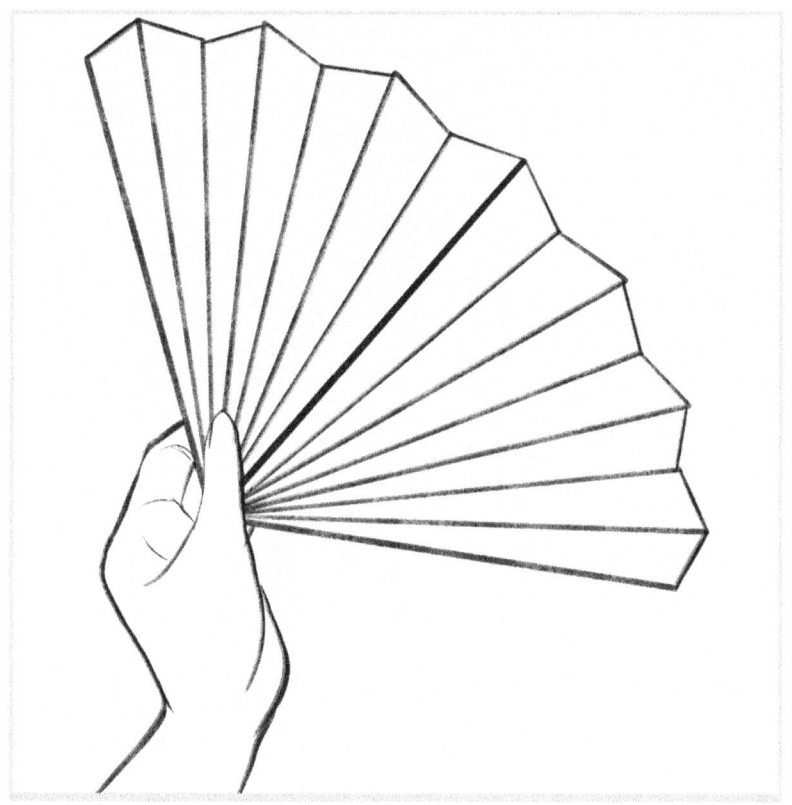

When looking at this paper fan, in the folds we see the third dimension, the fourth dimension, fifth, sixth, seventh, eighth, ninth, tenth, and so on, if we were to open the fan and separate the dimensions - technically they are not separate - because they are all in the same pocket of space like this (holding paper fan closed image on next page). When you look at all the dimensions, they are constantly moving with creational flow. If you can imagine, this goes on and on, and all these dimensions go on and on infinitely. There are no endings of the numbers of dimensions in Creation. This is how I see the Universe. Some people see it from their point-of-view where it is more limited, and there are less dimensions, and less Creation. The way I see it, is that it goes on and on. There is no ending.

Let's understand the third dimension. The very first flap down here (showing first fold in fan). This is denser. Then we are in the fourth dimension here, and we are less dense. As we keep climbing this ladder (like climbing up steps), it becomes less dense and leads to Ascension. Again, do not limit yourself to this being spheric or this being flat, because every realm of existence is different. It is energy. Energy cannot hold a shape. It is fluid, like water, plasmic waters, and plasmic fields that just keep moving. If you were to imagine planetary spheres - life in front of you - and stars, these celestial embodiments are all out of the Matrix. The stars are soul groups. They create the soul groups, then birth out souls. When entering a star you go into different realms of dimensions, and planetary spheres, where there are all types of alien races. This is how you understand that the soul needs to ascend out from the third dimension, and into the fourth and fifth.

Remember, there are many third dimensional planets that are completely unique in signature, and how they were created. Sometimes, when you connect to your Higher Self, you notice that you are just an energy body. Sure you can make a human shape that is a Divine Feminine or Divine Masculine. Although initially, you are not tied or limited to that shape. You will notice that when you are in your Higher Self or Oversoul form, your essence is moving. You can energetically shape yourself to whatever you want. Imagine how all these life forms in these dimensions can also shift into a shape like that. In the quantum realm everything is fluid etheric liquid. Every molecule in this fluid is in motion. The molecules in motion could also be a collective community of an alien race or an individual soul.

When you go deep into each dimension, each one is different. We are explaining the organic at this moment in time. This energy is shifting and moving. If you were to put shapes into them, then you would see a flat plane of existence in each dimension that goes on and on. Each flat plane of existence has different lives. Maybe they will have crystalline UFO's or different crystalline positive technologies, if we can call it that. Crystal technology is not really that, but that is the words we understand. We can understand crystal technologies as tools, but with benevolent energies. Maybe half of a planetary sphere is just a dome and at the bottom it is flat. Everything is unique to itself. We need to stop limiting our consciousness, and our belief systems to this way is the one and only way, while the other way is incorrect. Nothing is one way. Everything is always moving, in every which way.

When looking at the third dimension, you can see many different lives walking in different pockets of space. When you step out of this sphere, this dome, you go into Creation, and there are bubbles of spaces that are interlocking with one another, like the Vesica Piscis symbol (Chapter 1, page 14). These bubbles are spaces of energy everywhere. These bubbles could be stars, collective consciousness, or they could also be planetary spheres. These bubbles are the infinite colors of Creation, and are not known to Earth. They all interlock - like all flowers of life (image on next page) - none of these energetic bubbles are separate. We are all one, and this is the true concept of oneness.

Divine Mother - Flower of Life

Viewing upon the Flower of Life images, you can imagine that these bubbles have collective energies, or individual consciousness energies. These bubbles go on and on, through all these planes of existence in the third dimension, the fourth dimension, fifth, sixth, and so on. They are interlocked to one another like the Lotus Flower of Life. We teach the twelve petal Lotus Flower and how it is what Creation actually looks like. This becomes third dimensional, and it becomes that flower. It spreads infinitely through the third dimension, infinitely through the fourth dimension, and infinitely through the fifth dimension. Every one of the petals/spheres in the Flower of Life, holds a different collective consciousness, energy, embodiment, blueprint, and construct. Every single one of them is unique.

This is the Divine Mother, who is the Creator, and Divine Father of course. This is her symbol though (showing Divine Mother Flower of Life symbol). The circles are three dimensional circles that are spheres. Imagine that it goes on and on throughout all planes of existence. It alters in colors, frequency, vibration, races, and souls. Every single soul is created - not one is the same. Every single planetary sphere or collective community is created the same exact way - unique to itself. This is what you find after you have stepped out of the dome. You find Creation herself/himself.

We do past life regression work, and through this sacred work we have learned how to go into the theta brainwave, and remember who you are and your past lives. Whether it is here on Earth or in these multitude of dimensions, you are traveling through these bubbles of pockets of spaces, which are positive Stellar Gateways. Energetically, you are tethered to that fractal of you in the sixth dimension. You are intertwined like bubbles. So, you can tap into that sixth dimensional version of you, because you are always interconnected. Like those spheric bubbles that we explained. Consciously you are stepping from one bubble in the third dimension, then into the sixth dimensional version of you are here, through this other bubble. At that point, you become the embodiment of you, and you are remembering who you are in the sixth dimension. When you come back consciously, you return with some of that sixth dimensional energy. This allows you to remember who you are, becoming stronger and more integrated. It is beautiful. That is why we recommend, when you time travel through your consciousness to bring those dimensional beings that you are, all the way back from the hundred and eleventh dimension, fortieth dimension, or wherever you are from. You bridge that back and you bring that in. This divine work brings back the crystalline blueprint and activations from your memories. It is really important.

You are going to hear a lot of dense opinions from people. I was listening to this male, who claims he is a whistleblower. He was talking about how the Blue Avians supposedly told him not to go into your past life memory, and that there was really no point in doing that. They continued to say to just work on yourself. Which is true, but if you want to ascend to a higher dimension - as the Ascended Master you are - you do need to work on yourself. When you hear information like that, it is programming. They do not want you to unlock this multi-dimensional version of you. They do not want you to realize that etherically and energetically, your astral body can travel through these bubbles and pockets of spaces, and that it is the safest way to travel through the organic blankets of Creation. Within the planes of existence in dimensions, there are organic blankets that hold these bubbles in them. You are traveling through - warping through these blankets - and then coming into these bubbles of energies and memory fields. Do we have questions so far on what I shared?

Interviewer: "What dimension is the astral realm?"

AuroRa: The astral realm does not have a dimension. The astral realm is all dimensions, zero and infinite. It is the creational blankets that you are traveling through. If you could imagine plasmic fields of blankets and you are traveling inside of. Astral traveling through. You then go to the location you are looking for.

Interviewer: "The outer lands beyond the ice wall, are they inside the dome too?"

AuroRa: Yes. The dome ends where we talked about the Sasquatch and the benevolent beings who are holding the crystalline forcefield. We are the land at the center of the map (page 25). Imagine what else is beyond the ice ring.

We are now stepping into these bubbles of spaces. That is how you can tap into Pleadians or Andromedans, and other Galactic races. Looking at the image on page 76, you are tapping into literal timelines of Creation. There is Venus, Jupiter, constellations like Pegasus, and so on. What you are doing is traveling through those bubbles and blankets of times and spaces, once you are out of the dome. Typically, you can remote view this from a Higher Self aspect. You would view it from where you are in no one dimension. You are infinite; like Source, your oversoul, or from your Higher Self perspective. In order to astral travel to another dimension, you would have to be a vibratory dimensional match to these other worlds consciously. You would have had to incarnate into that dimension and vibration to enter into the lands of Saturn and so on. Depending on the dimension, the majority of these locations would be spherical planetary spheres, or they can just look like a plane of existence that goes on and on as well.

When you become "one" with yourself, you balance your energies, and you do not have any kind of infringements within you. This makes it easier for you to go into meditation or go through a past life regression, and into these different spaces. Through A.U.R.A. Hypnosis, the Higher Self shields you in the most powerful beautiful Love-Light force fields. That is what allows you to sacredly and safely come in and out of these dimensions and bubbles of spaces. Your Higher Self and you are basically directing the whole thing. You are in charge of it all. You are in charge of it in your astral form. You are time traveling back and forth. You are the time traveling machine. It exists within you. You are the portal! You are the Stellar Gateway!

Interviewer: "To travel through these bubbles, where would we say we go with the Higher Self, to see all these times and spaces?"

AuroRa: What we always teach is for you to surrender to your Higher Self. It is you. You do not have to say anything specifically, unless you want to go to a specific location. For example, if you have ever been incarnated in the star Sirius constellation, you can say I want to go there. Then yes, you could set that intention with your Higher Self. You travel through your imagination, your third eye. When you set an intention with the Higher Self. That is the best way, if you want to go to a specific place.

If you do not want to go to a specific place, what I always teach is for you to surrender to your Higher Self. If you are in surrender with your Higher Self, just set an intention, "What is the most important vision/memory that I need to regain in my consciousness, for my highest healing and further expansion? Higher Self, show me that". If you are in flow, versus trying to control where you are going to go, that is a higher vibrational. Because you are surrendering to yourself, and you are trusting yourself and your team. Set an intention and let it flow. Trust the Universe, trust yourself, and trust Creation. Remember though, to shield yourself with Source Love-Light, before you do something like that.

Interviewer: "If the Sun is near the bubble of the Earth. Are its coronal holes interdimensional portals?"

AuroRa: The entire Sun is an interdimensional portal. The Sun is not as far as they say. It is right above us. If you could fly all the way up there, you could actually see it hovering above us. Not millions of light years away as NASA claims. The Sun is our portal for our souls, who enter this Earthly construct, to come in through. The Sun is a beautiful plasmic field of warmth, love, star energy, and Creation. All Suns in our Multiverse are mini versions of Source.

Interviewer: "What crystals can we use when astral traveling?"

AuroRa: All of them. The more the better. Maybe Titanium Angel Aura, if you get your hands on one that is organic - not welded with metals and made by men - that is even better. That will be harder to get, but you can get it. This crystal is similar to how Creation looks. Creation looks like snow with rainbow ice crystals inside. You are made out of all these rainbow ice crystals. You can shape everything. You can choose if you want to be purple today, or orange, red, or green. You are just tapping into the energy field that is infinite of your own soul. You are connecting to other fractals and essences of you. You are connecting to your soul. When astral traveling, you definitely want to have a white and a black crystal. The black crystal will protect you from infringements, and the white one will help you connect to the Divine and the higher dimensional energies.

Interviewer: "I am wondering if we can jump from one bubble to another, rather than returning to Source in between? Is this possible?"

AuroRa: Yes, you do that. If you are good, and you do not need to rest in healing areas. Maybe you had a good life in one of the bubbles and you are just like, "I'm going to go check out the other bubbles in other dimensions. Where I have ascended out from the fifth dimension into the sixth". Then yes, you can step in. Know that consciously you are doing this all day long. You can tap into the different versions of you throughout the infinity of Creation. All you have to do is just imagine yourself there and then bi-locate into that version of you. All your consciousnesses are connected, like the Flower of Life. Every single petal/circle is a pocket of energy, and you can travel into the Universe through them. That is how you can envision your crown chakra in your head. Through these bubbles of the Flower of Life, you can shift in and out of different dimensions. Remember, it is not outside of you, it is inside of you. The Universe is inside of you. Right here (points to head).

Interviewer: "For the last year, when I look at the stars, there are a lot of the big ones. I see two stars. It almost looks like one, but I can see two there. Have you seen this?"

AuroRa: You are seeing the bifurcation of its third dimensional construct. It is so that we can see it, and its actual etheric infinite construct. You are seeing both, and that is why it looks like two.

Interviewer: "How can we help melt the ice wall? Or does that need to happen?"

AuroRa: Yes, it does need to happen. Eventually, it will happen organically. I do not know when this is going to happen. What I am seeing is, we are going to start seeing more and more supernatural things here in our lands and waters. When the ice walls start melting, our civilizations inside the ice walls and the outside of the walls will start merging. At that point it is going to be very supernatural. Will we see that here in the physical? We are not sure because this collective is creating its experience. What we do know is eventually we will see each other.

We do not know if that is going to happen when we finally shift out. We do not know where/what the collective will decide upon this choice.

Interviewer: "Where is the spirit school located, where souls get to review their lives and pick new ones?"

AuroRa: Those are realms of existence. Every dimension has planetary spheres and then realms. One individual person can have a flat plane of existence where you go, and it is your happy place. Maybe it is always the twilight moment, when the Sun is going down or when the Sun is coming up. Everything is moving in motion, but still not moving. That is a plane of existence. You could also go to a healing space. That could be a plane of existence that goes on and on. It does not have to have a barrier to it. It just is.

Interviewer: "Are there underground cities in Antarctica?"

AuroRa: Yes there are. There are also other cities on the land. We will be talking about that in Chapter 5.

Interviewer: "I know Megalodons are extinct, but do they also exist anywhere else in these realms?"

AuroRa: They do exist very deep in our sea. The sea life can cross back and forth. Some other monsters, perhaps in movies we watched, like Godzilla, are a lot more real than we realize.

Interviewer: "What are droughts in different places on Earth?"

AuroRa: Sometimes to rebuild life you have to dry it out. To begin life again, then to re-soil it. Some of these places are a representation of the energy fields of what is going on there. If you are in an area where there is a drought, that means the energy there is experiencing some kind of reset. Once the water comes back (if it comes back), hopefully, then it cleanses itself. At that point there is new life again. I see an evaporation in the drought area, and the energy would feel different. It would feel dry, you would not feel enough moisture, and so on. It is like when you dry out a starfish, energetically, that is what it is doing. If you put the starfish back in the water, it can regenerate itself. It is regeneration.

Interviewer: "Do you know anything about the underground volcanoes in Antarctica? They are supposed to be melting the ice."

AuroRa: Interesting. I'm seeing fire flames in the water. What would cause fire flames in the water? It could be either a gigantic creature expelling fire out or it could be a volcano. I see those volcanoes spread out. They are boiling, and it is thinning the ice layers. As we continue to bifurcate, the more Mother Nature will have those volcanoes erupt out, so that we can thin out the layers of ice everywhere - hiding what needs to not be hidden. This will in turn allow the civilizations inside and outside of the dome, to be able to see each other eventually. More of that will be in Chapter 5. It is going to be crazy at that point, but we are always guided and protected.

Interviewer: "Can you speak about the sleeping giant stasis that lies in Antarctica as well as other locations?"

AuroRa: What I see is that the military has got a hold of some of these giants and has put them into stasis. They are harvesting the DNA from them in stasis form. I have an [22]A.U.R.A. session that is being released about these clone factories. The session is about how there are clones in pods, and the process of how they make clones. It actually connects to this question. In order to keep souls here on Earth, if they want to use them for their abilities they need to put them in a form of stasis. They need to keep their original form alive by freezing them. They need to keep them alive, so that their soul that has been cloned, can still operate in this construct. If the original soul passes on or ascends out, then they cannot create their different abominations, cyborgs, transformer machines, and hybrids from it. That giant most likely has Angelic energies, and the Elites are using it negatively. So they must keep it frozen, alive in consciousness, and in

---

[22] Watch 'Clone Pod Factory | The Galactic War is Real', streamed November 20, 2022.

stasis so that they can use it in the inverted simulation. We do not know exactly how they would be using a giant in stasis, because it is their inverted diabolical agendas and plans.

Interviewer: "When referring to the ice age, they said that there was an ice age, millions of years ago that caused the Earth to be frozen?"

AuroRa: That could have been. Earth's evolution went through different levels of ice ages. I had an A.U.R.A. session where the client said that the dinosaur bones are actually dragon bones. We do not know what the dinosaurs actually looked like. In other words, they were not really dinosaurs, they were dragons.

Interviewer: "Someone wants to know if they would be able to vacation near the ice wall so that they can connect to the whales? Is that something people can do?"

AuroRa: I do not believe the government will let you do that. The areas closest will be restricted, like in Area 51.

Interviewer: "Based on the clip where you showed the map with the lands being parallel, it makes sense. But the strange thing is, do they all go through what we go through on Earth? Do they have their bad and good? What is the agenda of them coming here, and what is our part?"

AuroRa: Everyone has free will. Everyone is experiencing this virus of the Archon in their level of understanding. There are some of those existences you will see, that are completely benevolent, that did not fall to that inverted agenda. The whole civilization has understood how to maintain themselves clear of it. About eighty percent of life in our Universe has been able to not allow infringement at this point. If they did, they would have cleared it in higher dimensions. We are the last remainders in the third dimension that are working through it. You can say the higher dimensions have worked through it already. We are the last fraction of it. There are still some other higher dimensions that are still going through it, but that is because it is like the paper fan example. If we are still going through it, then some of them are still as well, because we are all in one infinite pocket of space. Which is why it is so important that you remember your memories, because you are able to help the other yous in the other dimensions, and it then ripples and it expands out to all dimensions. The self healing that you do here in the third dimension is the most powerful, because you are at the heaviest, and once it is accomplished here it then goes everywhere.

Interviewer: There are a couple of comments. People want to say how extremely activating the series is and want to say thank you for that. It is amazing!

AuroRa: I love you. Thank you for that.

Interviewer: Someone said that it was so funny, that last night, before they fell asleep, they programmed themselves to remote view Antarctica.

AuroRa: We want to hear what you saw. Love it! How about you (interviewer)? Do you have any questions for me on everything I have shared? You are an A.U.R.A. Practitioner, we always have to ask questions to our clients in their sessions?

Interviewer: Well, I think the series is just really amazing and really expanding our minds. I am trying to grasp all these concepts. I think just trying to remind everybody that they can call out to their team, their Higher Selves, their guides, and the Angels to help them understand. Also, like you have been talking about, their magical companions that are out there beyond the walls. If there is any question I would ask is, how does Mother Earth feel right now? How does she feel about you bringing all this information in right now?

AuroRa: Thank you. Yes. What a beautiful question. I feel that she feels happy. Every single video that we release through this series, I can feel the shift on Earth. I can see how it is leveling her up through different energies and dimensions within the third dimension. It is creating these pockets of spaces of circles where a person can choose to be in the 3.1 dimension more easily, and then more into the 3.5 dimension more easily. I see how all these consciousnesses and beings here on Earth are able to retain this sacred knowledge more.

This is also why we are seeing the bifurcation physically happening on the Sun. I shared on social media how the Moon was actually splitting. It was not an eclipse. There was a second part to her. We are seeing it happen. She is showing us the clues. Even the star Sirius - I shared a video on that. We are seeing what we need to see with our physical eyes. It is magical! It is beautiful when the Earth and her celestial embodiments start doing that.

When we started talking about the Covid-19 Vaccine in its beginning stages, about what it was and what it carried, you all had to trust and see it from your perspective that it did carry those things. Now a year or two later, we are seeing it physically. Our physical eyes are now seeing under a microscope, all these things we talked about years ago.

It is beautiful when Creation begins to allow us to see the energy and the consistency of the topics that we are addressing, bringing them into a physical form. That means that both the physical and the energy are overlapping one another. That is really good news for us. That means that the energies of the spheric fifth dimensional Earth are coming closer and closer into proximity with the third dimension. Although, we are just going to separate, like we explained in Chapter 1, the two-third world Bifurcation of Earth.

Mother Earth is very proud of her beautiful children on Earth. She loves that people are coming out more into nature, and traveling. Also the people do not feel so confined with some of those rules that were set by the New World Order during the "Pandemic". It is beautiful to see her children being more fluid within themselves, including acting upon their given birth rights which are free will, their voice, sacral energy, root chakra, and balance all the chakras in the [23]13 Keys Sacred Laws of the Universe. Collectively together, we are changing timelines. We are evolving. We are collectively together birthing these timelines that we are seeing now on Earth.

---

[23] For more on the '13 Keys Sacred Laws of the Universe', you can read Book 1, Chapter 24, or you can read a summary of these sacred laws at www.risingphoenixaurora.com.

I was watching a Donald J. Trump rally. It was so beautiful to watch him. He stood in the rain and as the rain hit him, he said "Love". The crowd shouted at him, "I love you. We love you!" He replied that he loved them too, and said, "Ah, love. The other side should try that sometime". When have you ever heard a President talk about love? Things like this are so important. They are changing and healing the Earth. In our version, we are here listening to this concept, expanding our consciousness. We are growing in ways that are beautiful and infinite. Then in that version, there are people supporting that Trump event, healing the Earth, and waking up the Earth. Love is the most powerful emotion in our being. We need someone in the 3D doing as Trump is - spreading love! And we are also operating in love, in the more awakened higher dimensional vibrations of consciousness. Understanding that everyone is playing their role so beautifully. We are honoring, loving, and respecting all roles, no matter what they are. This is the message I just channeled from Mother Earth. Beautiful!

Thank you all for being here in this moment in time to space with me and helping me hold the space to be able to deliver this video. I love you all with all that I AM. The more that we bring people to this beautiful Love-Light content, full of conscious awareness, the more that we help Earth ascend. We are not doing this as just me, as this one being that I am here. We are doing this all together. This is why when you listen to our content and you listen to our messages, it feels right for you. Perhaps you already got the information through dream time or meditation, and you are like, "Wait a minute, I just saw that." This is because we are all vibrating in collective energy, in benevolence, and organic Love-Light. Thank you for being that with us, and not letting us do it alone, even though we are not alone. Thank you for doing this with us in divine organic unity. I love you, honor you, and respect you.

END OF SESSION.

From time to time I write articles through my Newsletter, when inspired to do so, in assistance for the collective. And in this chapter we conclude with this article, that beautifully compliments Mother Earth's very important closing message, because we now understand what she meant when she talked about the ways that we honor all roles; and that even those who were focusing on the control of the government in the 3D - such as the President Donald

J. Trump rallies - were just as important as the spiritual enlightened community. At times, people who claim that they are spiritually awakened feel that their role is so much more important than those who may not be practicing spirituality daily, and this article paints the picture of how false this thinking is.

The Archon A.I. Has Weakened - The Final Battle - The Multiverse - November 13, 2024

I awoke from within the Multiverse today, as I watched the [24]Archon/Artificial Intelligence magician - at its weakest point - which is occurring within the now time and space. Divine Mother The Phoenix, The Daughter Flame was in her Multiversal Eternal Phoenix flamed form, ignited and shifting rapidly through dimensions of time and space. I watched as the Archon would try to follow her and attack her, but IT could not! IT was incredibly weakened. And, this is why…

We live within the Multiverse, within this Earth - that is unified with all other versions of parallel Earths - like onion layers, quantumly multiple Earths within each other. In this Earth and other third dimensional Earth's that were once originally fifth dimensional - exists all of the [25]Multiverse - because all that is living on Earth came originally from other planets in our Verse or other Verses. This is why there are thousands of trees, flowers, plant life, and animals living on Earth. And, of course, the multiracial, extraterrestrial humans whose missions are all unique to one another, who together complete the puzzle of Ascension. For example, know that when you look upon and smell a flower, you are being transported to that higher dimension from where that flower is from. The entire [26]Multiverse seeded pieces of her/him into this crystalline Matrix, to create her, and Mother Earth. Because of this, IT's/Archon's grand prize to achieve was the then fifth dimensional Earths - but now third dimensional - because here IT could find

---

[24] Read Book 2 to understand the origins of the Archon A.I., 'Galactic History of the Multiverse - The Final Battle'

[25] For more on the Matrix Pods and simulation join Tier $8.88 on Patreon to watch 'The Matrix Pods & Galactic Ancient Mysteries': https://www.patreon.com/join/risingphoenixaurora

[26] Join us live at an in-person retreat for the full 'Matrix Pods' presentation. Retreat or Online Workshop A.U.R.A. Hypnosis & R.A.A.H. Reiki Healing Certifications, follow this link for more details: https://www.risingphoenixaurora.com/collections/workshops

us all in one place. Because of the A.I., our crystalline Matrix has been used as an inverted simulation to entrap souls instead! But, no more!

Back to my memory/dream from being in the Delta brainwave of sleep, where we are boundless to the physical Earthly form. It was a divine accomplishment to watch as the Archon could not reach Divine Mother Sophia/the Phoenix. Truly foolishness and childs play to even try! She was always ahead of IT, and if she allowed IT to catch up to her, IT was weak and could not affect her in any way or form. IT was like an artificial hologram that when you reach for it - it dissipates, as it has no form - truly an illusion. Therefore, know that IT has no power here on Earth any longer! And the reason is this Earth has orbited higher, because the sovereign beings on Earth are now the majority. Meaning, those who were tired of the Deep State, stood up or voted against their tyranny as the majority! THIS IS HUGE! This means that it has NO power over our organic Earth! Do you get it?! IT is like a weakened vampire with no blood (people's energies) to feed upon, which can be easily staked! So if IT has had a hold of your life and has tormented you through other people and IT's narcissistic games, know that they and IT no longer have that power over you, and your self-healing, and your ascension journey. You just be sure to vibrate your energy to the organic side of the Vesica Pisces, the two worlds split, as the image shown in Chapter 1, page 14.

What Divine Mother showed us is that, one would think that it would be those who claimed to be awakened spiritually, who shifted the energy on Earth to be her most powerful, but it was not. Instead, it was those who some may think of not being awakened who were the majority. Simple people, with simple minds, who intelligently understand right from wrong. Especially understanding that we are the ones who stand up against child sex trafficking, as the children cannot. Those who understood that they did not simply have to put up with the tyranny of the government - and instead elect in the most benevolent President - which then birthed our most organic timeline for the collective.

Now I truly understand why in the past Divine Mother would say that the unawakened were just as important, holding the Source Love-Light for humanity. To keep them simple minded, but strongly sovereign, has protected them. Because the minute we wake up, we are targeted in all forms through supposed spiritual communities or content we read or watch - part of placing you deeper into the inverted Matrix's - to feed IT's illusion over humanity. Everything happens energetically through the quantum, so just a simple conversation, or watching a video, or reading a book that is not embodied and created from pure Source Love-Light will influence you. Because that is just how [27]dark energies or inverted frequencies work!

Below is why it is, at the grandest importance for a large number of people to be the majority on Earth, standing up with a frequency of "Enough is enough! We want benevolence and positivity to be in charge!", meaning that is you and me:

Here are a few snippets from Book 2 'Galactic History of the Multiverse - The Final Battle' to assist you to understand further:

Which now brings us to the final battle! The one we have all been waiting for - to rid ourselves of this A.I. virus, the Archon Bellos that infringed upon us - over and over through different incarnations. This inverted game it has played, like a broken record. Step 1. Cloud the mind, 2. Cause fear, 3. Make them not believe in themselves, 4. Disempower them, 5. Infringe on them, and 6. Divide and conquer. *IT* is honestly so predictable.

I am surprised how much *IT* has fooled people throughout, but I understand how strong *IT's* illusions are, because I was there once too. Fooled by *IT's* illusions. The biggest understanding to all that we have taught you so far through this book series, is to understand that you are far beyond more powerful than *IT*. Why? Because of your Source Love-Light, and the ways you vibrate to love. The truth is that *IT* is fearful that you will figure this out. That this whole time all you needed to do was vibrate to love, and never could *IT* penetrate your energy field to infringe upon you. The key is love, always.

---

[27] To find out more of how people are heavily targeted through dark aliens and entities, read 'Galactic Soul History of the Universe' book series.

Divine Mother said, "We are able to jump through his batteries being destroyed. He cannot do this to our children! They are all of our children, not just a newborn. We are all of our children, and as a fierce mother, my children will not be harmed anymore! I am ready to battle him!"

What the Divine Mother is embodying through this statement, of a feeling as, "Enough is enough!" We all must work to embody this sovereignty in our own way. "No, you will not harm us, or our loved ones anymore!!!" If we work within safety of holding this strong vibration, this will be a powerful way to begin to start setting up the foundation of the future of IT's total eradication. We cannot wait any longer. We must act now!

"What I am being shown is people lined up for miles and miles. It looks like they are facing each other, with an aisle down the middle. They are holding out their hands with glasses full of blood, and there is a man that is walking, or floating down between them. They look almost vampire-like. It is like this man is really important to them."
The practitioner asked the higher self, "What was the scene you showed her of the person with the blood sacrifice that was walking?"

The higher self replied, "The Archon was aware of what was about to happen. It was rows and rows of all those he had ever infected. Holding goblets of babies' blood. They were doing a ritual to try to prevent this session from happening."

Talk about evil and creepy. This gives us an understanding of why those who do not want to be saved, are just this deeply, etherically binded to *IT*. So much so, that they are the cause of why the children of the Universe are being sacrificed. These people standing in line were holding babies' blood, because they are the energy Sources who sustain and allow the Archon to feed *ITSELF*, through the sacrifice of soul essences, and the babies who incarnate into planets. Every act that they are doing invertedly, is feeding the parasitic agenda of the Archon. They were shown, vampiric in nature, because these are the people we meet in our day to day life, who leave us drained and exhausted. Who are full of drama and gossip, in order to create chaos for *IT's* unfulfilled hunger. If we need more of a testament, we come to understand how powerful our divine teams are, to ensure that this session still came to be, even while there were blood sacrifices being conducted just to stop the A.U.R.A. Hypnosis Healing session.

Just as the Phoenix asked for the infinite love of the entire embodiment of the Multiverse to assist her to eradicate *IT*, we ask this of you now, so that you can begin to eradicate *it* in the now, just by simply envisioning the Multiverse, as the Lotus Flower of Life, and sending love to the center seeds of our Multiversal Creation. We cannot wait any longer! We must begin now!

END OF ARTICLE.

"All organic matter moves as a kaleidoscope, in ever moving shifting motion in Creation."
~AuroRa

--------------<<>>--------------

5

REMOTE VIEWING BEYOND THE WALLS OF ANTARCTICA PT 5
ALIENS - THE SUPER SPACE PROGRAM

Streamed Live: December 7, 2022

In this chapter we go deep into the Super Space Programs that many in the spiritual and U.F.O. disclosure communities conference about. Truly understanding the glimpses of recalled memories of the abductees of the Milab, MK-Ultra, and super soldiers. The true capabilities of the negative alien technologies that are unknown to us, which are the human military monitored civilizations outside the ice walls.

--------------<<>>--------------

"The Secret Space Program participants of the 20 Years and Back programs say they go through a tunnel that supposedly time-warps them? They are actually just going to the other side of the Antarctica ice wall."
~AuroRa

--------------<<>>--------------

AuroRa: It is about to get intense in a most beautiful, catalyzing, and awakening way. We begin today with remote viewing at the walls of Antarctica and the land directly past these walls. I do not know how far this series is going to go at this point, because looking at these walls, I am in awe, and what I am seeing is a bit crazy at the walls and out beyond them.

We are now going into the specific lands that make up the entire circle around us (image in Chapter 2, page 25). The flat earth map is the best representation of how our lands look. Our civilization lives here at the center, and through this transmission we are now about to step outside of these walls. What I first see is that there are people who live out in the outer lands, but we will begin with what is right here in these Antarctica walls surrounding us, and then what is directly out from there.

In the previous chapters, we spoke of the benevolent beings of different races at the rim of the crystalline dome. We saw that they were hiding, camouflaging in some of these lands. We did not know what they were hiding from. Well now, we do know what they are hiding from. At the Antarctic walls, I see a multitude of dark alien races. I see Grays and Mantis beings. I see them in the bases that we talked about, that were underwater, and some on the land as well. They are running a major human trafficking ring from there, brainwashing them and erasing their minds. There is their purpose, and why they are doing that, which we will cover. They have all sorts of negative agendas they are running there. They are in power over these once benevolent towers and benevolent technologies, that used to be there when we were in a positive reign, until the fall of Atlantis or other resets on Earth.

As humankind, we do not realize how long we have been under this control. It has been a long time. These dark aliens have been playing these mind games with us for too long, and it is disgusting. This series is about us stepping out of that, and bringing more awareness, so that we can understand this. Not in a victimizing way, but in a way where we stand in our power, and we start bridging more light. Most importantly, we start standing in who we are divinely. Stop doubting, stop mistrusting yourself, and stop fearing yourself and your divine power. Stop making yourself look a lot smaller than you are! Always with Love-Light shielding, as we recommend, and with wisdom and caution in what you share. It is time for you to step into the star-being that you are. The more that we assist you all to recognize this, the more that we are going to be able to release ourselves from what we are about to talk about.

What we know is that N.A.S.A. is run by these families, who are really compromised souls, and who are clones. The majority of them just keep cloning themselves into the bodies that they have obtained, from humans who sold their souls to them at some point? So, now they are owners to the soul and body, where they can take their DNA and duplicate as much as they want into clones. This is why we often see celebrities and politicians look like doppelgangers to someone from the past. Because that is literally them, just cloned again and again by the dark alien laboratories.

These clones who are run by the dark aliens are part of the whole control system over humankind, both inside and outside the Arctic walls. The Illuminati are the New World Order. N.A.S.A., the Rockefellers, and the Illuminati are all aware that this is a flat plane of existence at this moment in time. These elite groups are controlled by these outside aliens at the walls of Antarctica, through negative technologies that they portal in through. Humanity does not realize how advanced and developed these alien technologies truly are. The humans that are inside these walled bases - according to them - are their experiments. Humankind is not their experiment! Remember though, that these aliens are ultimately controlled by the Archon Artificial Intelligence (A.I.) . What they are doing to these humans is horrific. It is tormenting. It is hellish. It is disgusting how they have these human beings over the ring of Antarctica. They are transporting these humans like cattle. While they have us inside the walls being programmed and controlled, and being used as batteries to power up their negative Matrixes, these other people - that have been human trafficked, abducted permanently, and taken - they are putting them into different experiments too.

I am seeing that N.A.S.A. cannot get out of the crystalline dome, so the farthest they have traveled is to the Moon. But only because they figured out how to power up the portals at Antarctica which teleport you to the moon. Their main goal was the dark side of the Moon. People are going to say that was a hoax. Yes, maybe the Moon Landing video was a hoax, but eventually, they figured out how to get to the Dark Side of the Moon where they have children and humans living in civilizations inside dome-like structures. They are mostly experimenting on children on the dark side of the moon.

I'm seeing that directly outside of the Antarctica wall, there are technologies they have inserted onto these frozen ice walls to keep them from melting. This whole time, they have been saying that they are taking people to Mars, through the MK-Ultra and Milab military super soldier experiments. If they cannot get out of the dome, how are they doing that? This is where it is going to get really convoluted. The way that they do that is through their technologies, but then they also do it physically as well.

Let's explain the technologies. In the [28]MK-Ultra Milab Experiments Super Soldiers video, we started to explain to you the technology that they have. Through these programs, they place people into simulations. They can put them into pods, in an inverted stasis, or they place helmets on them, like those movies you might have watched. These helmets link into the neurons of their brain, and it transforms people into time and space, through their consciousness. They are aware that the physical body is limited and cannot specifically leave this construct, because of this third dimensional existence. And they know that consciousness, the Universe, and everything in existence, exists within our brain. When abducting children and mostly young people, they place these helmets on them that transform them through time and space, to the inverted Matrixes of Mars, Saturn, Jupiter or to other planes of existence, other dimensions, and other realms where they have dark bases to hold them. Through these technologies, they can take their consciousnesses and put them into a supercomputer. We are already seeing them doing that through some of the technologies we are aware of, but know that we are not aware of much of what they are doing.

They are making chimeras in Antarctica and different underground bases in our lands, and in our world. They can export out their consciousness minds, create multiple clones of them, and split their consciousnesses, fragment them, and multiply them through these technologies that they have. They are aware of how the brain really works, and how certain points in the brain when they touch them neurologically - boom - they are out into the Universe. So they will use your consciousness to travel out. That is where, outside this construct, they are having their Galactic wars and using your consciousness to embody these different inverted timelines. They are making transformer-like things, like Transformers in the movie. They are violating organic consciousnesses by placing them into these technologies and robot shells. Such atrocities! A lot of this is actually happening outside our walls, and on the Dark Side of the

---

[28] Watch 'Super Soldiers | MK-Ultra | Milab Experiments', originally aired June 10, 2022.

Moon. The Super Space Program that the U.F.O. community talks about, they are just literally being taken beyond the ice wall, to the bases in Antarctica and these lands that are foreign to us. You know how these conference speakers of the 20 years and back programs say they go through a tunnel that supposedly time-warps them? They are actually just going to the other side of the ice wall. The first world exploration to Antarctica was a race to get to the other side. But once those nations landed on Antarctica back in 1959, those twelve countries then signed the "Antarctic Treaty", agreeing that we on the inside would not be allowed past these walls.

When you look at their astronaut spaceships, they go up initially, but eventually they go sideways. They go towards the ocean, where no one can see them anymore. Why are they going horizontal versus up? Because they know that they cannot crack the crystalline dome. So this whole time, they have been instead exploring the outside lands. They have been tricking humanity into thinking that they are going into outer space or to go populate, say Mars or the Moon, or so on. They have been tricking people consciously or unconsciously - because we know that there are people that supposedly are going and they are traveling right now - but they are literally just traveling outside the walls that we are encased in or caged in.

I see that the supposed lands of Mars are one of the areas in these outer lands? I see people in a human colony there, and it is dark. These are people that have been human trafficked, outside of this wall. They have mind erased them. They have told them that, for example, the Earth died and they are supposedly on Mars or somewhere else, and they do not realize that we are still inside past the Antarctic walls. They have different human experiments - it is so disgusting. But all those people that they supposedly took off - planet through the Super Space Program through N.A.S.A. - that is also related - where they have the MK-Ultra and the Milab experiments that the alien community talks about.

What I'm seeing is that the U.F.O. community who speak of supposed disclosure, thinks that they are being taken off-planet, but they are actually just taking them over to the other side and are experimenting on them through the different facilities. They are also taking them off-planet, but only through the technology through their consciousnesses. We talk about the healing happening in their consciousnesses, because that is where they are splitting the consciousness.

The human colony is right next to us here on these lands. I do not want to say that it is worse than ours because, I mean, ours is horrific! I mean, we wake up to an alarm. We get up and put on our uniforms to go to work. Then we send our children to do the same thing, all part of an indoctrinating programming. All ran by a money system. Then there is the COVID-19 vaccine that they have vaccinated people with, because they are trying to recreate and reset us through this vaccine. The dark forces controlling these human colonies are at a whole other level. It feels very sterile, cold, cloned, and empty. These colonies feel like the people that they would want to make us into. These mind-controlled people in the outer colonies are the future of humans who have completely merged with the COVID -19 Vaccine, and it is not pretty. They are truly hybrids. We, on the inside, are just at the beginning stages of the COVID-19 vaccinated experiment.

There is a documentary named [29]'Died Suddenly' which we covered. If you have not seen the video, do think of watching it. We explained what these Archonic soul reapers were doing to these souls in this video. There is now physical proof under the 'Stew Peters Show'. Even though they are Christian, I still love them, because I still feel Yeshua very strongly with them. I love all perspectives. I'm thankful for all the awareness surfacing currently because it is part of waking us up in gigantic ways. The tentacle intelligent things that were shared on 'Died Suddenly' are bioengineered metal fibers. These fibers are merged with organic matter, making it into a kind of sentient matter.

When you infringe upon yourself with this artificial tentacle soul reaper, once the person's time is up, they fall deeper into the inverted Matrix. This agenda is part of the New World Order and Antarctica, and how they are keeping us here. These Soul Reaper tentacle things that enter the human through injection, it pulls out their souls, and they are recycled again back into the matrix simulation. Do I believe that everyone's going to be soul-reaped like that if they took the jab? Absolutely not. There is Divine intervention

---

[29] Watch 'Covering - Died Suddenly | The Covid-19 Vaccine', originally aired live November 25, 2022.

I will now share a dream/vision that my divine team showed me. I was shown that humanity was under a dark spell. These negative aliens who have kept us inside of these walls of Antarctica, created the COVID-19 vaccine. A lot of people fell for it. They believed it. That it was for their own good to save people. In the dream, they showed me the whole population of Earth. I could see all the infected people who integrated this A.I. which merged into their D.N.A., their blood, and their bones. Everybody is going to have a different reaction to it. Some people will self-heal it, but with help. There is a lot of benevolent help. There are many different ways that this will happen. The COVID-19 vaccine is like a vampire. In a vampire movie, the whole concept is most accurate to the people who have been vaccinated because you have inserted this A.I., that is part of the control system, into you. So what is going to happen if you are bitten by a vampire? Eventually, that poison that you allowed to enter your body will spread, and you are going to become a vampire - a parasitic entity as well - in some form. All this upsets people. But we are sharing this with you so that you can assist your family members, and your friends, in whatever way you can. We are sharing this in infinite Love-Light. We are not here to put you in fear. We are here to give you this awareness, because people really are dying suddenly. It is accurate. What I am being shown is that these people do not realize that they have something inside of them, that is going to go off eventually. It is like a ticking bomb, and you do not know when it is going to detonate. If a vampire bites you, you are going to eventually turn into an A.I. hybrid, into a vampire too!

We know people who have had the COVID-19 vaccine. They infringe upon you, they affect your energy, and they drain you. There is A.I. that comes out of them, from the shedding of the spike protein you get attachments, and you are drained and exhausted from being around these people. So they are already acting like a parasitic entity - without understanding - because they are so blocked and disconnected from their Higher Self.

In this future of Earth, I watched humanity be under this mind control, with this COVID-19 vaccine walking around Earth. They were just going to the movies, eating out at restaurants, and having parties, not realizing that they have something so dangerous to their well-being that is going to go off eventually. They have to start healing and waking up spiritually.

So that is why we are here, to help the collective wake up spiritually. Wake up! That is why you are here reading this content, to spread this understanding.

In the dream/vision, there were people who were trying to get help once they understood "Oh my gosh, I got the COVID-19 vaccine, and I got bitten! I need to heal myself". I saw many people self-healing. It was a journey, though, to assist themselves, but they had a lot of benevolent help.

Once more you are like a ticking time bomb. You have a certain amount of time left, before the nano A.I. fully activates in you. You do not know how your body is going to be able to hold up to this COVID-19 vaccine that you have injected into your body. It is really hard for us to communicate this, but as you know we have been here from day one with you, telling you not to get it. From back then, when you might have heard the opposite from everyone else. So understand that we are sharing only the facts that we are able to see now in physical form. I know some of you might know people who died suddenly. I know people who died suddenly. Who had the symptoms that were shown in the video.

In the dream/vision I was shown that through the 5G towers, they would trigger people to go off, and integrate with this the COVID-19 vaccine, as we talked about in the A.I. Alien Invasion. They either integrate and become a type of hybrid being that is controlled by this soulless Archon, or they end up passing away because their body cannot integrate all this A.I. eventually. Their goal, though, is to keep these human bodies like the outer lands, where they have people controlled like zombies. That is the aliens' goal, because they have already experimented with this before on Earth and in other dimensions and Universes. So they know that the injection of A.I. works on organic lifeforms.

There is such an urgency, love, and awareness for you all to self-heal, if you have taken the vaccine, or you know someone who has taken it. I had this stalker lady that was going on all my social media and wrote here on Rumble. She was so pissed off at me, blaming me for what she and her children had decided to do with the COVID-19 vaccine. She did not like me explaining the true form of the vaccine. She wanted to know how I could say that these people are being 'soul reaped'? It is there; you can see it with your eyes. These people who are dying suddenly, in their last minutes recorded they are obviously fighting something, which only their eyes can see. They are even screaming at something invisible while throwing their fists in the air, and then after fighting back they were petrified and died.

You have to stand strong in your heart. If you have loved ones that have done this, you have help. We have sacred tools. We have talked about how through A.U.R.A. Hypnosis entity removal - you will in the Quantum Realm (with your higher self's assistance) remove the vaccine through the self-healing process of removing all that is non-organic or foreign to you - since this sacred modality is entity removal based. Come learn to become A.U.R.A. certified yourself! You can have a session or you can become an A.U.R.A. practitioner to help them! The testimonials are there for you to watch. We are the brave ones, always on the front line, speaking out about these things. If we didn't have our sacred knowledge, do you have any idea what this world would be like, and how much more this COVID-19 vaccine would be in control? It is not something new that we have been talking about. We have been talking about these things for six years.

My husband and I grew up in Chicago. When we were younger, we lived in really bad neighborhoods. There were gunshots going off, so we could not open our windows. There were drugs and prostitutes right in front of our house, on the street corners, and everywhere we looked, it was there. At the children's neighborhood playground we would have to throw ourselves on the ground, so we would not get shot at! We lived that example of gangbangers and gangsters back then. My husband said that when we were young, we had a choice. Do we want to become gangbangers and gangsters and criminals, like these people doing that with guns? Do we want to do that? We decided, of course, not to. He said, "But say you did choose to be a gangster, become a criminal and harm others like this, there will be repercussions. There is going to be something that will happen." It is a choice of what you make. People cannot expect to take something that is nano A.I. into their bodies and not have any kind of repercussions, and nothing that they have will balance and heal that. That is not how it works. With every action, there is a reaction. You chose an inverted choice, and now you need to karmically energetically balance this out. Understand and step out of your ego and your fear, and start working on yourself. All can self-heal, as we have always taught.

So why I'm bringing this up in this chapter is because that is what is going on here. That is what they want to turn humanity into, but we are not allowing it because there is too much Star Seed energy on Earth. There are too many Angels, too many benevolent beings, and too many benevolent alien races that have incarnated into these human bodies. The dark aliens are beginning to realize that they cannot control us and they are freaking out. They do not want us to go past these Antarctic walls to realize there are lands beyond them. This infinity of lands that are other worlds and where our ancestors exist. Some of the Ascended Masters left our lands, closest to the crystalline dome space, where people live a lot longer. We live perhaps a fraction of what they live nearest to the rim of the dome. I will go ahead and start taking questions.

Question: "Wow, they are telling them the Earth population has died?"

AuroRa: Yes. We have people here inside, who are unaware that there are people outside that wall. Then there are people outside those walls who are not aware that we are inside of here. They have been putting them into these dome-like structures, telling them all these false things, and taking their children and putting them in these different experiments of these Super Soldiers, MK-Ultra, and Milab, and it is all being run by these negative entities.

Question: Is the clone colony where they begin to turn them into Grays?

AuroRa: Yes. Since all time is linear to itself. We have explained what Grays are in other COVID-19 explanations. These experiments that we are talking about - they have been injecting different types of A.I. into people - and it morphs them. Then fast forwarding time and space, this is how our human mind can understand this, as this A.I. turns them into these future species of Grays. The Grays are the worst. You are hearing a lot of people who think Grays are good. They are absolutely not good. They are clones from the hybridization of the future of human life that can no longer reproduce. They are cold, highly intelligent beings that are soulless.

Question: Is the Super Space Program, the Twenty-and-Back program real? Is this part of the transhumanism agenda?

AuroRa: That is real. Remember, it is happening through their military bases and through their technologies. Then they are reversing them back by putting them back into their bodies, right when they were taken, when they took them away. Some people are not put back into their bodies, which could be the true reason why people are randomly dying in their sleep. But again, the Secret Space Program is part of that program that we talked about that is right outside the wall. It is not out in outer space. What I'm seeing is that Rover (where it is supposedly traveling on Mars), is actually traveling to the outside lands that human life inside the icewall cannot reach, or more like the aliens cannot reach because they are so negatively polarized. They would have to be positively polarized if they stepped foot on some of these further outside lands. This Rover has an organic consciousness that is merged into it. So some of these lands that NASA is supposedly exploring, that they are telling us that is Mars, are really just outside our Antarctic walls.

Question: What healing, if any, can be provided for the organic consciousnesses that were infringed upon to create these controlling A.I.s? Would their Higher Selves be available during one of these videos so that they can be talked to?

AuroRa: Through A.U.R.A. Hypnosis past life regression entity removal, we talk to these A.I. consciousnesses we find in people's bodies too. When the Higher Selves, the Archangels, and their guides scan their bodies, they are finding A.I. consciousnesses attached to them. These A.I. consciousnesses tell us their journey, "I was this organic consciousness, and all of a sudden, they vacuumed me up through their U.F.O. and put me into these cubes that were technology matrixes. Then they took my consciousness and started fusing it with A.I. injections like the COVID-19 vaccine. They did this to us. We were originally elemental beings on this other planet." With these A.I. injections they then became these A.I. consciousness infusions. Watch our A.U.R.A. regressions, and read the Book 1 and 2, Galactic Soul History of The

Universe, because that is going to help you start understanding these concepts. This is so important. Do your homework.

Question: I got a puppy. The breeder got their first round of shots. On the shot records they gave the puppy Coronavirus was checked off under vaccinations. Is this the same COVID-19 vaccine used in humans?

AuroRa: It seems like that, unfortunately. There has never been a more important time to become the healer. You are the healer. You are the Star Seed. You are the healer in every which way. Everyone heals in different forms. Some people heal through their eyes. Some people heal through their touch. Some people heal through their love. Some people heal through their whole auric field and embodiment. Discover how you are a healer because that is why you incarnated here to Earth. To volunteer to bring that light in so that these infringing things that we are talking about, that are happening to this beautiful human life - us in this world - we stop this. This comes to an end. It is time that we understand that we are the healers, and we need to become the healed healer. Because many of you still have a wounded child operating from your wounded childhood. It is time to release that and grow from this wounded trauma state. Again, all our courses help you and give you the foundation for that. Come on over, all of you. There has never been a more important time for you to come and learn these courses so that you can assist the collective, and most importantly, begin with healing yourself and your loved ones. So yes, your puppy will need healing. If you watch all the A.U.R.A. Hypnosis past life regression sessions that we share on our channels, the Higher Selves and their teams talk and give a lot of guidance on how to self-heal. Watch those sessions if you want to start doing it on your own. Take notes. Take it seriously.

Question: Is the Loch Ness monster real?

AuroRa: Yes, it is real, and it is a sea animal. It is a water dragon.

Question: What causes the sea levels to rise if the ice melts if we are in a dome?

AuroRa: The dome is not the ice walls. The dome extends out past the ice walls. The water levels as the ice melts will extend past our Earth, connecting and flowing into the infinite waters of Creation.

Question: What is the crack in the land that is going on in Antarctica about? It has been expanding more every year.

AuroRa: That is the passageway out.

Question: When they do their live feeds from space, where are they at?

AuroRa: I feel like it is mostly computer generated imagery (C.G.I.), but there is something else that is more to that. Some of these outside lands that they have gone to, I feel like they are just the ones that are right outside, that they could actually reach. I see that from that viewpoint they are looking back.

Question: Can you speak more about the dinosaurs and dragons? A light bulb went off for me when you mentioned that in the last video.

AuroRa: We talked about how the dinosaur bones that they claim are dinosaurs are not. They are dragon bones! Leumuria (Mu) when we were crystalline, this land is still coexisting in the original organic 5D bifurcation of the [30]2/3rd world perspective. Because this world was magical with giants, unicorns, dragons, and so on. So because of that, you will see the skeletal bone remains of these creatures - these magical beings are animals that went extinct. Real animals that had multiple tails or multiple horns, that looked beautiful. If you want to know more about dragons, watch our playlist on the Atlantean/Mayan series. We go into the Land of Mu, the Land of Pangea, and all of the history before we became the inverted 3D that we are in now - the Matrix.

Question: How many planets are free from infringement?

---

[30] *Watch the playlist on our channels titled '2/3rd World Split/Bifurcation'.*

AuRoRa: At least seventy to eighty percent, at this point, are free from infringement. What we are seeing through the map in Chapter 2, is that other dark planets that are 3D like us, are directly around us, because we are in the lowest dimension of the third dimension in the last role of dimensions of communal life. They are nearest and besides us. They have been so used to siphoning our energy, and us feeding their intoxication of Adrenochrome or light from us. So they don't want to let that go. Ultimately this energy goes to the [31]Archon that will never be fulfilled with light, because it is an absence of light. It is always going to be hungry for light until it is eradicated, when Ascension happens.

Question: How do we begin to get people to see that they have made an inverted choice, just like choosing to be in gangs like you described?

Answer: You hold love. When I am talking to the Angels, they explain that whenever you are in a situation like this, say you have a family member, a loved one that took the jab, and you are so worried, you are like, "Oh my God, (especially after watching the Died Suddenly documentary). Wow, what if they die? What if this happens to them? What if their soul is inserted back into the Matrix?" They are going to come back into another family, and who knows what that family is going to be like, because they are going to have to replay their karma again. Hopefully, they will come back to you, maybe as a grandchild. You do not know what will happen. But, we do know that there is a divine intervention. So even though they made the decision to be a part of the inverted, they will always be given a second choice.

The biggest thing that the Angels say is that when we let go, surrender, and we just send love, this is the most powerful. Because what happens is that when we get worried, and we are in fear, we are holding onto them with a tight grip, and that is not helping them. So when you release, and you let go, the Universe is going to ensure that they are taken care of. You should talk to their Higher Self constantly. Learn how to channel your Higher Self so that you can then talk to their Higher Self. Through the Isis Priestess/Priest course you will learn how to channel your Higher Self/yourself and then channel benevolent beings. Then, you will learn how

---

[31] Read Book 2 for more on the A.I. 'Galactic History of the Multiverse - The Final Battle'.

to safely start talking to their Higher Self. You can do this right now with your consciousness. Start asking them, "Higher Self, what can I do? I'm going to send love. Higher Self, I'm going to be in surrender, but know that I'm not giving up on them. I'm going to hold the strongest Love-Light I have ever held in my infinite creation for them. I am going to believe that they are healed. I am going to give them clues in whatever which way. I can help them. I know I can."

Send love-light shields to them - especially if they are your direct children and grandchildren - you can shield them. Just keep holding the organic blueprint they originally were with their Higher Self's permission. Believe it, know it, feel it, and breathe it. A lot of those answers you will find under the video where we covered 'Died Suddenly'. How I explained that people can self-heal themselves through it. Just hold the highest potential and no matter what, don't worry, and don't fear. Even if it arises, because it can happen in this third dimension. These lower emotions sometimes control us or infringe upon us. No matter what, you are going to hold the love-light up. The minute you feel the lower vibrational emotions, you are going to transmute it. You are going to do breathing exercises. You are going to talk to your inner child, your own human ego, balancing it out.

If you go to my Live Channeling videos, we have channeled so many different beautiful beings, like Archangels, who give us such a foundation for spirituality and how you can tap into and activate these infinite potentials of you. Unleash them, awaken them on Earth. So take these gifts that they have given us through these videos and literature that we have channeled throughout the years, and start working hard. You can do it. But no matter what, believe that all is possible. All is healable. But remember, no attachments. Love all but attach to none. Because that is the best way to surrender, release, and allow flow. That is really when healing occurs.

Question: Isn't that interesting how they say that if you go on the Moon, you bounce?

AuroRa: I never put it together until I realized that there were people outside the ice walls. Remember how we talked about the lighter you get closer to the edge of the crystalline dome? How you start bouncing? That is gravity. They are going through their spaceships and their shuttles underground to the other side of the ice walls. It is all hierarchical competition.

There is China, Russia, Ukraine, and the Americas, and they are all fighting for who is going to go out and conquer more of these lands. Just like the Spaniards or English went and conquered all the indigenous people, and spread out to the islands, and North and South America. It is that same concept. They are trying to get to the other side to see who they can conquer, and what further experiments they can then control humankind through.

Someone said in regards to Zen (AuroRa's husband) describing growing up in Chicago and choice of being in a gang: "Yes, I love that example. Thank you to Zen for that." So many are asleep that they are even in the harmful gangs. You can picture that as they are in the gang of the COVID-19 vaccinated, because they are so hateful and mean to you. They want you to get it too. Why? Because we know they are controlled by the A.I. system.

Someone said, "Oh no, I just adopted a puppy too. I need to look into the shot paperwork." Yes, start transmuting and healing them. You can do it. Use your hands, open up your hand chakras. Place your hands on them. Love them. Set intentions before you go to bed. You could do this as well with your children. That you are going to heal them as you go to bed. Meditate constantly, dream, and use sacred alchemy, colors, and symbols to help them heal. And of course, R.A.A.H. Reiki and A.U.R.A. Hypnosis certifications teach you deeply how to help assist others to remove the COVID-19 vaccine and all vaccines, and how to remove the A.I. Archons linked to it. You learn how to remove A.I. consciousness, Reptilians, and Grays from people and their timelines. How to heal people who fractured their souls and became clones because the military did that to them, as they are run by the Illuminati.

Somebody said: "So many people do not believe the COVID-19 Vaccine is bad." Eventually, they will understand, is what I can say to that. Eventually, it will be seen.

Question: Project Blue Beam is a program the military is testing to use a hologram of an alien, or whatever, for disclosure and to create fear in that area. This can be used to create a fake alien invasion.

AuroRa: Well, they do have that technology where they can project and make it seem like there are aliens invading, but the aliens are already inside. They are inside and attached to some human bodies. You have met these people, and they are really cold and lifeless sometimes. They are really programmed because they have alien attachments inside of them. They are the host of the parasitic alien.

Amazing! Thank you, everyone, who is assisting, and thank you to you in the future who will read this and share it. I love you, honor you, and respect you. My love to everyone.

END OF SESSION.

The disclosure is infinite in this Chapter! So many puzzle pieces are finally placed together through the knowledge shared. For those who have been searching for the true disclosure for so long, you know and feel how many lightbulbs went off in your brain, through the understanding of this remote viewing session. Get ready for more, as every chapter will continue to build upon one another!

"A healthy mind questions all reasons of what does not make sense in their environment. An unhealthy mind just follows what they are told by supposed superior authority under the pretense that it makes sense."
~AuroRa

--------------<<>>--------------

6

REMOTE VIEWING BEYOND THE WALLS OF ANTARCTICA PT 6
OUR ANCESTORS MAPS & KNOWLEDGE

Streamed Live: December 22, 2022

In this chapter we expand on our understanding of the Earth being flat, by looking back at the biggest clues of our ancestors' history left behind for us to unravel. We look into our ancestors' advanced knowledge and we discover, land by land, and page by page, what Earth looked like through the earliest maps found from the 1500's. How we as a collective are living through the aftermath of some of their choices in our now future time space.

--------------<<>>--------------

"When we go inwards, through our hearts, we connect inwards into Mother Earth's heart."

"We are the sunshine in our home and our family."
~AuroRa

--------------<<>>--------------

AuroRa: Through the previous chapter you learned that there is another human civilization, outside the ice wall in the lands of Antarctica. And they are not aware that we are here, and we were not aware that they were there. The military are performing experiments on them. Some really dark stuff. Now we are going to take it further into those specific lands.

I have been remote viewing into 1587 when this Urbano Monte map (Chapter 2, page 25) was made. The aliens used technology to freeze and make the Arctic wall, so that we could not see what is out there in these outer lands. Using the Urbano Monte map as a reference, these circling lands are directly at the Antarctica walls. Back then in the 1500's, 1400's, or even 1000 millenniums ago, there were rulers of royal men, as shown through their images at the petals of the edge of the map and inside the lands (image below). Some of them look similar to the races that are located right under them. For example, this man is darker skinned, and he is under the petal of Africa (image on page 118). These are the outer rims where these men were located and where they were ruling.

We thought that it was perhaps just the English and the Spaniards that spread out and conquered all the indigenous places they could find such as islands, and North and South America. Some of these royal ruling men were dark and dangerous. These families illustrated on the map, are basically the seven or nine dark founding families that we have heard about through disclosure. They did not come from England or Spain. What I am seeing in this time and space, is that they came from these outer lands - the ring of land around us. The indigenous people all over Earth were conquered by these outside races that were on these outskirts.

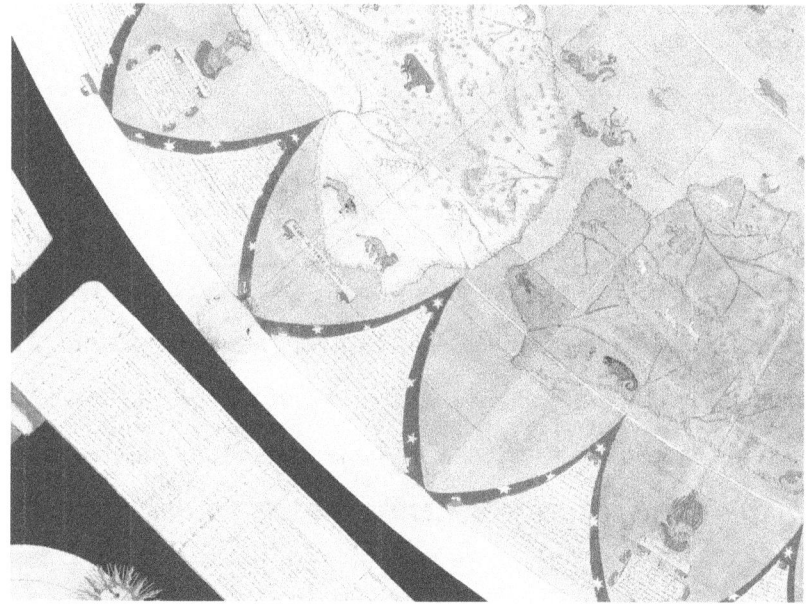

Close up of royal rules at the petals edge of the Urbano Monte Map.

Close up of African royal ruler.

When you look closer at these encircling lands, you can see a Centaur right under the America lands (image on next page), where all the Mayan and indigenous pyramids are at. At the lands directly under North America, you can see that there is no royal man designated to these lands. Every other land has a royal man at the lands directly parallel to them. This land for some reason is free. I do sense that there are some benevolent people still there, perhaps ancestors of ours that went out of this ring of land of control.

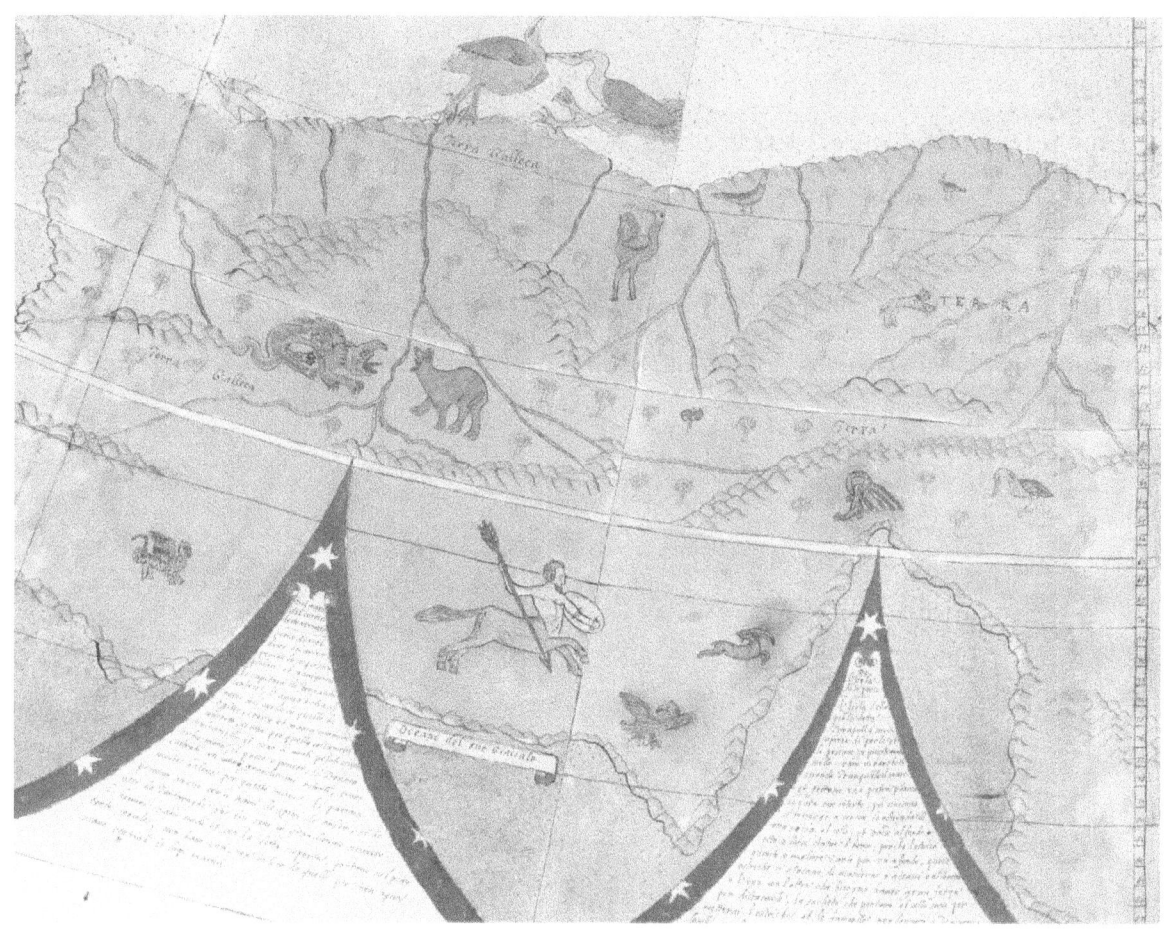

The Centaurs were the ones that were part of assisting all these indigenous people, specifically in Mexico and North America. They were their guardians. I am seeing this grand battle that happened. All of these dark forces - these royal men out there that rule these other lands - attacked this outer sacred land of where the Centaurs were. Remember time has been altered. Not much of what we say will match what they have written in Google and the history books. The Centaur land was providing a force field for the indigenous people to carry the [32]Atlantean information that we talked about in previous videos. Once they brought that forcefield shield of the Centaurs and benevolent beings down, they then were able to conquer them and go into Mexico and the Americas including anywhere there were still indigenous people who were one with the Earth and who were not programmed yet. They took them over. They indoctrinated them to the false religion, control systems, and the schooling. Once they attacked their energy there, they were able to go in and split up the continents. How many

---

[32] Watch the Mayan/Atlantean series on our channels.

continents do we have? We have seven. How many families are there supposedly? Seven? Once they came out from the outer lands, and they completely split up the lands inside, they then came up with the New World Order diabolical plans on how they were going to continue to control everything and everyone.

There is a direct connection from land to land here (image below) in the South America lands. You can literally walk into Antarctica through the lower part of South America.

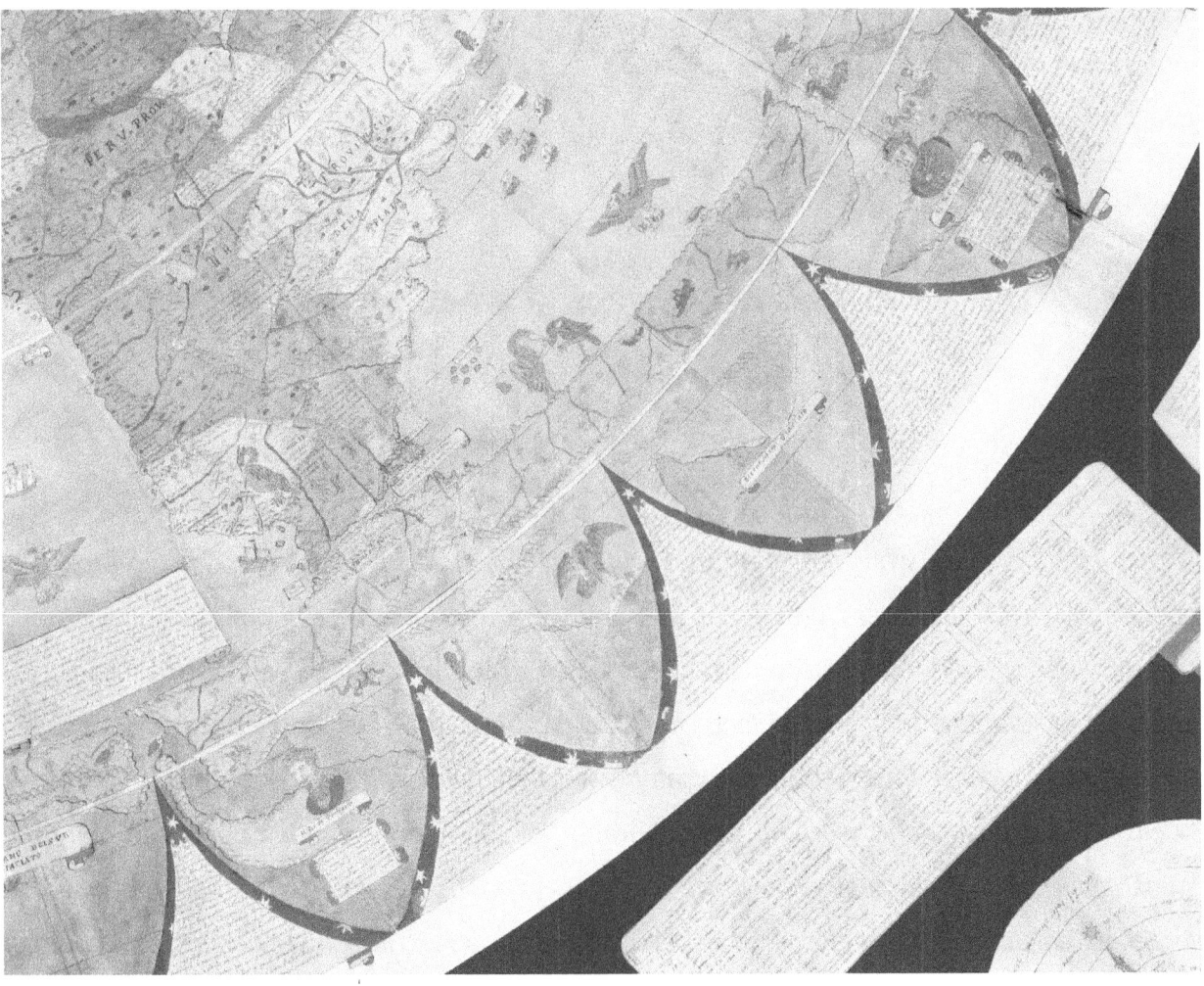

This map is in Italian. It is a little different from Spanish, so I can understand most of it. For example, all of these islands here feel like Australia (image on next page). These are the closest there besides South America where you could directly walk to Antarctica.

120

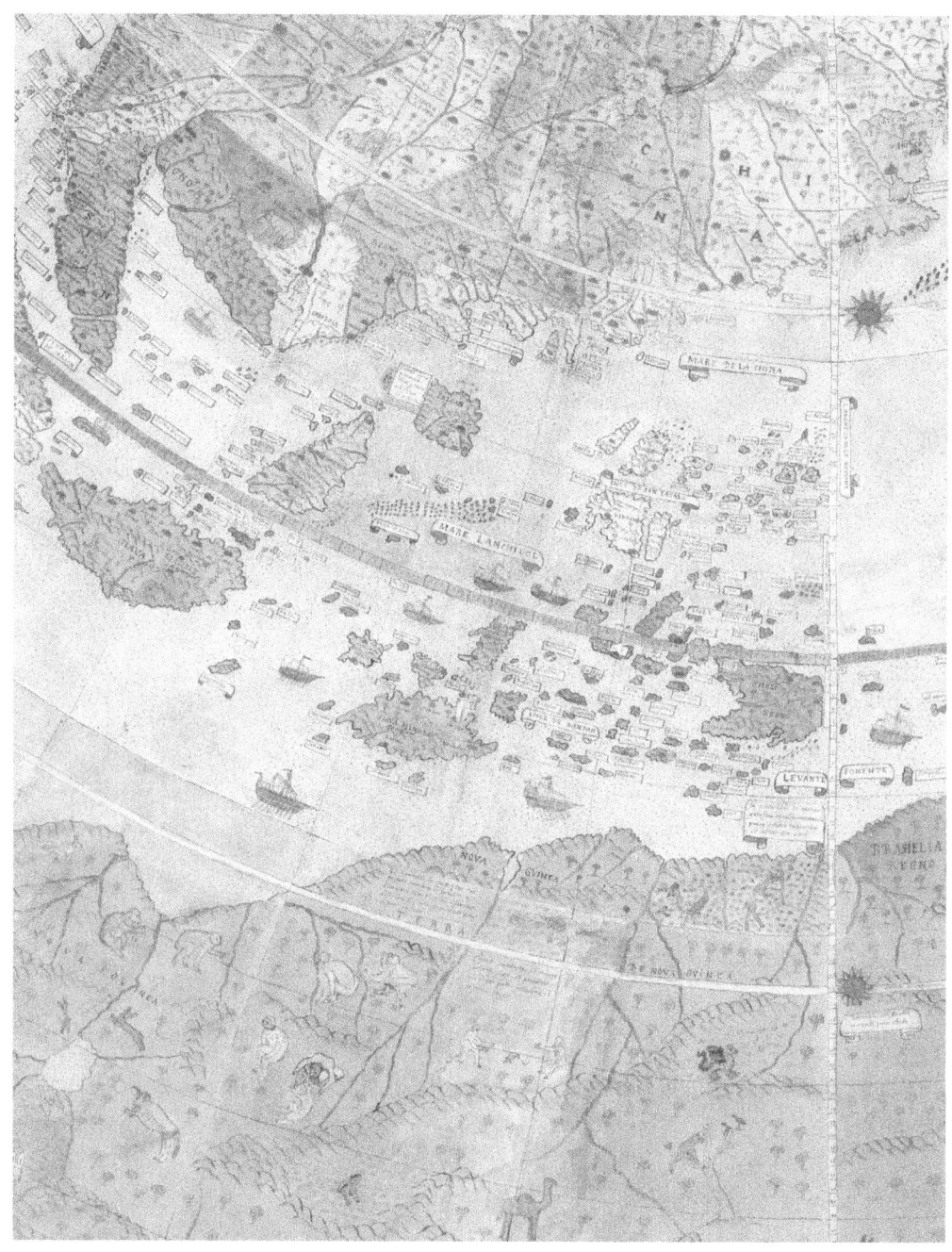

There are colder poles at the bottom of every single one of these lands, like the bottom of South America and Africa. Where they are closest to these ice walls. There are penguins and arctic animals closest to the ice wall. They are very much lying to us. There are so many more lands that we do not know about. Look at all these Islands here (image above). This map was exciting for me to look at and to be able to see energetically. It is just phenomenal. There is

even an image of an Angel there (image below). I have to meditate on that further, and I will speak of this in another chapter/book.

They came in from the outer lands and conquered all the inside. Then they started erasing our history, making us think that we are on a globe and there is nothing beyond the Arctic walls.

The colors show that this map is coded, as it seems like the red is more of the drier lands. If you look at this nasty man here (page 120) it seems like his lands were more desert-looking. If you look here, there is red in this area, and the energies where Arizona is. It is amazing to look at this map and how accurate it is, when we look at this actual document that matches what we have been speaking about.

Interviewer: "A military man had a near death experience and saw huge crystal structures very clearly. Is this the same thing as he was looking at the outer edges?"

AuroRa: I'm getting yes. That is what he was seeing. I can see these huge crystals that he saw. They have multiple points, like a raw crystal that has multiple points coming out of it, and are sharp at the ends. So interesting. There are definitely formations like that out there and in the sacred lands.

Going back to the Urbano Monte map and those royal men, they got compromised by negative aliens. The aliens started plaguing their minds. We talk about how these aliens try to weaponize humans against each other on the 'Cosmic Mother Rising' show that I co-host with Laura Eisenhower on Rumble. We talk about the A.I. Alien Invasion and how these dark Greys, Reptilians, and dark aliens compromised the men that were the rulers even before 1940. What we have explained, is during the late 1930's and 1940's the aliens landed on Earth by traveling through dark portals.

Through these dark portals on Earth they gave information to these men directly into their consciousnesses. The men were then downloading this information like you would do with a computer because they were a matching vibration to these dark forces. Especially, after they conquered, killed, raped, and burned to death the women and the children. I personally have Indigenous memories and they are horrific. They would take children, rape them, and them toss them into piles and burn them alive. The children were screaming, violated, and burning. This is how disgusting and horrible those men were. Christopher Columbus did not necessarily come from Spain or England, he actually came from the outer lands! It also was not just him. It was all these families that are part of the New World Order depopulation of Earth.

Interviewer: "Is there any information about the crystal skulls that workers claimed to have found in a pyramid in South America? Are the crystal skulls for real?"

AuroRa: Yes. I do feel that there were crystal skulls. They give me the creeps when I tap into that energy. It feels dark. It does not feel like it is a benevolent consciousness speaking through these crystals. Also, their heads are elongated. I know an alien race that is very dark that has an elongated head. They are part of the dark Anunnaki. I feel that they went through and placed these alien crystal heads in these locations to compromise them. I do not feel that they are positive in nature. I personally would never connect to any of these crystal heads. I do believe that there are other positive crystal heads, but any specific ones that have an elongated head like that would be typically negative. I feel that they are Zeta Grays that are tall, slender things with an elongated head. They have these huge mouths that have sharp pointy teeth inside of them. The mouth can expand almost as big as their face. Those specific crystal heads are related to these Zeta Grays, and were planted to invert the human race through different pyramids.

Crystal heads are important to us. We used to sculpt them ourselves in ancient times. Typically, you do not want someone to sculpt them for you. If you sculpt them yourself, there is sacred information that will be given to you through your soul signature. We have been taught to buy sculpted crystals from people, but they will be matching their frequencies. You don't know what type of frequencies they will be and what kind of entities are channeled to create those skulls, so they may be dangerous. But feel it out if one feels good for you. Do not feel fearful about this. If one feels good for you, and helps you connect to love, then that is all that matters. Maybe whoever sculpted that one would be a positive being. I am just a very highly intuitive developed being, so I can sense everything including all the timelines that might have been created, or energy that might have been fed into what someone else creates for you. Therefore, it is always best to create your own things. That is what we have always taught since Leumuria, Mu, Sumerian, Atlantis, and so on. Specifically for the skulls, why this is so important is because it is not just someone sculpting a guitar or something like that. No, this is something very sacred. A skull would directly link you to your Akashic and your memories. So how could someone sculpt you a skull? The skull would be a matching vibration to your Akashic, and you are the only one that is in charge and the Guardian of your Akashic. You do have Guardians in your Akashic Hall of Records. For example, some of my Guardians are benevolent beings from Egypt, like Thoth and Anubis, alchemical dragons guarding, along with the Archangels, and so on. So how could someone else sculpt that for you? The skull is a sacred memory of what your brain and your consciousness is throughout the multitude of the Universe and the Multiverse. So that is why someone cannot do that for you.

Interviewer: Someone said, "I know that Toth was putting his body into regeneration pods. I always thought that some of these Giants that we have found were already in stasis. How do we know that they are not soulless until a soul enters the body? Could they be incarnated bodies like [33]NPCs (Non Player Characters)? Could they upload consciousness when they are ready?"

AuroRa: Back to the Giants. Yes, I do feel that some of them went into a stasis. They were put into stasis by their own kind to protect them. I see that there are Giants still in some of these mountain ranges and people have actually seen them on TikTok. I saw a video that a man recorded a Giant climbing a mountain and the military came in. Unfortunately, I think they did something to the Giant in that video, and then guess what? That man came up missing shortly after, which is really sad. There is always going to be both. Wherever there is a negative, we also find a positive to it. Nothing will always be directly negative, as there must always be light with the darkness. I do see that the military, and these negative founding families from these outer lands, do have advanced technology that can place Giants and other people into stasis.

The last chapter in Book One 'Galactic Soul History of the Universe', we talk about the Matrix pods. In these Matrix pods, they have technologies in the alien bases on Earth where they are keeping people asleep. If they find for example, a benevolent being like a fractal of a Seraphim Angel that incarnated on Earth, or any type of higher vibrational being that carries these crystalline codes in their DNA, they tend to make genetically clones out of them. They will abduct these beings and then put them into the pods. Then they could do all sorts of experiments by creating clones and different dark things from this being, or they want to study it by experimenting on it. Like all of those experiments that we have watched in our Earth's history. We have only seen glimpses of some of what they do, through our life experiences that we see, such as when Adolf Hitler started doing experiments on people.

Going back to the map, we see how these royal families invaded all of these countries and the seven continents that they reign over, by looking at whoever is placed at the ring on the

---

[33] A Non-Player Character (NCP) is a human that does not have an actual consciousness. They are under programs written by the inverted Matrix simulation, like a character in a video game that is just there to fill in space. Instead the NPC's fill up our world and are at times used to distract real human beings.

map (Page 117) at the bottom. The ones that are running these circled lands, are the ones on the maps closest to the seven continents that they ended up possessing. This is because they allowed parasitic alien entities to attach inside of them in the astral realm. The dark aliens convinced these royal families through their mind in that specific moment in time, to go in and start the takeover through these wars. Not all royal families were convinced, as some were too benevolent. So those that allowed the inverted conquer through negative soul-binding contracts with the dark forces, teamed up against those who would not turn against their people, and the dark royals took them out and their bloodlines.

Through the negative portals that were open on Earth in our time and space in the late 1930's and early 1940's, at that point, they had landed officially in their own alien bodies. The military was then given the negative technology that we talked about in the A.I. Alien Invasion video. The aliens were then able to spread out, wherever they could reach on Earth - once they were given permission by these royal families - once more in our time and space. These negative aliens who came through these dark portals on Earth, targeted these seven families again. Especially because in their bloodlines, those original negative contracts of their ancestors from the 1500's royal families still remained. These families have been cloned over and over in Earth's History by these negative aliens. These clone bodies cannot live too long, so they have to keep remaking them. The soul is just being replaced into these different bodies. The consciousness is being taken back and forth into these bodies. It was at that point, they started to build the ice wall some time in the 1800's. This was because the aliens started giving them the alien technology to do so. They then started changing all of the history of Earth. And here we are in the 1900's and 2000's where everything has been erased from our memory, because of the indoctrination of our Ancestors who would be the seeders of organic memory and knowledge. But we still carry the memory in our DNA, as our DNA will always hold these memories.

Interviewer: "What is going on with the Grey aliens A.I. they are breeding in Chicago? Since they are inorganic, besides keeping one's frequency high, how do we get rid of these as they are controlling the people and causing them to harm others?"

AuroRa: The Greys are half organic and half A.I. These alien military bases can just make them through the process of clones with artificial wombs in their labs. We definitely want to stop that from being allowed in any form. After they make them in these artificial wombs, they then spread them out in different locations. A lot of them are placed in Grey UFO disk ships, so that they can abduct people constantly. I do not think people realize how much their neighborhood or their town has been abducted. If you are not shielding, according to them you are consenting. Just about all of your neighbors are being abducted and are being experimented on.

The Archon A.I. thing (IT), is an abomination. Ultimately, these aliens are puppets to this thing. They are just on a program that IT has downloaded into them. So because they are part A.I., IT can download these programs of what IT wants them to do. How it wants them to eat off Light on IT's behalf. IT is never going to get full because IT is an emptiness of Light. No matter how much Light IT feeds into itself, ultimately, IT is never going to be Light again, because IT separated itself from Source Love-Light long ago and this cannot be reversed.

The biggest thing we can do is to continue to communicate about these dark aliens that are harming people and abducting them. These aliens do all sorts of experiments with the people and their eggs and their sperm. There is a lot of confusion about hybrids. Some people think that they made contracts and agreements with these aliens to supposedly have Grey baby hybrids or hybrid babies overall. This is false. Be very careful if you are a hybrid Mother. Do not go to any site where they are supposedly a hybrid community for mothers. They are going to target you even more, and you are basically contracting yourself for further abductions. Treat yourself sacredly. Sacredness comes with a lot of secretive information that you really want to guard for yourself. A lot of people have memories of these Greys. They have seen them in dream states of mind. They have erased memories that seem so familiar. They are trying to remember them. We are the advocates, and we have to continue to use our voice.

Interviewer: "If every divine and Universal law has been broken here, why and how could an advanced civilization watch the continual abuses?"

AuroRa: It is not that they are allowing it. What is going on is that we have free will, and we have to honor our choices. If you are being abducted, most likely you decided to allow that in some form. You may be accidentally abducted when you were sleeping, because you are not shielded by Source Love-Light, and you do not have enough crystals around you and so on for protection. Or, when you were astral traveling in time and space through your consciousness, they saw you and "made" you make a contract with them. Have you ever had a dream where they try to give you papers and you have to sign it? Do not ever sign those! Through supposed spiritual teachings and communities, you have been taught that shielding with your own Source Love-Light is fear based, which is ridiculous.

If you start shielding, you will be able to recognize when they try to do this to you, enough to not consent to it. If you are not using your Source Love-Light around you, then this is what is allowing them to just scan you and then infringe upon you. It is your choice. Now, the minute that you start shielding, what happens is you start remembering your dreams. You start remembering, "Oh my God, there was this dark entity that tried to infringe upon me last night, but because I had my shields, I was able to remember what they tried to do, and I was able to stop it." The reason why is because you are not stepping into your empowerment - your sovereignty. Therefore, you are choosing that dark path in some way. Whether you want to admit this or not. You are in some form. You cannot blame anyone. When you blame that is when you become narcissistic or a victim. The greatest narcissists are the biggest blamers and the biggest liars. You do not want to be that energy embodiment. Instead, you want to take ownership and responsibility upon your decisions - whether they were this life or a past life - that you are working out in this time and space in the now. Once you understand this, you can then start really releasing yourself from these inversions.

Many have been programmed to think that you are being a pest or pain to call for assistance from your Angels, Guardians, or Source. It is like you are bothering them. You need to get past all of this negative Archonic New World Order programming, and start stepping into your power. When you are matching your benevolent team's vibration, you are up there in high vibration. Until then, you are stuck in this lower vibration infringement. Your guides cannot overstep your boundaries of benevolence. They are who you must ask for help. That is when *they are allowed to come in. Only negative entities do not need you to ask them for help. They are the ones that overstep your boundaries, by not needing permission.*

Benevolence has to follow the sacred Laws of the Universe. When you allow the entities to break these sacred laws upon you by choosing that path, they still eventually have to respect your free will once you figure them out. If the benevolence oversteps your free will, then they become Archonic and parasitic in nature themselves. So they cannot. They have to let you do what you want to do. We are not dictatorships or hierarchy. They must respect your choice. All they can do is keep sending you love, and keep sending you synchronicities up until you start the embodiment of Source. Then you start seeing this gigantic team around you. Circles and circles of these benevolent beings around you. They have always been by you, but you could not hear them and see them. They were always there. You just were not the matching vibration to hear them or to see them. It is not that they are not there or not trying to assist you. They are there, but you need to raise your vibration to be able to hear them.

Interviewer: In regards to the Vesica Pisces, someone says they have always seen the Universe that has bubbles and bubbles, like the Vesica Pisces and they are really large. Are these all testatory fields?

Aurora: I am not familiar with testatory fields, but they are toroidal spheres in form. They have a donut shaped consciousness as bubbles, for both collective consciousness or individual consciousness.

Interviewer: There are a couple of questions about the space program. "What secrets, if any, do you think the new James Webb Space Telescope will uncover?"

Aurora: What they are seeing through these beautiful telescopes is the projection of the Universe beyond the dome. I think it would be grand and beautiful. We are going to learn more about how expansive our Multiverse is through this series. Those of us who can remote view will see more into these images that they will zoom in on, as far as they can, as they call it, many light years away. These places will be Verses within the Multiverse. I am seeing pockets of spaces of Verses within the Multiverse as well. I think many beauties will be found with that telescope.

Interviewer: "The Artemis space rocket that was just announced, where was it going?"

Aurora: It was definitely going into the outer lands, as we explained prior. I am seeing this land right here under Australia (image below). It was heading in that direction. I know that there are experiments going on back and forth. I see technology structures that are very extraterrestrial looking. It reminds me of the Archon technology. It looks like multiple beams, and they are all sticking out. It is really creepy.

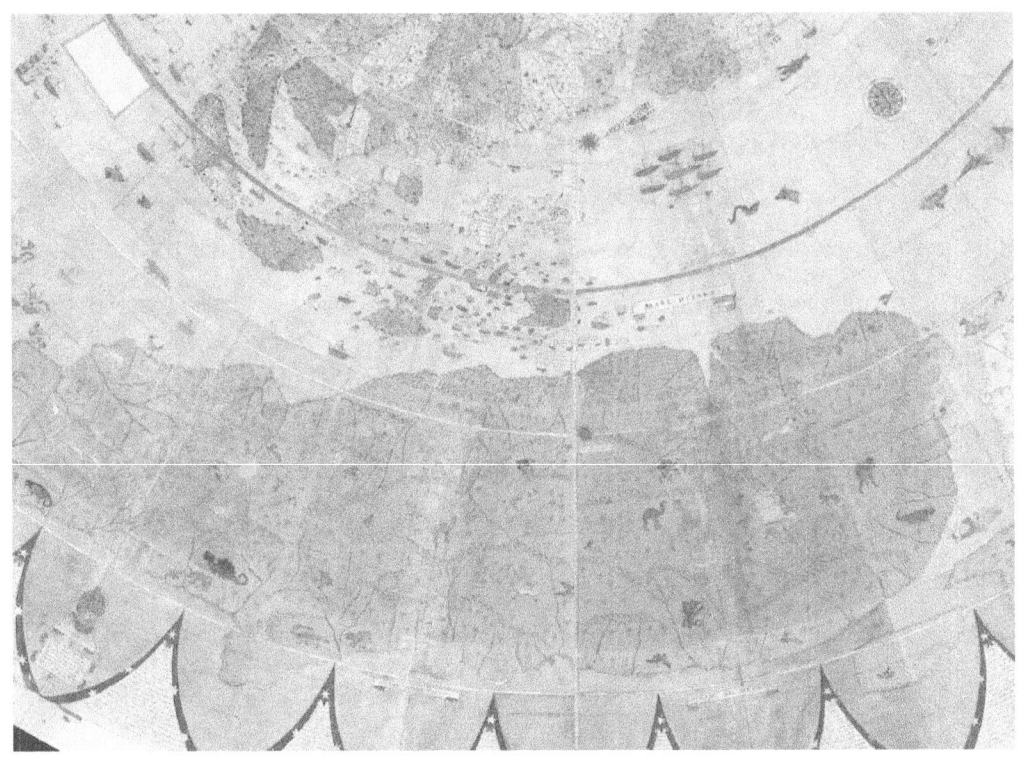

Interviewer: I am seeing the same beams you are. They curve over and project a projection.

Aurora: Why did they send the spaceships over to these lands? What do they carry in the spaceships? Well one, they have to keep on the persona that supposedly we are going to outer space through these spaceships. But really, they are going out to the outskirts of these lands. This place is a black market. They are storing something in that spaceship that is bringing something out from here to there. But why do they have to go across to these lands?

Interviewer: What I'm seeing is that they are carrying it over. Those are the specific portals to the areas that they need to go to, so they can just transport them there. Similar to the people who say they have had experiences on Mars through the Secret Space programs. They use those portals.

Aurora: I agree. There must be a negative portal there that they are working through. I'm seeing an important metal or mineral that they are taking on this other ship. That is as far as I'm going to go there. It is too dark to look further.

Interviewer: Someone asked, "Are there two suns? Some people say that the second sun would be something called Nibiru. Is that a part of the outer lands or is it a planet?"

Aurora: There are two suns on the map (image below). There is a sun here and a sun here. One of the suns goes around what we would call the equator and the other near the Antarctica ring of land (image below).

The sun moves in a circular motion on the land. At the center near the Arctic, the sun does not go down. Some countries, like Norway, will have months where the sun never goes down. This is the same in the highest portions of Canada, Iceland, Alaska, Finland and Sweden. Some of them will have full dark days. The other sun is out here, and it spins around for these outer lands. I see that the sun has been bifurcating energetically just like the Earth and the Moon. I'm wondering if sometimes the suns would energetically somehow align? (In November 2023, at the Nashville Retreats we got to see this incredible sight, as the two suns aligned and overlaid each other, while creating two rays of light in opposite directions. (The image below) There is a false cloud filter over the sun that [34]H.A.A.R.P. pumps into our atmosphere daily, that tries to block us from receiving the sun's healing properties. But since we are in the organic Earth, we can feel the sun's potency and beauty, and we know that Source channels through the sun no matter what they try.

---

[34] H.A.A.R.P. is a government derived program and technology that is used throughout Earth to make artificial man-made clouds and fogs in our skies, which are soaked with chemicals to try to control the human mind, keeping it dense and asleep. One of the biggest problems that causes illness and disease to humankind.

Interviewer: Someone would like to ask what you thought about the videos of the different volcanoes that are erupting in Indonesia? They saw a face of what they say is a Goddess. They want to know if all those eruptions around the world are a good thing for cleansing the Earth? Or are they a bad thing with the dark forces trying to destroy the land to have control? Also what is the symbology of the Goddess appearing in a good natural event?

Aurora: That is Mother Pele or Divine Mother that you are seeing through the volcanoes. She does not just connect to Hawaii, she connects to all volcanoes. There are different Goddesses that are essences of these mountains. The volcanoes are trying to transmute the negative energy on Earth. As they erupt they spread energy through their eruptions to transmute the dark energy on Earth. That is why you are seeing Goddesses in the formations within the volcano eruptions. Through the volcanoes Mother Earth is balancing herself.

In Mexico, there is a mountain that is in the shape of a [35]Goddess. She is really beautiful. They are reminding us that they are the Goddesses. The one in Mexico is laying down. She was a Giant that fell asleep and became a mountain in ancient times. I do feel that it is positive. I personally love lava and fire myself. The energy from these elements just feels so wonderful. When I went to Hawaii, I laid on the lava rocks on the beach, and they completely rejuvenated and gave me rebirthing energies like the Phoenix. We know though that the Illuminati have taken these beautiful benevolent symbols such as the Phoenix, and have tried to invert them. They call themselves the Order of the Phoenix - which is disgusting! The Phoenix is the embodiment of the most sacred symbols known. They are trying to invert dark magic into the Phoenix divinity, which is not possible, and so disrespectful.

Interviewer: "We live in an illusion, like The Matrix. What individual event will trigger our ability to see what is real beyond the green screen?"

Aurora: The biggest thing is the Flat Earth awareness. When we start looking at it, and we realize that if it is a globe, why would the Arctic areas have the sun up for that amount of

---

[35] Mayan/Aztec Goddess Iztaccihuatl is the Sacromonte Mountain located in Mexico City. Here she lays in slumber. Iztaccihuatl means flame, and she is the Goddess of day, heat, fire and queen of the volcanoes.

time, and sometimes for months on end? Technically, wouldn't it be darker there, if the supposed North and South poles are further away from the Sun through the Earth being a globe? We need to start questioning and looking at all of these things that make absolutely no sense. The divine has told me it is really important to realize that we are on a Flat Earth, because we are in the third dimension. This is because planes of existence are layered on top of one another. It is interesting, because the minute that you talk about Earth being flat - the people who are so programmed to it being a globe - they attack you. They get so pissed off! They think you are insane and mock you like bullies. Which is classic and common acts when you are indoctrinated to a false system. They refuse to listen to what you are saying. Along with what was found in our ancestors' hieroglyphics and knowledge left behind, this should be common sense to us.

Interviewer: My guides just asked me to show you something with this globe that I have right here. We have been told all of our lives that Antarctica is the largest continent, because we can reach Antarctica through all counties - if we go opposite of the North, which is instead South. If that is true. Why is it so miniscule shown on the bottom of the globe? It is a very small area depicted. If it is the largest out of every continent, why would it be shown like that?

Aurora: Yes, I agree. So keep questioning, keep looking, and keep searching yourself as you are meant to. This series is about expanding your consciousness through your mind. Continue activating your heart so you can start questioning these things that make no sense.

Interviewer: Someone wanted to ask, "Can we not see the ancestors that we have unless we are in the fifth dimensional body consciousness? Is that correct?"

Aurora: It depends on which ancestors you are speaking of. Are you speaking about the ones that are directly outside the ice rim? No, they would be more like third dimensional beings like us, right outside the Antarctic circle. But the ones that are outside yes, they would be more of a fifth and fourth dimensional beings. You can see them, when you are operating in the fifth dimension, in your imagination, your third eye, and your consciousness. The other ones you can see physically, if we ever make it out of these ice walls, this Antarctica ring. Which I feel we eventually will someday. I think that would be the biggest part, catalyzing us, so that we will start collectively ascending out.

Interviewer: This next question ties in about the ancestors and the sun. "Some believe that going into the light after death is a trap. To me, I always feel it was through the sun or wherever it is we need to go. What do you think?"

Aurora: I feel that through the heart, inside, inwards into Mother Earth is how we are ascending out. Though souls and soul groups do come in through the portal of the sun, and then we go inwards, out into our hearts. It is always inwards, right? When we go inwards, through our hearts, we connect inwards into Mother Earth's heart. It is the gateway that society calls the underworld, but again, false programming. Through the Egyptian teachings, the Guardians that guard these sacred energies, they are guarding her in this moment in time, and they will guard this sacred energy until we ascend out. Once you are a matching vibration - your heart to that portal - that will ascend you out. I feel we used to go out through the sun in the past, but then it changed with the fall of Atlantis. It shifted, and then we went inwards through her heart of Mother.

We are the sunshine in our home and our family. It is a very important role that we play. Think about you being that sunshine for your family and how you are doing that. So whether you are male or female, become more of the embodiment of that sunshine to Source energy and be the heart for your family. Every family should have a beautiful heart.

Interviewer: There were several people who were saying how they love the series, and they were letting us know how activating it is, and also confirming lots of the different things that have been seen. They are just absorbing it all, very grateful, and sending lots of love. Also, another A.U.R.A. practitioner was talking about the dream that you shared previously. It was upsetting that they saw what the COVID-19 vaccine is doing to clients and different family members, but they are grateful everyday for your teachings. The truths that you are sharing, and that Part Five of the series was really expansive. This practitioner also had a session with a client who worked on clearing certain negative Mars energies that were also linked to the royal family. They also talked with a client who had spoken of negative aliens under the ice in Antarctica.

Aurora: That is amazing! The more that we come into this awareness within this Rumble channel, the more that this will then spread throughout Earth. You are going to see people coming into more awareness and being able to tap into this knowledge, because that is how we work. When a person gets an idea or a sacred download, we share it with the collective and then it spreads. Then all of a sudden everyone is getting information about it because it is time for it to unveil itself. So this is a time where we are here speaking to you and communicating this to you, because it is time for us to start unveiling these secrets that they keep us in.

Interviewer: Is there anything important you want to share in regards to wrapping up the end of this year?

Aurora: Were you all working very hard this week? Especially right before the twenty-first portal happened? Maybe in dream time? Were you having some powerful dreams? We are all collectively working in these times and spaces, shifting not only the collective energy, but also our individual timelines. So keep on working. Keep setting your intentions. Keep shielding with your Source Love-Light. It is so beautiful, because you then receive continual information from your Higher Self when you shield with love. It will be easier for them to connect to you and actually reach you. Just like a phone call way, and they can connect to you. Keep growing. Let's all continue to grow. Question everything. Love one another. Continue to send love to Earth.

I want to share with you this Lemurian word, the original 5D language of Earth, Crystalline language. Light language that was given to us by a star child. Lorona - Lo-Ro-Na. L O R O N A means "I'm free"! Be the embodiment of that! When you are doing your shielding - your sovereignty - state it with an intention of "I am free. I have attachments to none". In Spanish, Llorona means weeping Mother, but actually, it means you are free in Crystalline light language. Thank you for being here with us. I love you, honor you, and respect you. Lo-Ro-Na! We are free! I am free! Free your spirit!

END OF SESSION.

"All that has been forgotten can be found in the memory of the clues left behind for us, from those who walked before us. Those who oppress can retrieve and delete or alter the remnants left behind for us, but they will never be able to find it all to dispose of. The truth shall always be revealed, simply because of the lightness that is held within it. What is lighter in density, must always scientifically float up to the surface."
~AuroRa

--------------<<>>--------------

7

THE RESISTANCE AT THE NORTH POLE

Session #531: Recorded in February 2023
Never before shared.

We will change it up a bit through this chapter by providing a glimpse into the detailed sacred knowledge obtained when conducting an [36]A.U.R.A. Hypnosis Healing session, which you have heard being referenced throughout this book. Step into the world of the exponential work in the theta brainwave of hypnosis, and the true power of our minds and consciousness.

---

[36] Read 'Galactic Soul History of the Universe' book series for more memories of people from all over the world of who they have been in this dimension and others.

In this online A.U.R.A. Hypnosis Healing session, Cynthia the client takes us on the journey of understanding how much underground benevolence there is whether this Earth or another. What is hidden at the North Pole? But, before that we remember a life that Starseeds most often have had to live of persecution. What it is like before we incarnate into a planet, and instead express ourselves as the energy of Source. This session provides us a view into how vast the Earth and other Earths can be, much of "What if an Earth is being controlled by a form of a Deep State?", and the obstacles that the resistance can come up against.

--------------<<>>--------------

"Because it's a parallel dimension it is like a mirror. So what is happening on one sphere or one spherical dimension of the Earth, can be felt as a reflection on another. It's like an echo in another time and space."

~Cynthia

--------------<<>>--------------

A: *[AuroRa] What is it that you feel around you?*

C: [Cynthia] Darkness, like a blanket. I feel heavy, it is almost like I'm covered in something. I think it is Earth. I'm on the ground.

A: *Feel yourself, are you able to move within the space?*

C: No, it feels really claustrophobic, like I'm in a box. I think I'm underground.

A: *Let's go back in time, to right before this happens, where you end up being underground. You are there now. Tell me what you see and sense.*

C: There are people around me, an angry mob shouting.

A: *Look at yourself. What do you look like?*

C: I'm young. I have a dress on and I've got long hair. I'm dirty, and I'm being dragged to something, dug under the ground.

A: *How old do you feel?*

C: Maybe sixteen or seventeen.

A: *Who's dragging you?*

C: Men. They are being cheered on by people watching. It is at night and they think I'm bad.

A: *How do you feel about that? Are you bad?*

C: I'm scared. They are putting me in the ground. They are covering me. It is not in the ground.

A: *Where is it?*

C: I think they are going to put me in water. Put me in a box, they are weighing it down. Pushing it into the water. I'm going down, down, down, down. I cannot get out.

A: *What happens to you there?*

C: I'm trying to get out. I am scratching the box. There is some water getting in. I die.

A: *Let's go back in time. Before these people thought that you were dangerous. We are there now. Tell me what is going on.*

C: I'm in the garden and I'm picking herbs. I have a pouch. I'm putting things in my pouch. I think I'm collecting medicines or things that can be made. I'm with an older lady. I think she is my grandmother. She is showing me how to mix the flowers and the herbs, to make remedies. People used to come see my grandmother to be healed with different kinds of ailments. When they get boils or open wounds, or pains in the head. She showed me how to make the medicine. Not everybody knew about her, because I think it's kind of a secret. I think it was frowned upon, what she was doing, and she showed me how to do it from a little girl. So, I was helping her. Then my grandmother got sick herself. She was old and she died. I was left to do the work. So people then used to come to me, to help them with their children. They had sick children, so they brought them. I would help them with my hands, but also use plants. Then they would be okay. Then somebody told some people about what I was doing. I'm walking and a mob came out, a group of angry people from the village. They took me. They were shouting, saying I was a witch and I was evil. They dragged me out into the… Where am I? I know where I am. It's not a big town and it's a river.

A: *What are the people dressed like that came and grabbed you?*

C: There's an older man, with a black hat with a brass buckle on front. It's like a Pilgrims hat; it would be the closest that I could think of. It's got a wide brim and then it goes up like a plant pot on top of it. It's black and it's got a square buckle on the front. He's got a really skinny face, big nose, and gray hair. They don't have torches, so it must be pretty old. They have a piece of wood with a flame at the top. There's some people shouting at the dogs. They tie my hands around my back, so I can't move. They drag me to a makeshift, small box. It's not a coffin or anything like that, it's much smaller. So I had to be bundled in, they sealed it, and dragged it. They are laughing and shouting. Dragging it through a bridge over the river. I was crying and they didn't care. Then they just tip me over the edge, and down, down, down. I drowned. Water got into the box and I drowned. I can't get out.

A: *What are your last thoughts as you are taking your last breath?*

C: They judge me for something they know nothing about. They made a big mistake, and I just wanted to help people. It's too late.

A: *Let's go ahead and leave that scene. Let's go to another important time where we will find answers that we seek for your highest healing. We are there now, tell me what you see and sense.*

C: A bright light, like the sun. It's so bright and warm. I think I'm part of the sun. I'm in the sun. There's a door in the sun, and I'm in it. Recharging my batteries (laughs). It gives me energy. I think I almost just exploded. I was charged up in the sun, and then just burst out. It's like I'm not a person, I'm just an energy. Like a starburst happening. I'm just floating down. I'm not actually on a planet or anything like that. I think I'm just in space. There's nothing there. Just a big yellow ball that had a doorway in it. I was in there, and then I could just feel like this charge. It felt really good, then *pfft!* I ejected out and I just went through it. I am matter. I'm not a person, I'm just an energy. I have just carried on out into space. I don't know what my purpose is for that experience. It felt good, but I don't know where it's going. It's like I'm everywhere. It's like I'm nothing but I'm everything. Just like part of the Universe. It's freeing and peaceful. I don't know where I'm going, I'm just going everywhere. Part of all that is. No worries, no cares, just be.

A: *Beautiful. Let's go ahead and leave that time and space there. We are going to another space, an important time where we will find answers that we seek for your highest healing. We are there now. Tell me what you see and sense.*

C: Cold, very cold, snow everywhere. Nobody is around. There is nobody. It's just snow and cold. Walking and trying to get somewhere. I'm in the North. The ground, the snow is split into four, and there's a hole in the middle. There's like a vacuum in the middle. It's a portal. I'm at the center of the world and there's snow that is divided in four directions.

A: *Look at yourself do you feel like you have a body? What do you look like?*

C: I'm male. I'm wearing heavy snow protective clothing for the weather. It's very cold and I have got a coat and a hood. I have a bag with me. I'm putting something in it. I'm hiding something, and I'm throwing it into the hole. I think it's a portal out. I think it is a gateway out. There is a big energy around this hole. I'm throwing what looks like gold out through this hole, but I don't think it's gold. You can't get to the edge. You will get sucked in if you go too close to the edge of snow. It looks like it's a black hole, but I think it's a portal out. It's the way out.

A: *What is the purpose of you throwing that in? Why do you think you're doing it now?*

C: I'm hiding something that they're looking for. Is it a crystal? It looked like gold. I don't know what it is. It's shining. I don't think it is gold. It's like a metal, but I don't know what the metal is. I think it's important and I'm trying to get it off the planet. You throw it into the hole and it zips its way out. I think it's way out of that realm. I think that it's something that if it falls into the wrong people. It's very bad for … I just feel like I'm on a mission to get rid of it, to hide it, to get it off the planet. I think that's the way off the planet through this hole. I need to get it off the planet, to protect the planet.

A: *How many pieces are you throwing into this place?*

C: I've got a bag, bigger than a satchel. I'm trying to get this off through this portal. The only way off is through this hole. I think there are people not far behind me. I think I'm doing it in quite a hurry. It's not like I've got all the time in the world. I feel there are people coming for me, because they know I have it, and they are trying to stop me from putting it in, but I did manage to get it all out. It looks like metal, but it's not metal. I don't know if it's from this planet.

A: *What color is it?*

C: It's gold, but light shines through it. It's weird, like clusters of crystals, but it's not glass. It's solid. So it looks a bit like clusters, but it's of color gold, but it's not gold. It's not dense like gold, gold ingots or things like that. There are parts where you can see lights through it. It does vibrate, when you hold it, you can feel an energy off of it. Anyway, it's gone through the hole. I've emptied the bag and it's gone. I've got to get out of the area because there are people coming. People wanted to stop me from doing it, but it's too late. When you put this stuff in the hole, a glow of light shoots out, and then you put another piece in, and then it shoots out, and then it's gone. Now, I'm trying to get out there. There is nowhere really to hide. It's white everywhere, you can't see any places to hide. It's like you are sitting on an iceberg I suppose. It's just flat. I know I'm going to have to walk far. I'm glad the stuff is gone. I've managed to do it, and now I've got to get out and find my way back. To get away from the people coming. This place has really big energy and is amazing. It's helpful in this void. Part of me is tempted to see what happens if I jump in, but I don't. I'm too scared to. I'm moving off. I have done my job.

A: *Can you keep explaining, how do you get out of this place?*

C: I'm just walking. It appears to be east. I keep having to check behind me because I don't think they're that far behind. Maybe they are farther than I thought, because I don't see anybody. I know that there are people coming because they didn't want me to get rid of this gold. Now it's out of their reach. It's gone. They needed this material to be used to make a light beam that could destroy areas. It's not my job to know what it's for, I just had to take it to where it needed to go. I think it was something to do with a part that can create a real concentrated beam of light. Not a laser, more like something that could destroy large chunks of land, whether it's buildings or chunks of the ground. It was something important to help complete this weapon, and we needed to get it off the planet. This was a gateway. It is a way out.

A: *So are you able to escape?*

C: Yeah, I'm walking, there is snow everywhere. It's just open space. I'm heading towards the east. I know that there is a point where I'm going to be picked up by people who are waiting for me to get there, so I can get home. I'm walking east and I will meet up with them and have transportation that I can get away. It's not a transport, like a car, it can levitate. It's not a spaceship. It's very small, very fast, and it hovers. It's metallic. It's got a glass front. It doesn't look anything like an airplane, and it's really small. You could fit three or four people max in it. It's like a bobsleigh that hovers and it's sealed with a glass thing on the front. It has four seats. I don't know what powers it. It's like vloop! I wish I could draw it.

A: *It's okay. You will be able to remember it when you wake up, so you can draw it.*

C: It's really cool. It's not a car because it's above the ground. It doesn't fly, but it doesn't move along the snow. It's maybe a foot off the ground. Maybe not quite a foot. It can move really fast, and it can hold about four people. I got picked up by this vehicle, and I'm going back to the base. There are three other people, there are two men and a woman. We are going off back to base to report on the mission being completed, but we are still mindful that there are people who are following who could intercept us. I think it's got camouflage. This vehicle is so cool. With the glass on the side it can be reflected with the light, so it actually hides. Not quite stealth. It literally makes it hard for it to be seen. So it's got a form of camouflage where it's using the light from the Sun. It deflects which makes it invisible. Does that make sense? It makes it so that it cannot be seen. I don't know if it's done with mirrors the way the light reflects from the Sun that it actually makes us very difficult to be seen. Almost like we disappear and we are going back to base (the image on the next page).

A: *These people, do they look like you? What are they wearing?*

C: They are wearing really thick kind of outdoor clothing for cold weather. Not like Eskimo kind of stuff, fur lined hoods, but they are orange and white. You think orange is a really stupid color to have if you are trying to blend in with the snow. Mostly white. They are in big heavy boots, really thick for the cold kind of coats and trousers. Not quite how you go skiing, but like ski clothes. The heavy duty kind for really cold weather, like minus forty. They have got goggles, black with orange glass. It's like eye protection that you can see through, and gloves. So they are kitted out for winter, really cold weather. We have, not masks, but inside the hoods. There's an earpiece, a hearing piece so that we can hear each other well when we are speaking. We are speaking through something we can hear through the hood of the jacket. We are saying that the mission has been completed, we are moving off back to base so we can report back to tell them that the evidence is gone. The material has gone. So it means that they won't be able to get hold of this substance to finish this type of technology that I don't know. It's beyond my grade, I was just the deliverer of the stuff. I'm not a scientist who knows how it works.

They just needed to get it off the planet because it could be a BIG problem. It could destroy the planet and the people. It could just disintegrate people. It was their goal. You are not evaporating them. It's not like incinerating them, because there would still be evidence that they are there. It's like, they just disappear. It just breaks down the matter into nothing, like they were never there. It can make big craters in the land, on the Earth. It can literally destroy parts of the Earth. There's no evidence that the Earth bed was there. It's all gone like it never was. You would never know that, that hole in the ground was not there before. Like, there's no trace. That's what this machine does: it wipes out the people, the ground, the building. Which is why we need to hide the important mineral, or whatever it was, so that they couldn't make the weapon.

A: *You said that they are taking you back to base?*
C: Yeah, and the base is underground. The vehicle is going across. It's going really fast, we can't be seen. Looks like it's snow, but then it isn't. It's like an optical illusion, because there's a way that you can go under, so you are actually going under into the ground. Then you are in the ground and it's huge. There's other vehicles like ours. There's lots of people. There's other vehicles that look kind of spacey. It's quite a lot of people underground. They all are getting on with whatever jobs it is that they are doing. Then we dock, get out, and we are going up the stairs, round through this tunnel bit. Then we are in and doing a debriefing. I'm in a room with people talking about the stuff that I had and got rid of. There's another batch of stuff coming in that's been found somewhere else that needs to be repeated to dispose of. So in different parts of the planet, there is this substance. I just know that there's more of it. They are excavating more of it, it's in the Earth. It comes into this space. Then another soldier like me goes out on the mission and takes it to the portal in the north. It's all to get it off the planet. So

we gotta get this stuff off the planet because more stuff is coming in. I was just one of many people who are doing this job. I'm not the only one doing the same thing. There is a military, a kind of militia that is trying to find us and intercept us. They don't know the exact location of where the portal void is. That's why they need to try and intercept us. So they can find out where it is, to stop us from getting rid of this important raw material for their weapon. This base, they don't know about it. Obviously, it's a secret base and there are lots of people that work in it. These other people, the ones who want to do the damage, are trying to find this base and the portal. They don't know where either is. They just know that the resource they are looking for, for their weapon, it's been found. They are trying to intercept it and get hold of it. The whereabouts of this place is protected and a closely guarded secret. My mission is completed, and then I'm waiting for my next assignment, which will probably be to collect another batch of those minerals, repeat the process, and don't get caught.

A: *Can you describe what this base looks like inside?*

C: Yeah, it's enormous, immense like twenty hangers in one space underneath. There's metal, rock and walkways. Stairways leading down into the main base where the transports come in. The openings are quite cavernous. Almost like a big underground cave that's been decked out with a proper floor, metal stairways and railings to get down to the big base. There is white rock around the inside that gets darker as you go down, and there's a hover train that runs around a track around the inside where people can get in and go off through the tunnels to different parts of the base. They have different vehicles and big containers where things are being put into the containers. Then they get them put into blocks on this harbor train and then transported around. It goes off to be delivered to someone who's doing what I was doing. There's not just that going on, there's other stuff going on as well. Other mineral mining is going on in this space as well. Things are coming into places within the base where you go much further down into the Earth. Mining pulls out resources, minerals from the Earth. They are collecting those and moving them out. There's control rooms where decision-makers are deciding who's going where and what's going where. Liaising with whoever they need to liaise with, but I'm not important enough to get access to those control rooms. I'm just one of the foot soldiers to get them out. I'm quite expendable. There's quite a lot of people doing what I do. I'm not part of the higher hierarchy. I just do my job and wait for my next mission. We live within the base, not in apartments. They are very basic, almost like pods. People who stay there a longer time, they get to be all together. But you have got your own separate sleeping pod. The guys who do what I do are kept all together. Then you have got other areas where maybe more important people get better digs than me. I'm happy I managed to get back. I wasn't sure if I was going to make this particular mission. You don't want to get caught.

A: *Keep moving time. Let's see what happens next of importance.*

C: I'm going out again. I've got another bag of minerals. I'm going a different route this time because the people that are looking for us are starting to find a better way to track us. I've been left by my crew because you attract even less attention if you are on your own. The others are waiting back quite far and I have got a long walk across this time. I'm coming from the north this time going down towards the portal. I've been seen by something. It looks like a drone. It's quite small with a camera. It's found me. It has a beacon on it. Now I'm trying to run back the way I came, because I don't want to lead the drone to the portal. So I'm now changing my direction away from the portal but there's nowhere to go. There's white snow everywhere. There's people that have found me.

A: *How did they find you?*

C: With their drone, they are coming. They have a bigger vehicle than the one I was in with my crew. It's a similar style, but theirs doesn't hover. It's almost got legs and skis. It glides through the snow so it leaves tracks in the snow. I'm trying to get rid of my bag. I'm trying to dig. The drone can see me and see what I'm doing. I have been caught, I had a good role but it's not gonna end well for me. I'm trying to dig. I'm trying to bury the bag. I know it's pointless because they are gonna see it. The drone is recording everything, and they are going to be able to dig it up. I can't let them know where the base is. I have taken something, put something in my mouth. Then I'm gone.

A: *Were you able to hide the material?*

C: I buried it, but I know they're going to dig it up. The drone sees everything. I tried to hide it in the snow. They are going to get some. They're going to pick that up. It's not enough to make their weapon, but they have got the technology now. I couldn't let them find the base.

A: *So you took something that ended you? Is what you are saying? It made you pass away?*

C: Yes.

A: *You are able to still see. Go ahead and leave your body. Keep following the scene. Tell me what happens. Do they get there?*

C: Yes. The drone comes down, people arrive. They see where I am and they go over my body. They are checking my vitals and realize I'm no longer there. They are taking off my coat, checking if I have any tracking devices, any kind of communication tool. Then there's another person that's just digging where I was digging. They find the bag.

A: *What do they look like? These people that are doing this to you?*

C: Men with the same kind of coats as me, but not the same color. They are dressed for winter, and they have a weapon strapped over their back, but it is not a gun. They have dogs with them. The dogs are grabbing me and ripping me. I tasted good. They have goggles, dressed for deep snow and they have a weapon longer than their back. Dogs are helping with the digging. Some of them are just grabbing at my body. They find the bag and they take it back. So my mission that time didn't pan out, but they didn't get to know where the base was. I'm happy.

A: *How many times have you done that before?*

C: Loads and loads of times. I've been doing it for years.

A: *How do you think that they were able to spot you, if you've done it several times before and weren't caught before?*

C: They were using more clever technology to locate us. They knew it was in the north, they just didn't have the coordinates to find it. So they haven't found the portal. I wasn't anywhere near the portal, but they had set up drones to scour the area. They had an idea of a general area because we have been doing it for so long. Eventually, with their technologies and with their scouts, they are going to coordinate with a map. Where they pinpoint to get a rough idea of the area of where you could potentially be. They are getting more and more soldiers working for them. So they have more teams, and we go out in very small groups. That's why we keep it as a single, because it's harder to track one person. You are easier to spot when there's more than one. I guess I got caught that time. I've been doing it for a long time. We managed to get a lot of this particular mineral off the planet. That's why we only take a bag in smaller quantities. We could move loads in one go, if we used other technology like a trailer. It would be easier to spot if we got caught and they would have much more of the materials. Therefore they would be much closer to building their weapon. We do things in bits, so it keeps us more stealth like where we can't be easily tracked. If one of us gets intercepted, it's only a small amount. It's not enough for them to do such huge damage. So that's why we go out and there's several people doing what I do at different times. That's why eventually someone with their tracking drones, their technology they have, one of us could get caught. I'm not the first person to get caught. There were other people. We're expendable, as long as we do what is more important. I don't know if they managed to get the mineral from other people who were caught before. I don't know because I wasn't on that mission.

The Higher Self is called forth.

A: *Can I please speak to the Higher Self of Cynthia?*

Higher Self: Yes.

A: *Greetings Higher Self.*

Higher Self: Hello.

A: *Wow! Phenomenal session so far. Thank you. Higher Self, I know that you hold all the records to Cynthia's different lives, so may I ask questions about them?*

Higher Self: Yes.

A: *In the first life you took her to a life where they thought she was a witch. They put her in the water and drowned her. What are the lessons you wanted her to learn?*

Higher Self: She's been dealing with a lot in this life. She's feeling a lot about injustice, and I wanted her to realize that it wasn't from this life. It actually stemmed from previous lives. It's a past life trauma that the contracts about it are over and she needs to heal from that. It is passing into this life because of what she's experiencing with the situation, with everything that's happening right now on your planet. She has a real sense of righteousness, trying to right the wrongs. When she sees injustice that stems back, it makes her really angry. Obviously, this emotion depends on how she challenges this emotion, for it to be either positive or it can be negative. It stems back from other lives that she has had, where she has been persecuted and wrongly accused. So this is deep within her DNA that she needs to heal.

A: *Thank you. Go ahead and start healing this Higher Self. Thank you for showing her that. From there you took her to this life that we just viewed. Was that on Earth?*

Higher Self: Yes it was on Earth.

A: *What Pole was that?*

Higher Self: She was at the North Pole.

A: *Can you explain when she said that there were four directions separated. What does that mean?*

Higher Self: This is a portal, out of the Earth. You have got the four corners of the Universe - the four points, North, South, East, West. This is a portal that goes direct to Source, straight out into the Universe. They needed to remove this mineral to get it off the planet. That is the quickest way from where they were based to get it off the planet.

A: *Can anyone go through that portal? Do you have to be a matching vibration to go out?*

Higher Self: Yes you do. First you need to be a matching vibration to find it. Then you need to be a matching vibration to be able to penetrate it to get out.

A: *So if a person who was negatively polarized would they be able to find it?*

Higher Self: No. This is why they have been looking at trying to track the people.

A: *Have they been able to find it?*

Higher Self: No.

A: *Good. So basically, the portal takes you to other dimensions.*

Higher Self: Yes.

A: *This mineral, where is it mined from?*

Higher Self: It's coming in from the centers. It's within the rock surface. It's really, really deep into the Earth. So they dug really, really deep. It's within the crusts of the layers of the Earth, as you go through. It's maybe about a quarter of the way down before the center of the Earth. So it's about a quarter of the way down from the molten rock. There's a thin band of it around within the interior in between the crustacean. They are just chiseling it out because it has very powerful energy within it. When it is concentrated and put under immense heat, it can cause a very big heat. The atoms go so fast that it causes a big explosion, but it's not an explosion. It's basically so strong and powerful that it can actually just blast through anything. It's a very dangerous mineral that can cause craters on the Earth, that we think has been hit with meteorite from outer space. This weapon can cause the same kind of damage., It literally can blast out and obliterate the matter. It's very important that they don't get enough of this mineral that can basically wipe out cities, people, large areas and make the area uninhabitable. It's mass destruction. It's wiping out history. It's wiping out evidence. It's like it was never there, and leaves no evidence or trace behind. It just leaves a hole or a crater.

A: *It erases?*

Higher Self: Yes, it erases. There's no matter. The particles are so small. Even bones, they just disappear. There's no evidence, there's no remnants of what was there before.

A: *Have the negative polarized entities used it in the past, leaving craters behind on Earth?*

Higher Self: Yes, they have. This is one of the ways that they rewrite by obliterating areas and changing your histories. It can literally wipe out huge chunks of the population, the planets, the towns, the mountains. They can make it be gone.

A: *Are there areas on Earth that you can share with us where they have used this technology to erase populations as you are saying? Show us a time and space where they did this to a certain civilization. What does that look like? How are they doing this?*

Higher Self: They are beaming something out through, it's not a satellite. They have done this in parts of the Midwest in America. It caused a flood in the mid west area. This technology created a tsunami and wiped out huge chunks. Then it creates a canyon where people think it was just a meteorite or something like that. But it wasn't, it was with this technology that they created.

A: *Like the Grand Canyon, is that what you are talking about?*

Higher Self: No, it wasn't the Grand Canyon. There was a tsunami that caused a flood that wiped out the whole area.

A: *Why were they trying to wipe out that civilization? What time and space is it that you're talking about?*

Higher Self: It was only a few hundred years ago that it was wiped out. There was a tsunami that came through and then there was an Earthquake on the other side in Asia. It's cause and effect. You got the tsunami and quake, cause and effect, and then wiped out. It's not the Grand Canyon, but I think part of the Grand Canyon was actually not created by meteorites or whatever they say. It's technology that actually blasts out huge chunks. It wasn't from outer space. It was from here in our space and not from outer space. The technology that actually created it. But, they make it sound like things that came from outside, that caused the damage, creating these huge craters across certain parts of the Earth, in the Americas, in Australia and across Asia. These are pockets of things that have happened all around the world. They are being explained by things coming in from outer space but actually it's not, it's A.I. technology that is here, that has the capacity to do that. It wipes out certain civilizations, and then everything gets rebooted. So they can wipe out a whole civilization and then they can just repopulate and rewrite history. It's three cycles. Like starting again, on repeat, but each time with new people.

A: *I have been to some of these places where it's a canyon of sorts. There are chunks of land missing in America where there's younger trees in these locations. It's weird, because why are there new trees there? All lands should have ancient trees on them. The new life grows, and the trees aren't old because new life recently grew on these lands.*

Higher Self: Mother Nature will be able to regenerate.

A: *Thank you for explaining that. So then the good guys are mining it and trying to get it off the Earth, so that these dark entities stop using it like this. How about the bad guys? Are they able to mine it?*

Higher Self: No, they don't know where it is. It can only be found in certain parts of the Earth - only mined in certain parts. They haven't been able to track it themselves. They have heard about it, but they don't know where it is. Which is why they are using their A.I. to track the carriers and the porters. They don't know where this portal is. They can't get to it because as you see their vibration is not a match. But that doesn't stop them from trying. They think if they intercept enough of the soldiers on foot who are carrying the minerals that they will get enough. That's why they're doing it in such small quantities. If they get this mineral in such high quantities, then it could be catastrophic. So the carriers are their target, that's the only way to get it. If they can locate the foot soldiers and intercept them.

A: *You said that they were wiping out a civilization a couple hundred years ago. What civilization was that?*

Higher Self: They do swathes of it in other civilizations. The people who were there in America before the settlers came from other lands, wiped out the people who were there before.

A: *Who were those people? Is there a name for them?*

Higher Self: Yeah. They were settlers who were there before. This was way after the Mayans and the Incas and those civilizations. These are people that had found and moved over to the new Earth, who were wiped and erased then restarted again. It's like they don't want the people to be there long enough to remember their history. If things start getting discovered too early, they just make a clean slate. They keep the little ones and then get rid of the rest. Then they restart it again and restart again.

A: *They are able to do this through technology with this matter?*

Higher Self: Yes they can do this with technology.

A: *With this material?*

Higher Self: Not necessarily not with this material. They have other materials to do that. With this material they can wipe out big chunks of the Earth, where they can take over the people. They have other technologies for erasing memories of the young ones. So they don't know and then they are left to repopulate the area. Like, starting from scratch.

A: *When was the last time they did that on Earth?*

Higher Self: Just a few hundred years ago.

A: *So, is that why she says she took something in her mouth to kill herself?*

Higher Self: Yes, she did. They were going to get the minerals anyway. She did it because she didn't want to be interrogated for them to find the underground base where they are mining it. Obviously, they aren't going to have the vibration for the portal, but they would be able to discover the base if they had managed to capture her. They will not get caught, it is part of their mission. If they do, then they know they have to to prevent themselves from being interrogated at all costs. They are expendable, they know that.

A: *Do these bases exist now?*

Higher Self: Yes.

A: *They are doing this actively now?*

Higher Self: Yes.

A: *Who are these people in this positive base, that's helping humanity like this?*

Higher Self: It is people from certain military governments on Earth, and also with some Galactic help from other beings that are here on Earth. It's a collaboration. So it's a mixture between some of the underground military operations that are happening in certain countries around this planet, and outside sources from other planetary influences.

A: *How long have they been trying to assist Earth?*

Higher Self: Many eons. They have been here a very long time and it's their mission to try and help.

A: *This vehicle that they were driving, it was hovering. It reminds me of a lot of what we have been talking about about Tartaria technology that they had. Do they have any connection to Tartaria?*

Higher Self: A lot of information that was given to Nikola Tesla was here before Tesla. Tesla was bringing it more to this generation, but this technology has been around before. It was kind of gifted to Tesla. He was able to transmit this information during his time, but this technology has been around for a very long time. It's just that people don't know about it. This is a very old technology. It's not new technology. This is something that used to be an abundance on this planet.

A: *What is this type of gold mineral but not gold? What is its benevolence divine purpose? Why was it made? They are trying to use it negatively but what is its real purpose?*

Higher Self: It's actually an important layer within the Earth and it is part of its magnetic field. When it's been mixed with a certain A.I. technology, it concentrates it, which can then make it very volatile and destructive because it's a very powerful energy. That's why it can be destructive. If it's been manipulated it can then be used for great destruction. When it's used in its natural essence it is actually there as protection. It is a very important part of the structure of the Inner Earth, which helps with its magnetism. It helps with the electromagnetic field.

A: *Thank you. Anything else you can tell us about why you showed her this life?*

Higher Self: It's actually important for her to know that part of her mission is always to be healing and protecting. It's done in not just looking after the people, but it's also looking after the planet. It's the same with the energy from the sun, when she was shown that she was this burst of energy. We're all a part of all things. We don't always come back as a person. We don't always come back as the same matter, we can come back as other things. It could be a mineral, it could be a star, it could be a person, or it could be a tree. It could be a piece of the ground. It could be water. That was showing her that she's experienced in many lifetimes, different aspects of being. It's not always a human experience. It is always an element of protection to the Earth and protection of humanity, is one of the reasons why she's here.

A: *Similar to that life that you showed her where she was part of the sun and then she just kind of exploded? And became everything.*

Higher Self: Yes, she is a part of everything. We are all a part of everything.

A: *Anything else you want to tell us about that life with those craters and those minerals?*

Higher Self: No, this wasn't in the present time and space. This was in another parallel dimension. It wasn't something that's happening right this moment on the planet. It is Earth but there are many Earth's. It's not the one that we are occupying now. It was another time and space.

A: *Okay, so another parallel Earth.*

Higher Self: We are everywhere. We are all things. There's a part of us in all dimensions. We are not just this one being - we have a multitude - we are everywhere having an experience in different times and space.

A: *Since this was a parallel Earth, it's a different Earth. Did that happen here? Using this material to completely remove and reset Earth? How does that work?*

Higher Self: Because it's a parallel dimension it is like a mirror. So what is happening on one sphere or one spherical dimension of the Earth, can be felt as a reflection on another. It's like an echo in another time and space. Something that was projected from one Earth can actually also be reflected onto another. So it's a vibrational echo. This is something that you can have a multitude of experiences within one dimension because Earth is a reflection. When it's crossing through the dimensions, it is like a mirror, like an echo. You can experience something that's happening over here, in this dimension, of what is happening on that Earth. It can have a reflection back, which then has an impact. Different choices that are made by the energies within that Earth, that can then be transferred to another dimension. It is all one. We are all one.

A: *I understand, so it's like layers all happening in the same layers.*

Higher Self: Yes, like an onion layer. It's superimposing, which is why sometimes you see the remnants on one dimensional Earth to the other. It's an echo reverberation, which can then show up on the other. It doesn't necessarily mean that everyone is experiencing what happened on that parallel Earth. It's a vibration that is multi-layered.

A: *Can they do that here with that type of mineral or just on that Earth?*

Higher Self: No. I don't see the probability of this timeline coming on this Earth, it is very small. The timeline for this Earth is not on that trajectory for it to be in this space and time.

The Body Scan begins.

A: *Thank you Higher Self. I feel that we have asked plenty of questions with those lives. We can now begin her body scan. If you can start scanning her now. Tell me who would you like to call forth, Higher self? Any Archangels or benevolent beings to assist during the body scan?*

Higher Self: I would like to call on the Divine Mother.

A: *Higher Self, connect us to Divine Mother now. Greetings Divine Mother.*

Divine Mother: Greetings.

A: *I love you, honor you and respect you. Thank you for being here.*

Divine Mother: Thank you AuroRa.

A: *Higher Self and Divine Mother, if you can both now start working together scanning her body from head to toe? Looking for any energies, entities, technologies. Where would you like to begin in her body?*

Divine Mother: Start the scan from the head. She's been doing a lot of work on herself. There's not really a lot to remove. There's something in her womb space.

A: *Let's scan her womb now. Let's look for any energy, entities, or technologies. What's there?*

Divine Mother: An energy that's like an entity.

A: *What kind of entity is it? Reptilian, Archon, Earthbound, or something else?*

Divine Mother: Not Reptilian, it's not Archonic. I think it's just an Entity or something that's been here before.

A: *It's been there before this life? Is it like an Alien Entity or an Earthbound Entity? What is it?*

Divine Mother: It's an Earth Entity.

A: *Go ahead and contain that Earth Entity with the symbols in her womb. Let me know when it's contained. Let's keep scanning her for any other entities. Are there any other entities in her hiding?*

Divine Mother: There's something on her kidneys.

A: *What kind of entity is that? Reptilian, Archon, Earthbound or something else?*

Divine Mother: I think it's Reptilian.

A: *Contain it now, in her kidneys. Let me know, when it's contained?*

Divine Mother: It's contained.

A: *Scan her one more time together, Divine Mother and Higher Self. Are there any other entities in her?*

Divine Mother: No.

A: *Beautiful. She has an Earthbound Entity in her womb. Let me go ahead and speak to it. If you could help it come up, up now please. Greetings.*

Entity: Greetings.

A: *Thank you for speaking to us. Love you, honor you, and respect you. May we ask you questions?*

Entity: Yes.

A: *Thank you. If you could tell us when it was that you were attached in her womb? They said it was prior to this life?*

Entity: Yes

A: *What was going on with her then, that allowed you to attach to her?*

Entity: She was being abused. So she was full of pain and fear. I just decided that I had to help her and I tried to protect her.

A: *Thank you. Did you have a body before you became this Entity?*

Entity: Yes.

A: *Were you female or male?*

Entity: I was a female.

A: *How was it that you passed away?*

Entity: I was in a house fire.

A: *Thank you for sharing that. We are looking to assist you, as we assist entities throughout the Universe. Entities like you who have been stuck or attached to others. We would love to assist you to find your light and spread it and become free no longer having to attach to her or anyone else. Would you like for us to help you find the light and become free?*

Entity: Yes.

A: *Beautiful. Find that light inside of you now, spread it to all that is you that you have attached to her womb. Let us know when you are fully out and you are all light, making sure you don't leave any piece of yourself behind.*

Entity: I'm out.

A: *Beautiful Do you have a message for her before you go?*

Entity: Yes, I wanted to say that I love her and that she kept me safe. I think I was causing her some damage in her womb space and I'm sorry for that.

A: *Thank you. If we can call on Archangel Azrael now Higher Self. Archangel Azrael, we love you, honor you, and respect you. If you can assist the now positively polarized Entity where it's meant to go divinely? Ensuring it doesn't get tricked along the way.*

AA Azrael: Yes, it is done.

A: *Thank you. May you be surrounded by the love-light of the Universe. Blessings to you, thank you Azrael. Higher Self what was the entity causing by being there in her womb?*

Divine Mother: It was causing her burning in her womb space and down into her joints at the top of her pubic bone. That was causing an aggravation and it was making her quite acidic inside and burning inside.

A: *Higher Self and Divine Mother let's direct Phoenix Fire and Love-Light there. Healing all the trauma it has caused in this life beginning from the time and space when it is attached. She had certain things happen in her life, like the abortion that she had. If we could provide healing for the abortion, as well as the I.V.F. (In Vitro Fertilization) that she had to conceive her beautiful children. Making sure she doesn't have any residue left behind from either the abortion or the I.V.F. Can you scan her for that?*

Divine Mother: Scanning. Any residue is cleared. She's cleared.

A: *Since we are speaking of her creations, her beautiful children, as she birthed them in. Can we provide any healing to her boys to what might have caused autism? We know that everything is self-healable. If you can tell us, is there something that is causing this in her boys?*

Divine Mother: Yes. With Eli, the eldest boy, this is part of a contract. The anxiety linked to his autism was aggravated by his immunizations when he was small. Taking some of it into his brain, like the metals from these jabs that crossed his blood brain barrier which then made his condition more acute. He has a former contract that he needs to deal with, which is causing him to have to manage his fear. So the fear that he needs to overcome in this life also has an impact on his autism. It gets in the way of his processing and his communication. He needs to keep the contract in place for now to overcome his fear, so that he can live a more simple life spreading joy. He spreads joy, with who he is.

A: *Beautiful. Go ahead and provide healing for him for that whenever he's ready to release that contract. I know that his mother will assist him along his path. She says she's going to start practicing A.U.R.A. Hypnosis Healing, and I'm sure she will be given how to assist him with that. Since he was conceived through In Vitro Artificial insemination. Can we provide healing for him, when his initial conception happened?*

Divine Mother: Yes.

A: *If there's any A.I. or anything related to the I.V.F. procedure, can we clear that from him?*

Divine Mother: Yes, absolutely.

The Body Scan continues and completes.

For every A.U.R.A. Hypnosis healing session we ask that the Higher Self and team ensure to remove and heal all as listed from the clients Tree of Life: entities (Grays, Mantis, Reptilians, Archons…), dark portals, repair and crystallize DNA, negative cords, technologies (implants, metals, hooks, wires, nano, vaccines), illnesses, vision, dental health, regrow teeth, age regress 5-15 years, blocked or misaligned chakras, open-up the third eye and activate abilities, expand heart, issues with auric field, fractured soul, contracts, deletion of inverted timelines, and trauma from current or past life.

END OF SESSION

Through this session we witness human kind's savaged dark nature when consumed by their fears. All it takes is one person to become fearful and this fear spreads like a virus to those who are a lower vibratory match to fear. A young witch drowned by the village people, who she loved and assisted. She just wanted to help them, but when people are taken over by fear and do not want help, they will turn on those who are what they feel they cannot be. Threatened by others' beauty. Sounds silly, but a recurring theme with those who shine too bright, who hold the antidote in unlocking others hearts. Ultimately, why people stay in fear depends on how long they have been within it. The high of fear is most familiar to them, and once more people fear the unknown of releasing the fear, because what will come next if they no longer have the familiarity of fear? In their eyes they do not know, but in ours we know that what comes after fear is strength.

The celestial energies of the sun are truly divine. When connecting and recharging with the sun's energy we are connecting to the Universe, because in that moment as you gaze in awe at the sun, so too are you gazing simultaneously on all the suns in our Universe since they are all interlinked as ONE. The Sun is the portal into our Universe and the Multiverse that is in constant echo dispersing out these celestial energies from above us onto us, being that every sun/star is connected to its own star soul groupings from its galaxy. This is the way we can feel the love and support which is being channeled down onto us everyday from the higher dimensional beings of creation. These energies are showering onto us a waterfall made of love-light codes from the benevolence of the races in the Universe. Any time we feel low in energy or feel like we are astraying from our soul mission, let us simply look upon the sun for the sun's soul recalibration healing powers. Recentered we will be once more.

At our [37]Hawaii retreat in 2025 we witnessed and recorded everyday the sunsets at the Pacific Ocean. We watched the most tremendous acts echo out from the sun. We caught on camera the sun opening up at its edges, and Father Ra portaling/walking out and back in - in his gigantic humanoid form of light. So too did the sun turn from spheric into a Phoenix Egg shape - displaying the Hawaiian islands (image on the next page) and lands within it - setting itself three times in the sky, and vibrating out sacred geometry from within. The magic is real! The image below is right before Father Ra steps out of the sun from the bottom right opening. Ensure to watch the video mentioned in the footnotes.

Such incredible knowledge shared of what is at the North Pole! Assisting us to understand further on why the Deep State restricts areas such as the North Pole and Antarctica, because they know Earth's true shape is flat physically and that there are ascension exit points at these locations. However, energetically the Earth is a toroidal in shape as the image on the next page. The reason why at the center of the Earth, at the North Pole there is a portal which connects you into the Universe, because at the center of the toroidal sphere, there is an opening. This opening is a wormhole, and cosmic communication and teleportation. This

---

[37] For the videos of the Sun's magic mentioned watch 'CURSE LANDS | CURSE GODS | Vampires, Werewolves, Skinwalkers, Witches & Ghosts' recorded live February 21, 2025.

opening is the actual Universal portal. When viewing the image of the toroidal sphere you see how you too are a multi-dimensional being because you are the energetic wormhole vortex at the center. YOU having the powers within, as this Universal portal that connects and transports you into the infinite cosmic realms.

Here is an updated excerpt from Book 2 'Galactic History of The Multiverse' to further understand the science to a toroidal sphere in how you are in constant Multiversal communications:

"Scientifically speaking, through the Quantum world we all harness a natural energetic magnetic field containment, which is our toroidal sphere that is our entire being, as shown in the image on the next page. Our toroidal sphere is what holds our entire memory of who we are as a consciousness. That being our Akashic, experiences, lessons and crystalline DNA genetic makeup. To further understand our toroidal sphere, though organic, can be seen as a computer, with its memory, which is held in its hard drive. When you hold too much memory, the hard drive becomes full, and you are then required to delete data from your hard drive, or you can upgrade to one that holds more memory. What Divine Mother means, in regards to us needing to release what is toxic in order to reconstruct ourselves, is if our toroidal sphere is filled up with things, thoughts and people that no longer serve us for our highest good, we can't expand and grow because we are too weighed down and full. These things, thoughts and people are taking up that space in the memory/hard drives of our toroidal sphere. So, just like ever so often we go through our devices to delete what is no longer needed, taking up the space, we too have to do this with things and people in our lives to free up our space to create from that space and upgrade ourselves energetically. Ensuring that we are able to keep up with Mother Earth's upgrades."

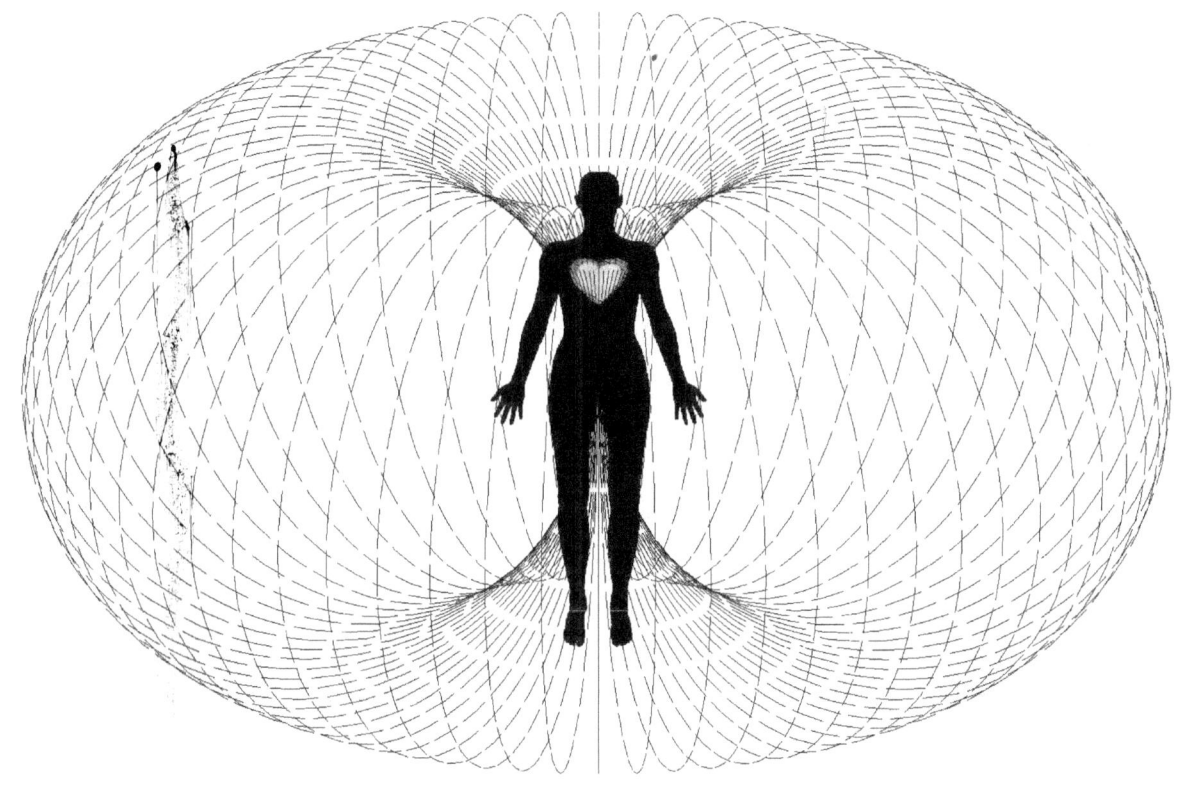

Our plasmic light photons and atoms are the material and framing to our toroidal sphere. The photons are the communicators within the magnetic field/toroidal sphere to all the cells in our bodies, our nervous system, and most importantly our neurons in our brain. Photons are scientifically made up of only light, therefore within each photon is found as God Source. Being that photons only consist of light, they are one of the only particles that travel at the speed of light as explained in [38]Einstein's theory of relativity. The photons carry the light codes to all that is alive within us. The photons are what assist us in our communications to the Divine through sacred ideas, manifestations, and creations. The photons are what allows us to always be in communication with the Universe, whether we believe that the Universe hears us word by word or not. The Universe will always manifest what we ask of it in some form, because energy once thought of must always create.

---

[38] To watch AuroRa channel Albert Einstein, go to Patreon 'Rising Phoenix Aurora' and join the Tier 'Extra Sensitive' series. Here you will also find channeling Nikola Tesla, Abraham Lincoln, Remote Viewing Area 51, The Philadelphia Experiment, The Grand Canyon...

Photons are hard to photograph microscopically, but here are two images I found on an internet search of a photon.

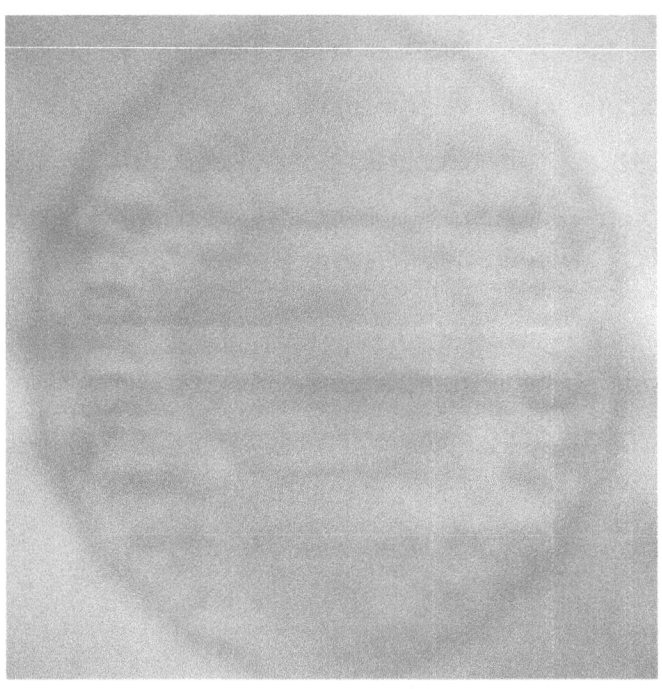

Why is it that we must release what is too dense within our magnetic field in order to rebuild our everyday organic living timelines? Because otherwise our hard drive is too full, unable to accommodate expansion. You can understand this density within you as a negative polarization and negatively charged magnet field that is pulling you down heavily, and if there is a majority of a negative field emitting out from within you, the negative will attract more negative charge. Photons then will be limited to expand, evolve or ascend further. Which is why we recommend an A.U.R.A. session, just as you read through Cynthia's session, she removed the attachments within her field that held her too heavy to raise in vibration. When we understand this scientifically it's quite simple. Maintaining denser compresses us into a denser plasmic light, versus an ideally lighter essence expansive and evolving.

What an incredibly exciting journey we went through as Cynthia undisclosed some of the work of the "Resistance" of this Earth and parallel Earths. In the time/space of me writing this chapter in March 2025, President Donald J. Trump has been elected. It is an exciting time as we have seen the most progress in the United States in just over a month, then we have seen in the history of the presidents of the United States. President Trump and his team are in the beginning process of tackling what matters to us the most through his Executive Orders. One of that being saving the children in all ways possible from trafficking or the grooming and indoctrination of transhumanism through the lesbian, gay, transgender, bisexual (LGTB) guise in the school system.

We are in the aftermath of the psychological warfare that has been pushed upon us for four years by the previous party, ultimately run and controlled by the [39]Antichrist Barack Hussein Obama. There is so much work to be done to now realign and shift into a higher Collective timeline. But what matters the most is that we are finally here, and yet they wanted us in the Federal Emergency Management Agency (F.E.M.A.) camps just four years ago. That inversion just could not pan out for them being that there is too much light now on Earth. As the Elites infuriated us starting from the COVID-19 plandemic of 2020 with every restriction and

---

[39] Watch 'THE ANTICHRIST | The World If Trump Is Not President | Dolores and Nostradamus', originally aired live September 27th, 2024.

ludicrous rule, they truly instead pushed us into such a powerful human alliance who wants the best for their families, themselves and others. It is very apparent that the Deep State has no power here anymore. They are cowering now running around, and they can't escape, because we have them contained inside the crystalline firmament. Ha ha.

We too within this Earth have an underground Earth Alliance run by some of the very people that have been elected in the year of 2025. So too do they have advanced technologies from Nikola Tesla's era, and prior, as humanity has always been advanced and not primitive. We are reflections of the fallen Isles of Atlantis, the originally advanced futuristic crystalline cities. We are now heading towards the trajectory of the advancement of humankind and the support towards the young scientists being born right now!

The reset and reseeding of the people on Earth, how they wipe our memories or simply densify us with metals and chemicals into our bodies through immunizations so that our neurons struggle to connect into the Universal of all that is, because our toroidal spheres are just too heavy to raise in photon light to achieve intelligence into enlightenment. The Elite has studied the human natural design and they know if they inject and insert as many foreign alien substances into the humans it compromises them into sheeple, so that *they* can instead be of higher intelligence over us. The Elite has ensured for too long that they would be the intelligence on Earth. However, no more, as everyday they look more and more ridiculous with their immature New World Order agendas that we see right through.

What one Earth goes through the others will feel in some form, reminding us how we have explained through this book that our Earth and the Universe exist within dimensional spheric pockets of spaces within one another. As Cynthia said "It doesn't necessarily mean that everyone is experiencing what happened on that parallel Earth. It's a vibration that is multi-layered." When timelines occur that are not livable within our current timelines they are like a fading dream that is not quite remembered, that feels like a distant memory. We will see echoes of these timelines, like a feeling of deja vu, but not live them ourselves. When one parallel Earth goes through a collective challenge, then another Earth most often doesn't and can't repeat the exact act because of the way timelines work. Like how your Higher Self got you to be reading this book at this exact moment, all that came before you as lessons learned needed to come first, so that all could be aligned for you to be reading this book right now at your highest vibrational light. Otherwise, divine timing can be delayed until you are in alignment to each lesson and choice to grow in your earthly path.

Cynthia explained as she threw the gold mineral out through the North Pole portal, that it shot out light, meaning that the high potency of photons within the mineral and the wormhole, assisted the mineral to travel at the speed of light to exit. So happy that in our Earth this timeline cannot be, where the Deep State aliens are dematerializing and deleting civilizations and lands. Most likely because that parallel Earth has taken care of it for the other Earths, including ours, by living it. Which means that what is happening in our Earth as the death ray laser technology stolen from [40]Nikola Tesla's patents that are being used to start forest fires artificially all over Earth, won't happen exactly like this on other Earths. See how important each Earth is to one another? Though we have not and will not see this play out here on this Earth, could it be that some of the locations on Earth where there seems to be smaller canyons or meteorite locations with missing chunks of land, are we seeing the Earth we spoke of through this session missing pieces of land? As at times when looking at these lands, it feels like you are being pulled into another point in time and space which could be a parallel Earth.

The light that this mineral was creating was being used invertedly to dematerialize matter by a concentrated beam of light. Cynthia explained that it was not a laser, instead something that completely destroys large chunks, whether it's buildings or chunks of the Earth. She said the beam dematerialized all matter like it never was there - even humans - leaving no residue left behind, just craters, and big holes in the land. As I teach courses of Quantum Physics through channeling Albert Einstein, he has taught us that when a particle becomes heated to extreme temperatures it oscillates faster and faster until it seems to reach a high state of being, which at that point is uncontrollable through the particle accelerator technology used in C.E.R.N. Which makes sense, as the element fire runs in heat from 1400-1800 degrees Fahrenheit, Source materializes and exists within the fire. Which means Source within the fire is naturally oscillating so high that it creates heat from within it, creating the element of fire that

---

[40] This knowledge is covered in Patreon 'Rising Phoenix Aurora' through the 'Extra Sensitive' seriesTier.

warms our bodies and homes. Through the heating of this mineral they were getting it to oscillate to extreme agitation where it dematerialised its environment and what came into contact with the mineral. One must be careful with these types of violating technologies, as the scientists themselves perhaps may make themselves no longer be.

Einstein taught us that what takes up space is matter, so it is insane to know that on that Earth they can make someone or something no longer be. This technology would have to go into the core of every atom within the matter of the subject and completely erase it from the space it is taking up as matter. What takes up space whether it is a more developed being as a human or a chair all has matter. It is the nucleus (image next page) within the atom that tells us how developed and intelligent the entity is to materialize into its form. The more protons and neutrons within the atom, the higher dimensional in intelligence the entity will be. Inside each atom at the nucleus is the soul and the DNA of the being. We are a kinetic energy that has grown into infinite atoms to make us up within the materialization of the third dimension. As the divine process of blastocyst cells (image on the next page) that grow into a human fetus.

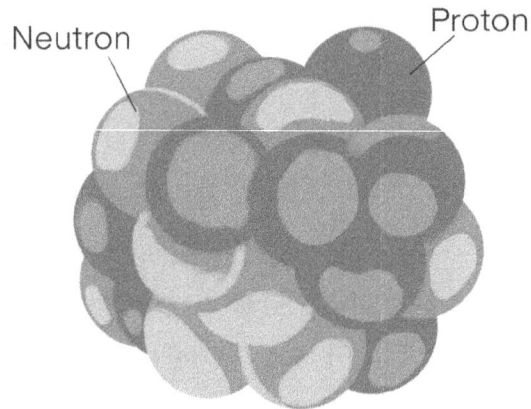

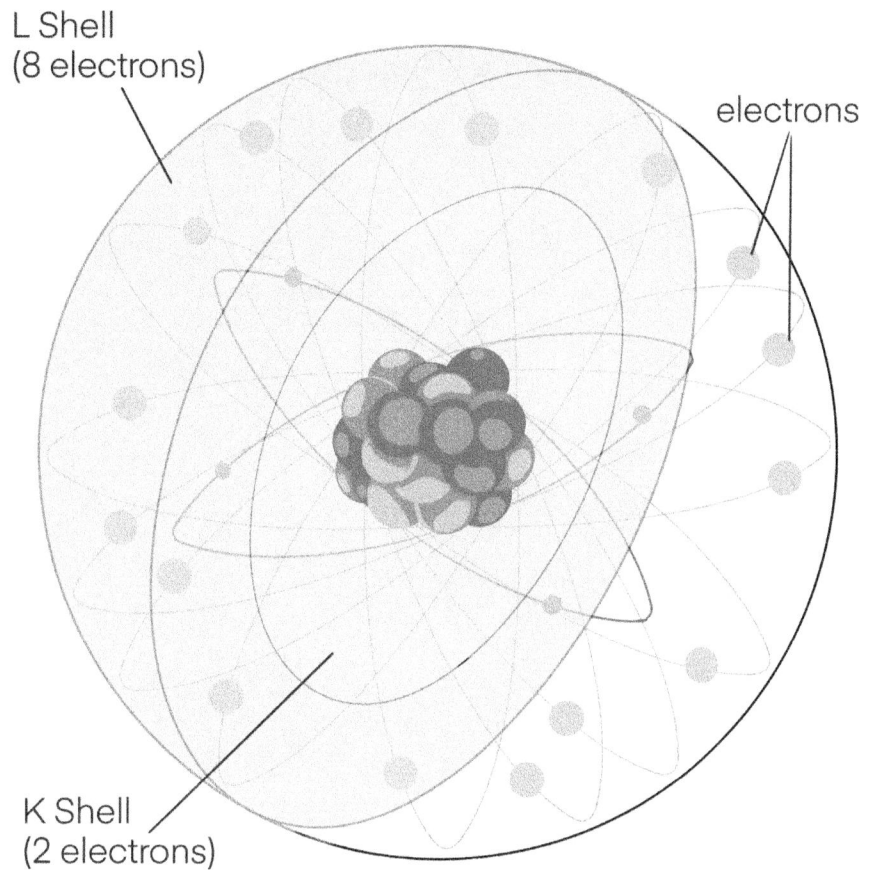

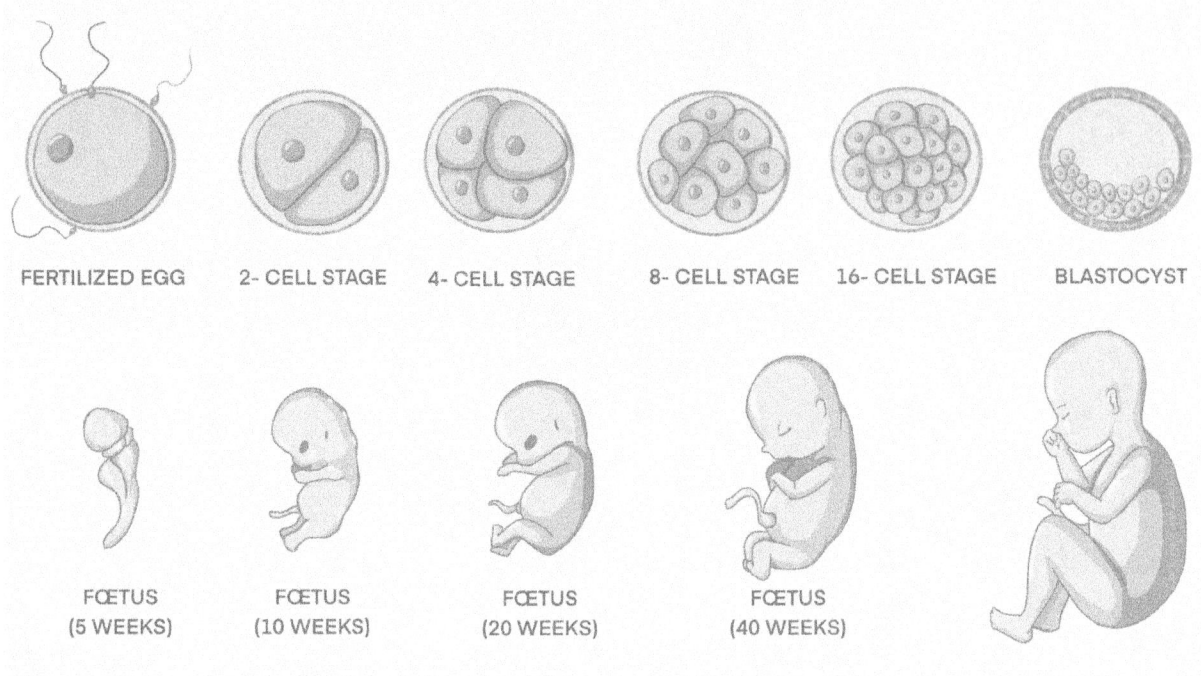

This parallel Earth had an incinerator technology, but on our Earth there is another type of technology being used. When we look to our past when everything was giant, there was an alien laser technology that was used on the people, giant humans and giant animals, but instead of dematerializing them into no longer being, these entities became petrified into stone. There is much more to this story of the petrification of giants which we will be covering deeply in Book 2 of this series.

On our Earth, we are seeing through the Deep State agenda of what they have been able to get their hands on as far as advanced technology. They think that they are still in a time where they can trick us by saying that it is global warming and climate change, but we know that it is instead their HAARP Weather Modification technology violating Mother Earth, and WE DO NOT CONSENT!

When they catch Cynthia and take the mineral she carries, she ends up killing herself so that they won't know the location of their underground base. This reminds me in the ways that through our clients and their memories of A.U.R.A. Hypnosis Healing sessions how Yeshua's students and disciples, how they would commit suicide if they were about to be caught by the Romans/Illuminati, just to protect the sacred teachings they carried with or within, so that the dark forces would not forcebly interrogate them and take them. This is how important the divine work of the benevolent lightworkers on Earth are. We know that if they get their hands on sacred teachings that it would not be good. However, our teachings through A.U.R.A. Hypnosis and R.A.A.H. Reiki Healing is set up so that if they were able to get their hands on them, they just wouldn't be able to use them. If they tried, it would positively polarize them to look or touch upon them or simply they just couldn't, because they would not retain the high enough vibration to comprehend them. Repelled they would become!

To conclude this chapter, it is most important to speak of artificial insemination, such as [41]IVF (In Vitro Fertilisation) being pushed onto humans, especially since the COVID-19 plandemic. This marked a time of a direct target to the reproductive systems of both female and males who got the COVID-19 vaccine, or those affected by the vaccinated Spike Protein discharge. Making people infertile so that the Elites can begin their intended inverted timeline to grow babies in artificial wombs to hybridize the next breed of the human race, instead of naturally growing in a mothers womb. To begin the protocol of having to go to a clinic to order your baby, like how you do so when ordering a package to be delivered.

The autism rise within children on Earth is felt all over the world and it will continue to rise if we continue to feed and inject hazardous chemicals into the children. Beginning from artificially inseminating them into conception, to hours being born vaccinating them with metals and foreign properties into their bloodstream, or feeding them chemical water and food that is bioengineered. As Robert Kennedy Jr. speaks of bringing awareness to Autism, it will continue to grow in population among children if we continue down this path of conforming. We, in the present, are the only ones that can change this timeline for the collective of all future human children. However, this topic is one deeply covered through our other book series 'Galactic

---

[41] In Book 2 of 'Galactic Soul History of the Universe' series, we touch on this very important subject in Chapter 13 "Lab Babies".

Soul History of Universe' and in our monthly video content. Hope to see you in our next live Friday video at 1pm Central Time!

We finish this chapter with an update from Cynthia and her beloved children:

"I have been having the boys join your [42]monthly group A.U.R.A. sessions a couple of times, alongside Gilbert a couple of times with the view that if anyone can help them connect to their Higher Self it would be you!

With both Gilbert and Oscar, my youngest, both can tune into the sound bath, but as soon as you start the script, they can't seem to stay in the theta brainwave and then don't connect to anything. My eldest, Eli on the other hand goes into theta and tells me he saw a dragon, went off flying and saw forests etc. So definitely more connected.

They have both made a lot of progress in their independence skills – now travelling independently on public transportation to and from college – and they can prepare simple meals including cooking the dog's food."

"Within every atom exists the memory of all that we are. If ever needing to heal oneself, all we have to do is speak to this memory so that what needs to be retrieved shall be."
~AuroRa♥

--------------<<>>--------------

---

[42] AuroRa hosts monthly group A.U.R.A. regressions on Patreon every fourth Monday of the Month at 1pm central time! Ensure to sign-up to that Tier to join us! These group sessions can harness deep self-healing just as a one on one A.U.R.A. session with AuroRa.

8

REMOTE VIEWING THE LOST CITIES OF TARTARIA PT 1
NIKOLA TESLA TARTARIA DISCOVERED

Streamed Live: December 30, 2022

In this chapter we dive deep into the civilization that came before us. Who were they and what happened to them? At the time we began to speak of the Tartarian civilization, not many knew of Tartaria, but in the current time in 2025, many do because as we began the series a big part of the population awakened to it and were ready to see with eyes unveiled. The Tartarian remembrance brings us to the deepest understanding of a distant memory within us of this world and how it was once so much more gigantic and magical.

--------------<<>>--------------

"These buildings were already there, long ago, thousands of years ago. It isn't just Egypt that we need to be in awe of. We don't realize that we have these ancient buildings among us, because there seems to have been a veil over them when we walked through them in the past. We now know that the veil has been lifted."
~AuroRa

--------------<<>>--------------

AuroRa: A lot of people have been asking, "How do I remote view?" The way that you can learn how to remote view in order to travel the Akashic for the history of Earth and our Universe, is through the courses of the ISIS Priestess/Priest and Quantum Galactic Akashic Reading. These courses are for both females and males.

Get ready and hang on to your Unicorns, Griffins and Dragons because you are going to freak out! What's about to come out through this chapter is pretty radical!

As we have been viewing the Urbano Monte map, it has allowed for me to go into these lands unknown to us at this time, and for me to travel through time and space through my third eye. We are continuing from Antarctica, Chapter 6, when we talked about the men that ruled these outside walls.

The dark aliens froze the ice walls with their HAARP Weather Modification technology. There is also benevolence to this, because everything I talk about will be benevolent as well. Viewing from an organic point-of-view of the two-third world bifurcation, Vesica Piscis, I also view things that are inverted. I am viewing both and I am bringing them into balance. That's why you will hear often the negative - the inverted - but then I will also tell you the positive. The ice that they have made, we have crystallized that with all the benevolence and the light on Earth, so that it holds coding within it.

We are now viewing the outside walls. These dark men have come up with a diabolical plan, which begins to wipe out the civilizations of the Indigenous, especially in the United States (map in chapter 6). Do you ever wonder why the United States were so targeted? Why were there not many people in the United States besides the indigenous people? Well, for that exact answer it will take time to unveil. It will be covered in the next book of this series or you can watch our Tartaria/Antarctica series live on our channels.

These men murdered most of the population of the Indigenous in these lands, but there were more people than just Indigenous living here spread out throughout the Earth (image on page 25). If we zoom in here, on the other side across from the United States, there is a Griffin right here (image on the next page). That is what we are talking about. We are talking about the Tartarian people. Tartaria. I knew when I saw the Griffin on the map in the previous chapters, that it was something really important. Now I understand why. We began to talk about it in Chapter 6, I didn't understand what the angels meant by it, when they channeled it over to me then. They told me that the 1900's were really important and now I know why.

On the other side of the United States, you can literally just walk across these lands, and at the North Pole the lands are all connected (image below).

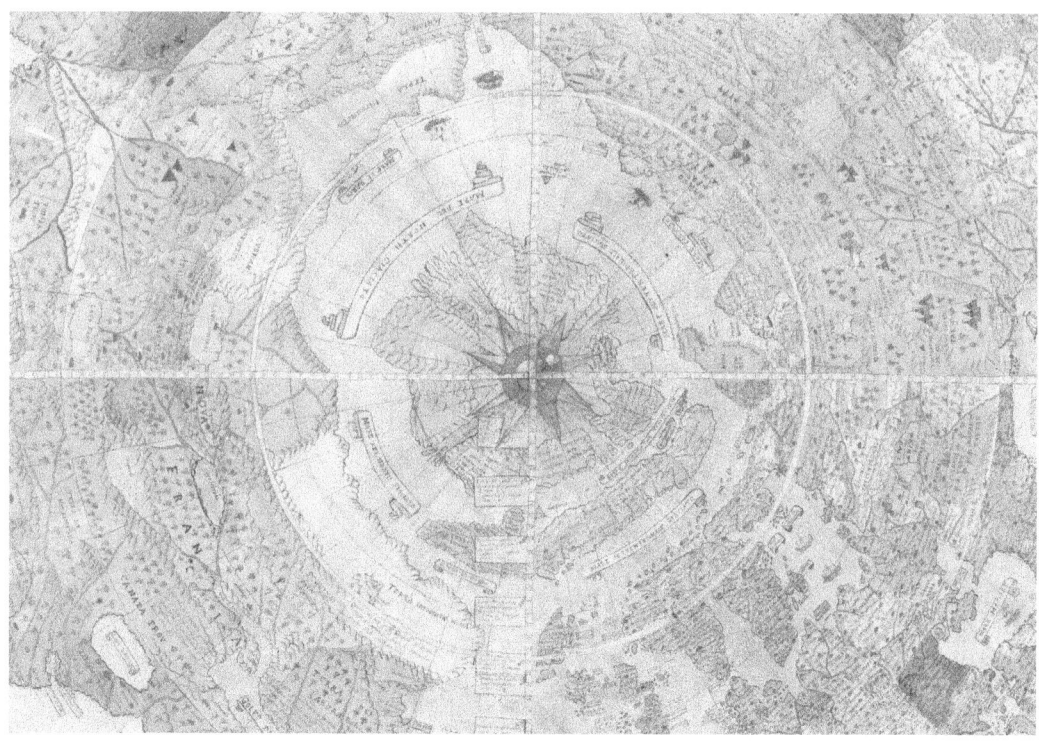

These lands used to be Tartaria. It's known now as Russia (Image below).

You can see some of the remnants of the Great Wall of China through this map (image below), but it's not the Great Wall of China. It is actually a Tartarian Wall. Why did they have a wall there and what were they trying to keep out? It's not a Chinese wall. It actually faces out towards China, as if they are guarding themselves from China. Tartarian people, wow!

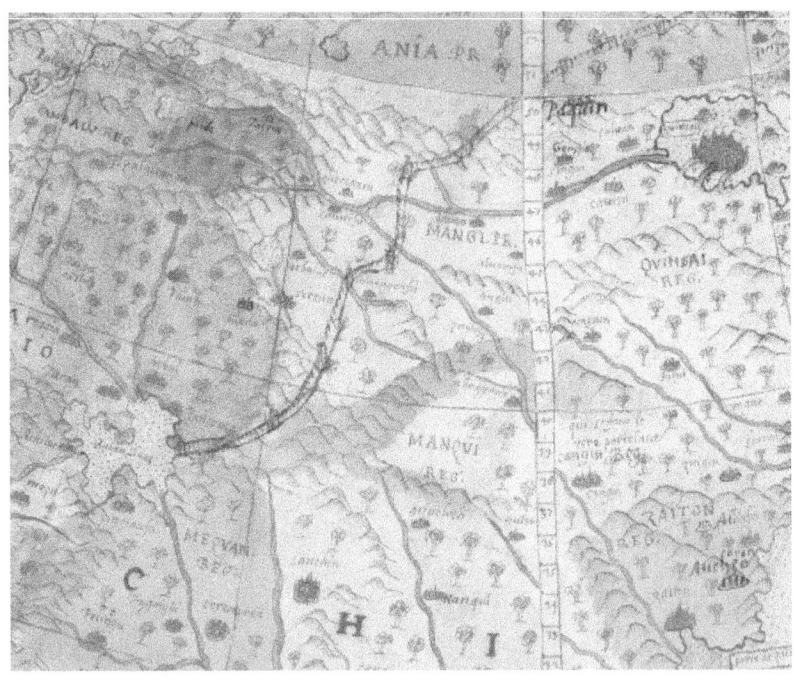

Nikola Tesla has been coming in and talking to me from time to time, but now he has completely come. He started talking to me as I was remote viewing this map. He told me that he was Tartarian. He was of these people who were from an advanced civilization that are erased from all our history. Up until the late 1800s and early 1900s, they were still there. Something happened to them. This was part of the diabolical plan of the dark alien entities, Grays, Mantis, and Reptilians. They targeted the consciousnesses of these men who were in a positive reign.

I also started talking to the angel that we see here on the map of that time and space (image below). What does this image of the Angel mean? They have names here. What they explained was that the Elohim were still very much in benevolence in the 1800s. Specifically in this map, which was made in 1587. We are going to explain how that is. The way that the dark entities were able to get to the indigenous people took a couple of centuries. They started going after the Tartarians and the land we spoke of in Chapter 6 (page 116). Where there was a Centaur depicted, and there was no man ruling over the land.

As I continued to talk to Nikola Tesla, he explained to me that is where his technology was coming from, it was part of his Tartarian bloodline. He was part of creating and bringing forth some of the positive technology that the Tartarians used.

As the dark entities spread out into those lands, first they needed to start taking down the indigenous people, but then they were protected by the benevolence of the Angelics. Then they went after the Tartarian people in the Russian lands and spread out. Where the [43]Law of Polarity is located in Russia, which is one of the Sacred Laws of the Universe, the Tartarians were overseeing that law and key. Their role was very important because it kept the Earth in balance by keeping the dark and light balanced. They were not just located in those Tartarian/Russian lands. They were also located in different energy vortexes, where there were gigantic crystal beds that they constructed their buildings and civilizations over. I am going to go ahead and share with you what that looked like. I am very excited!

I was born and raised in Chicago. What a phenomenal time I had. It was tough, but it taught me everything that I am, to be as strong and fierce as I am. I remember when I was younger, we used to go on field trips or adventure into downtown Chicago, and you would come across these gigantic buildings. I remember feeling very activated in these buildings. The majority of them are museums. I remember looking up and feeling so minuscule. I am only five feet-one tall. I am pretty short already, but the doorways to these museums were gigantic. The architecture seemed like it was out of place. It seemed like it was from ancient times. Here are images that I found, which is so exciting, to back up what we are talking about. Thank you to all the people who made these images and videos available that I will be showing. This is Chicago in 1893 (image on the next page).

---

[43] The Law of Polarity is one of the Universal Laws of the Universe of the 13 Keys spoken of in Book 1, 'Galactic Soul History of the Universe'.

Can you believe that it looked like that? Some of these buildings still remain. They are now museums. Look at the female statue (image above). Isn't she beautiful? She has her hair in a bun, and she has Angels at the top of the sphere. She is telling us that at that moment in time, there are Angels seen flying in the skies. If you search on channel platforms 'Angels', you are going to see videos of Angels in the skies. People record footage of them. The Angels are still here, of course. What is she holding up? Seems like some kind of unity symbol.

---

[44] All Images shown for the rest of this chapter were found in public web searches and channels. You can watch the origins of each if it is shown on the original streamed video of this chapter.

Do you remember the first chapters of this book? I said that there were some special buildings beyond the Antarctica walls. I didn't know then what they were. I just knew that we were going to talk about them later. Boom! This is what the buildings look like, over the wall. I said that they had pointed structures and some had dome-like structures. Like some of the structures that we see in India (image below) and different places where Tartaria had spread throughout Earth. It's quite phenomenal. The schools make it seem like we were so primitive in the past.

The indigenous were spread out throughout the United States, but there were civilizations like these in different parts of the land that are the biggest cities in our United States. These cities were not just here in the United States, they were in other locations of the world too. These are some of the buildings that are still standing today (image on the next page). If you look to the right or behind them, look at how out of place those modern buildings are. The older ones look phenomenal. They were a self-sustainable community. They were known to be [45]breatharians. Tesla told me that he didn't eat much. He would just sleep and recharge himself off the energy of the ether and the cosmos.

---

[45] A breatharian is a person who does not need to eat food to survive. They use the energy of the sun or the ether to sustain life on Earth.

At the tip of all of these buildings, they used to have pointed structures, but they took them off. They replaced a lot of them with crosses, or with their religious programming. Look at this architecture, and look at the buildings right behind them. These buildings stand out. They are ancient.

Why were these buildings created with domes? We have talked about how dome structures harness energy. Square structures contain energy and it stops the flow. Dome structures at the top pull in the ether energy. These buildings are very beautiful architectural energetic vortices. In the [46]'Remote Viewing the Pyramids' we spoke of stone, and how each brick is a conduit of energy. You have many components that are making up these buildings, that are drawing in energy to this one civilization, like I showed you that Chicago was.

I once took a field trip on a boat on this river (image above). I remember while on the boat feeling like there was something really out of place. I felt like I was in a different dimension, when I was surrounded by this river, this bridge, and these buildings. Now I know why. I was seeing timelines shifting of the civilization that came before us. The Tartarians, and the water was acting as the 'conduit of energy' for me to feel myself at another time and space.

---

[46] Watch 'Remote Viewing The Pyramids | The Mayan | 12.2.22 | 12.12.22 | 12.21.22 | Galactic Update' aired December 9, 2022.

Look at these (image below). I think the majority of them are from Chicago. Aren't they beautiful? Don't these remind you of churches? The churches were actually Tartarian temples, and they added crosses to them. That's why when you look at them, you are like, 'Wow.' A lot of you feel motivated to travel the churches. What do you think you are doing? You are working on Tartarian energy, because that is where your original blueprint is, from our past.

When the sun shines on them, they turn red like this (image below). Here are some more buildings (continues to show more images).

This is the Field Museum (image below).

There are eight goddesses and two Angel statues above the entrance (image above). Phenomenal. They look Greek. There is a Griffin on the roof. Griffins are the sign of Tartaria. There are also mermaid type carvings decorated all over as well.

Do you see these columns, ceilings and arches? It is all gigantic! Why did we have gigantic structures? You build a home or building for the size of the people, don't you? Look at how tall these ceilings are. See how tiny the people are walking on the ground. When you go into the Field Museum, there are these huge arches. They are as tall as those pillars. Why would we have buildings like this? Because a lot of the Tartarians were giants. When you walk in there, it feels like another dimension.

When looking upon the entrance of the Field Museum, the stone of the stairs going up all the way at the bottom is different (image below). It's not from the time of its original construction, as it is more recent. They added these stairs later for little people to climb, like us. I guess we will call ourselves little people (laughs).

Here is a map of Tartaria (image below). You see the supposed Great Wall of China again. Why were the Tartarians trying to keep [47]China out? The towers on the wall face into China, like they were protecting themselves from China.

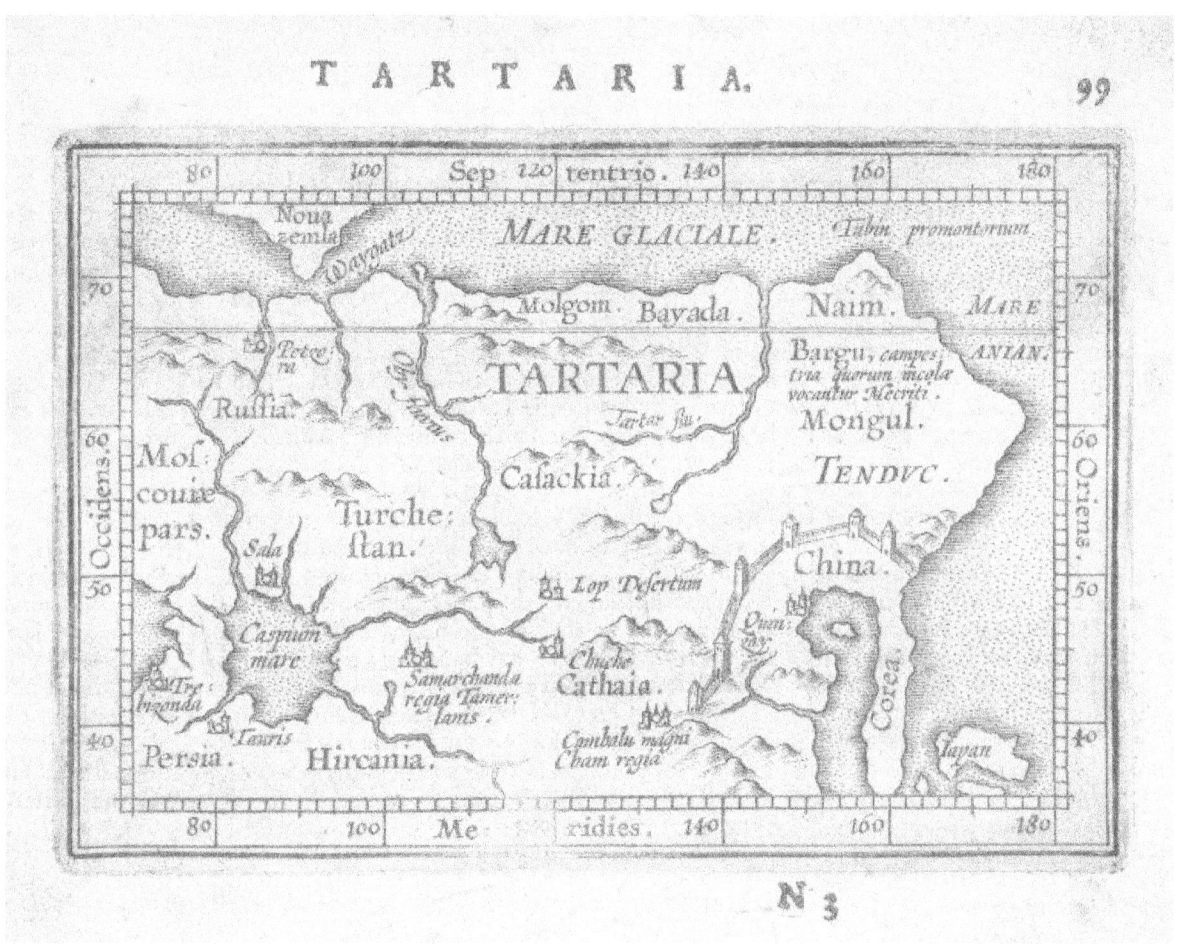

When looking at archived flags of our past the Tartarian flag had the symbol of a griffin. Here are some more images that I found of more Tartarian civilizations and what they look like. These buildings were already there thousands of years ago. It is not just Egypt that we need to be in awe of. We did not realize that we have these ancient buildings among us, because there seems to have been a veil over them when we walked them in the past. We now know that the veil has been lifted.

---

[47] This topic is covered in an entire episode, which will be in the next book or watch it now 'GHENGHIS KHAN | The Great Mongolian Empire and Wall'.

Angels are often on these Tartarian buildings. We know that we all have essences of fractals of Angels within us. You will hear people say that Angels are not real or that they are not incarnated. They are lying to you. That is false programming. They don't want you to realize you have essences of Angels within you. We all birth from Angels who are the first essences out from Source. They are Source's multiversal all seeing selves. So we all have these essences. We are incarnates of Angels.

When we look at this map, the red part is the most populated area, the greenest parts are where there are not so many people. Look at how most of the civilization is on the East Coast. I want to point out the difference in energies, and how in some of those towns that I have shown you in the images that were Tartarian, they replaced the population in them. We the people are now living in the same once populated cities before us. That's why they had us all migrate. The Deep State makes us think that we are overpopulated, but that is a lie. Look at all *these lands in green that are not populated. We only feel overpopulated because they further build our cities and houses side-by-side next to each other, with barely any land around us.*

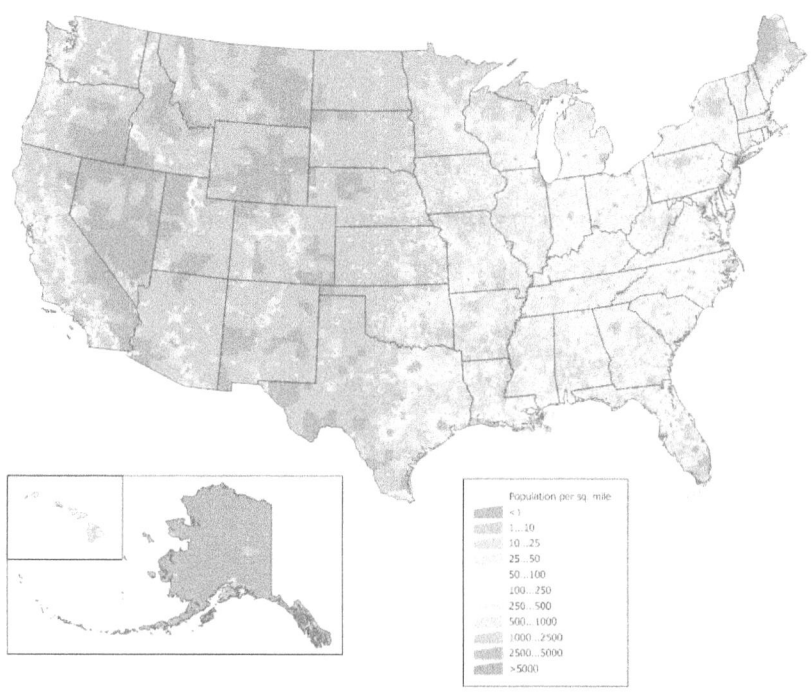

They have completely congested us in these vortex locations. Why are all the people mostly in the east or to the far west? Because there are energetic vortexes that keep you energetically powered up like the people in the Tartarian civilization who were breatharian, because they instead were kept alive by light, like a plant. Through these high energetic vortex cities is how the people kept energetically in high potency. What the Deep State has done is inverted our cities by placing negative technologies in them. Through the antennas on top of buildings they are emitting negative, hazardous frequencies that make these into [48]negative towers that we talked about in the past throughout our content.

How did we get here? It was the 'Fall of Tartaria', and before that, it was [49]the 'Fall of Atlantis'. The first initial degression of humankind, where we went from the fifth dimension into the fourth dimension. After that they began to take control through the New World Order agenda of depopulating Earth.

---

[48] Watch 'The Matrix' playlist found on our channels.
[49] Watch 'The Atlantis/Mayan' playlist on our channels.

There were not just gigantic people in Russia/Tartaria. They were everywhere! You can find their images on many channel platforms. Divine Mother told me that the Giants were basically Atlantean beings. We talked about in the Atlantis series, how the seer/the elder had left Atlantis and gone to the Mayan locations to help construct all the pyramids? We talked about how she was tall and glowing, and they thought she was a God? It was just that Atlantean beings were gigantic. They were ten to twenty feet tall, and all different sizes. The remainder of the lands around our Atlantean islands were more like indigenous shorter people, and other races as well. There were also dragons and all the [50]magical creatures that we have spoken of. There were smaller people, even tiny little people that you hear about in Ireland that are real. There was a diverse size of humans on Earth.

With Laura Eisenhower, who is the great-granddaughter of President Dwight D. Eisenhower, we broadcasted a video called 'The Alien A.I. Invasion' speaking of how the most recent alien takeover began. In 1959 the treaty of Antarctica was signed. It began with just twelve countries, and then it turned into a total of fifty-eight parties. Once they brought the Tartarians down, and the Indigenous down, then it was just about getting all these countries to align and to allow for the New World Order to reign over everyone. They signed a Treaty to never go past Antarctica, because the aliens are there, and we are not supposed to know that.

I was looking into the underground tunnel system that we talked about in the Antarctica previous chapters. How the [51]'Secret Space Program' thinks that they are going over to Mars, but they are really just going over to the outside lands beyond Antarctica. These MK-Ultra people have supposed memories of how they travel through these tunnel systems where they think they are going outwardly, but it really is just farther away from where we are at. Nikola Tesla told me that it was the Tartarian civilization that created all of these tunnels. All those dark entities that went into human bodies, compromised them, and then took over. These tunnels were not originally negative. They were positive transportation within Earth, but the negative took possession of them.

---

[50] Watch 'Mystical Creatures, Dragons, Griffins, Unicorns, Pixies' series on our channels.
[51] The Secret Space Program, SSP is the negative military UFO abductions they perform on humanity using negative technologies to wipe their memory of what they are doing to their victims.

Similar to how we talk about Egypt and how we had positive times of reign when the Divine Mothers or Fathers, Gods and Goddesses incarnated into their times and space. But, then there were times when the Illuminati (who were the original dark Anunnaki), continued their infringement that began in Atlantis upon the beautiful beings that were alive in those times. The benevolence was always there to guide us. Thank you to Nikola Tesla. I love you. He was an essence of an Archangel. He was Archangel Raziel, which is the architectural Angel.

I am going to show you some images of the Tartarian technology that has been erased, but some people found this content. This is the type of technology that they had back then. Look at this man hovering around (image below). They claim that this was new technology when they portrayed it in movies. This is old technology that was stolen. Just like Nikola Tesla's technology was stolen after the negative military killed him off. Something for you to look into further.

[52] These next couple images are screenshots taken from videos found on TikTok.

He's listening to something strongly here. His guides or Angels?

Here is an iPad perhaps? This lady is talking to their grandchildren through something called 'PICTUREPHONE' service.

The Tartarian people would ride around in these transportation vehicles alongside with electric cars.

This is a screenshot from a video of a child riding in his wheeled motorcycle, while his father runs alongside him.

He's like, "Yes, I can climb stairs."

Here's an image (image below) of Chicago in 1893. After 1893 it seems as if they built all the modern buildings that look out of place surrounding the older buildings in the now time. In the future we will cover more on why there were so many orphans. Why was Chicago empty, as shown in this image? Because they murdered the Tartarian adults when they introduced depopulation programs through alien-made diseases introduced through vaccinations. There were orphans because they were repopulating Earth. We are talking about centuries or one-thousand years of battle against Earth and humanity. The history dates and what they are teaching in their indoctrinating school systems have been written incorrectly. Once we fell from the fourth dimension into the third dimension, the actual 'Time Construct' began. It is more like [53]1,000 years since we entered the third dimension. When we were in the fourth dimension, there was no time in our Earthly construct.

---

[53] This topic will be covered in detail in the next book, or you can watch 'Yeshua Just Walked This Earth'.

I have been talking to the Giants ever since I began the Antarctica series. I have been preparing for a channeling of them in the upcoming chapters. Here is the physical proof. Thank you to all these 'Flat Earth' theories, because they helped us understand all of this. Look at these gigantic people (images below).

Look at where the arrows are pointing, see the giant female and a normal size person at the bottom.

Here is a gigantic man on the bottom right and again you see the smaller people walking around this monument.

The giants would just walk around like it was normal. But the Elites erased this memory from us. Do you ever wonder why there are and were constant UFO abductions of the population of Earth? They were erasing our memories of this, because it just happened a century ago. Why do you think that they give babies vaccination shots when they are born? They are erasing their memory of the magic that was once here by densifying the babies with an integration of foreign toxins into them through injection. We hold this memory in our DNA codex.

Look at that indigenous man. He is so beautiful.

You look at him, he is fishing with his smaller buddies. He probably needs a bigger fish to fill up his belly, and he probably uses larger hooks to catch them.

The giants were just walking around, running errands, just as normal size people are. People are going to try to say this is C.G.I. No, you can tell these are old pictures. You can't mess with pictures like this. You can see his reflection in the glass and his shadow is going in the same direction with alignment to the sun as the shorter people.

A huge part of my awakening was watching Japanese animation. I remember one of my favorite Anime was 'Fullmetal Alchemist', because they were Alchemists. There is the Brotherhood, and then there is the original one - two different versions of the series. I started off with 'Dragonball Z', but then I found Fullmetal Alchemist. I remember there is a part where Edward, one of the brothers in the series, discovers a city under a city. This felt so real to me. Like a distant memory, without knowing then. That was so activating for me.

The Tartarian buildings which are now Museums are not just one or a couple floors, there is way more beneath them that is under the ground that we don't see. These modern cities were built on top of ancient cities. We are only seeing the surface of the buildings. When *you dig under, there is way more to that building (image below). They made everything look miniature, but in actuality it was gigantic. Our world was gigantic!*

What questions do we have?

Interviewer: The first one we have is, 'Were there civilizations covering the whole Earth?'

AuroRa: They were powered by the ether of Elohim energy. Yes, they were spread out all over. Some of them were in Paris. These buildings are now churches as well. The Vatican was a sacred space. Now they have dark priests involved with the churches that are pedophiles. Disgusting. They are in this most sacred space.

Interviewer: "Did they build tremendous architectural buildings, ones with domes?"

AuroRa: Yes, that was them. They needed to have domes because most of them were breatharians. They needed to bring in the energy into their spaces, their homes, or their sacred spiritual places where they would go to recharge their energy.

I wonder who lived in the Field Museum (image on page 182). I am seeing that Giants lived there. I see giant Angels. I see them walking around, in their moment in time and space, before all the infringements happened.

Interviewer: "Did they build the Great Wall of China to separate from China? Do we have more information on that?"

AuroRa: They did, but it was not the 'Wall of China'. It was the Tartarian wall to keep them out. What I was told is that China was highly populated and China was starting to begin to show signs that they were becoming compromised. That is where the dark aliens went to target first. The Grays, as we talked about in the A.I. Alien Invasion on Cosmic Mother Rising Show, because they have an enormous amount of population versus everywhere else. The aliens went there so they could then infringe upon these people and use them to attack others. Why were they keeping the Chinese out? Something very dark was going on there.

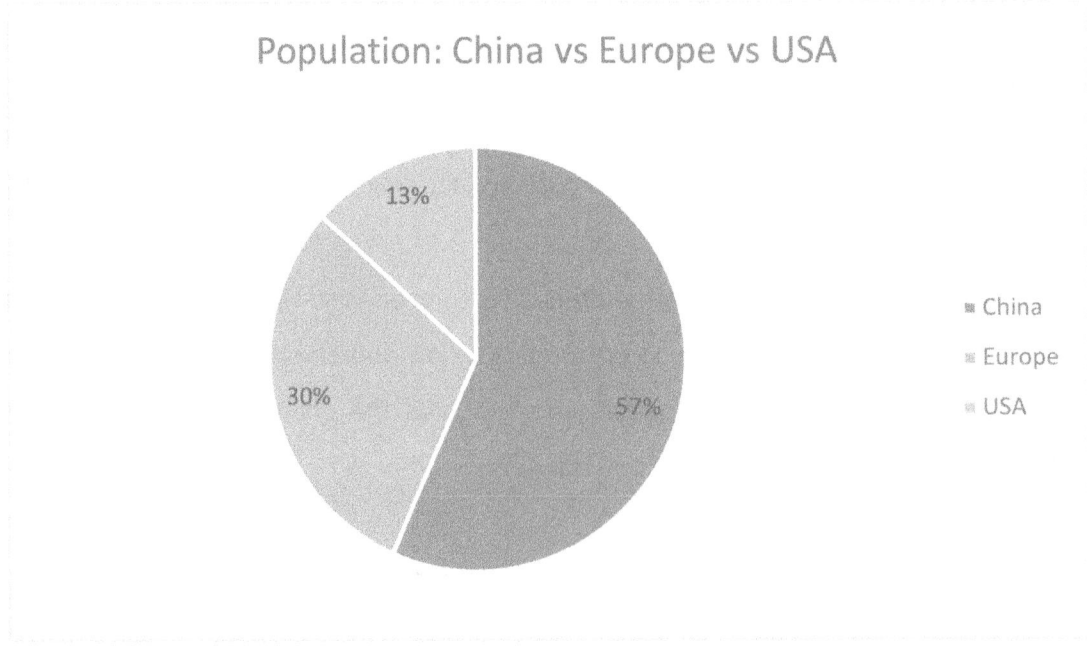

If you were a bad entity, imagine if you go in and compromise these leaders with big populations, then you have that population at best under your control. Same reason why leaders of all kinds, whether political or spiritual, are targeted. The graph above shows the population of China. Look at the difference in population in comparison to the U.S.A. Why did we need to repopulate the U.S.A.? Because they wiped them out. This is why America is made up of immigrants. Someone needed to come reseed these lands. They call it the Land of the Free, the Land of Immigrants. Everyone had to migrate over because the lands were emptied out. It was a massacre.

I was reading the comments on one of the videos I referenced and somebody said, "I used to live next to an older man, a neighbor, in Chicago. He said that he was Tartarian and he would show us these books and they looked really strange. Old to us. He said that he was 180 years old." You will find homes like that. They still have the similar architecture. The Tartarians are among us, but they are in hiding. Those that were able to survive, they are here, or their descendents, just like the Giants. They are here, but the military targets them for their experimentations.

Interviewer: When you were talking about all the buildings in the beginning, somebody asked, was all of that a part of the mini resets?

AuroRa: Yes. But I think that one was a gigantic reset. Part of one. There have been gradual stages to get us to where we are currently in the third dimension.

Interviewer: "Do magical creatures still live in Tartaria?"

AuroRa: They do. I remember when I started waking up and I became an Usui Reiki Master. When I woke up, I attracted Griffins. I was lying in bed with my children and all of a sudden the lights started flickering, and it felt like this gigantic energy filled up the room. It felt very majestic and noble. I knew that it was something very benevolent and positive. I said, "Who are you?" Just by me asking that, that night I went to bed and a Griffin Prince came to me. He told me that he traveled from far away, near Asia. I didn't know where that was, but now

I know that it was Mongolia, The Tartarian Empire of [54]Genghis Khan. Griffins do exist! We just can't see them in the third dimension because they are within the fourth dimension and higher. They are still on this Earth, and are parallel to us. We are starting to see the mermaids and the dragons in the waters in the skies. People are sharing recordings of them. They are still here. They are in the mountains and the oceanshiding.

Interviewer: "So are Tartarians human, or what exactly are they?"

AuroRa: Tartarians were human. We are the descendants of them. Whoever was able to survive until now. When I was scanning and remote viewing, I saw that the leader of Tartaria somehow became compromised and was taken down. That is why they were able to bring down the civilization. There was this one male named Grigori Rasputin back then, and he has incarnated now in Russia as is President Vladimir Putin. That same man who turned dark - compromised the King and Queen back then - and now he's back again. One of the reasons why he is interested in going past Antarctica is because they knew about these things from back then. They have all that information logged. They still have it in their histories, because they were some of the original lands to Tartaria. You can't destroy everything in just one century. There's no way. There are going to be things that are going to resurface, just like the Chicago man who had a neighbor who had the Tartaria books. They are there. Let's hope these people come out more, as we are seeing already.

Interviewer: "If China was becoming dark when the Tartarians built the wall and now the majority of items in the world are made in China, does this mean that the items coming from China are carrying dark energy?"

AuroRa: They can, but that's alright. It's just physical. It's good for us to be aware, but then we can't completely freak out because just about everything is made in China. What are you going to do? It's fine. Just shield everything you have. Positively polarize everything that you use. Clear that energy. Even if it's physical, it does have matter within it that makes up its

---

[54] Again Genghis Khan will be covered in the next books of this series or watch it now on our channels 'GHENGHIS KHAN | The Great Mongolian Empire and Wall'.

physical construct to be physicality. Just cleanse everything you do. It's fine. Shield everything and you are good. Once you start shielding your home, everything becomes energetically etheric.

People always wonder, "AuroRa, how do you do all that you do?" That is because I'm literally bringing in the ether energy into my space every day and I am slowing down time. Some of the days that are just one day to others, could be three-five days to me. We all need to become masterful like that, like Nikola Tesla taught us back then. That's how they were self-sustainable. He showed me there were Tesla coil structures that were at the top of the buildings that would draw in the etheric energy. We weren't primitive. The current Earth History teaches that we didn't have electricity. That's a lie. We had electricity even back then, just like you saw the advanced technology in the images.

There are older buildings in Chicago and I also saw them in New Orleans, and I was asking Tesla about them. There are fireplaces, but they say that they were not workable fireplaces, but yet in these older buildings, every room has a mantle and fireplace. What he explained is that they would draw in energy through those points at the top of the homes and buildings into the fireplaces, and the ether energy would literally run through these canals into the buildings. They kept themselves constantly charged in the building through the ether energy. He is showing me the structure right now in the building. The ether is coming in through the points and through the domes, zapping into the brick. Then it goes through all the tunnels or canals of the fireplace, and then I see this plasmic ether energy coming out of the fireplaces. It then charges the whole space. Every room. That was one of the main reasons why we lived hundreds of years back then. These were times of the Tartarians, before the Elites had implemented all these chemicals and chemtrails.

In our previous content we started talking about how winters were going to change. Are you noticing it? The recent freeze that just happened, supposedly from the North Pole, was false. It was created by HAARP and it is not actual snow. They were using the water from the North Pole and making it into this fake snow that is not truly snowflakes anymore. If you are at a location where everything became like an icicle, it wasn't organic. The Elites are freaking out *because they are seeing the change in the weather. They are going to say it is global warming. We are bringing the winters back to how they were. I always wondered how the indigenous were able to survive in their teepees in below zero weather. They didn't have below-zero weather! What they told me is that they had maybe fifties to forties Fahrenheit, max temperatures. How they do this is if you look up at the clouds, if you are in a winter state or winter country right now, there is a fake thick blanket of supposed clouds. It is coming from the North Pole, through this technology that we have been talking about for years, and the chemtrails. The weather modification technology is what makes this fake blanket, because they don't want the sun to wake us up and heal us. They don't want us to see that there is more than one sun or moon.*

I feel that there are days that are energetically heightened because there are actual eclipses that are happening, that they are blocking out so we won't see them. There are more eclipses than they claim. Right now they claim that there is not going to be an Eclipse until 2025 (I am now in 2025, and this is inaccurate. There have been several solar and lunar eclipses since 2022). There are multiple, because the moon and the sun align constantly and they create lunar and solar eclipses all the time. That makes no sense within the flat earth understanding, where we are within a plane of existence.

More than ever, call your dragons. Call on the elements and your benevolent team to keep transmuting these fake clouds that are above us that are made up of chemicals. The Elites are keeping the population asleep, feeding all these chemicals and hazardous metals into us. The reason they want it cold is because in the warmer climates such as spring and summer, there are more beautiful blue skies. The heat transmutes these chemicals. They can't hide the sun in heat because the sun melts these fake clouds. So they want it arctic cold. Antarctica cold - fake cold - so that they can keep the sun out which is part of the whole New World Order agenda. Keeping us asleep because the sun heals everyone and everything.

Interviewer: Wow! "Is there a way we can anchor these Tartarian energies into structures on our own property?"

AuroRa: Yes, crystals are a huge part to do that. Points in your home are important. You can get crystal points such as obelisk types of crystals. Tower crystals that could bring in that energy. If you have a brick home, it is an easier way that you can change the energy in your home and land. Theoretically, when you are doing your shields, envision etheric energy coming out of all points of your home. If you have a fireplace you can start drawing in the ether energy through it. Drawing it in through the chimney and any other vents that breathe out and circulate the air in your home. Start bringing the ether in. We need to become Alchemists now, bringing in the energy through all forms of the ether possible. You can get statues of Goddesses and Angels. Anything with points or holding points. The trees can now be the points for us. The trees on your land can draw in that ether energy for you and expand it out through the roots. Embodying the ancient symbol of the 'Tree of Life' and its roots and branches. Any part where the roof becomes points, you should be drawing in energy through there. Make your entire home into points like pyramids, that draw in that ether energy.

Interviewer: "What crystals are connected to the Tatarian people?"

AuroRa: It's hidden from us. I see it's like a silver. It looks extraterrestrial. It is solid like crystals, and has multiple points coming out of it. I think they have harvested it out and taken a lot of these. It looks a little bit like hematite. I think the closest one to it would be hematite. Look into what crystals are found in Russian and Asian areas, because those will be Tartarian crystals. The crystal which is Tartarian is very important. It's magnetic. Hematite is magnetic. You could use it for scientific experiments because of its natural magnetism. What can you do with that if you are a scientist? Black Tourmaline with hematite is very powerful too.

Interviewer: "Does the Law of Three play into the structure of any of these Tartarian buildings around us?"

AuroRa: I believe you are speaking of The Law of Three, where benevolent beings can only speak if they say their name three times in a row, without change. Only benevolent beings can say their name three times. Malevolent cannot say it three times. They will alter how they say their supposed name, or if they are posing as a benevolent being saying their name.

Pertaining with three - I see triangles and sacred geometry everywhere. Again, visit Tartarian buildings and churches, and you will find the architecture that's 'Hidden in Plain Sight'.

Interviewer: "Do we know where all these statues went? Were they destroyed?"

AuroRa: They destroyed them. They broke them off and they crushed them into rubble. Then they replaced them with their crosses and different demon-looking gargoyles. Those are not positive. There are gargoyles that are so cute. They are doggies with wings. Those are Angel dogs. Those are the real gargoyles. The fake ones are where they put their demons with their wings and they claim that they are protecting. No, they are part of the black magic. That is their entities, false deities that are Archon demonic things that they worship.

Interviewer: "What is the true age of all of these buildings shown to us? The history books are inaccurate."

AuroRa: Thousands of years. I would say two, or three thousand. It's hard to read time because there is no time in space. All there is, is now! Understanding our Earthly Time Construct is in Book Two, 'Galactic History of the Multiverse - The Final Battle'. This is information that I received in 2021, when I started to channel the Flat Earth module and the flat earth map. Time is kept by the sun. In quantum physics, Earth is a clock. Looking at the Urbano Monte Map in Chapter 1, the North Pole is our center of the clock. As the time turns, the hour hand turns, and the sun and moon cycles turn too. Energetically, this is a formula that is used in CERN European Organization for Nuclear Research. They stole it. They know that the Earth is flat and that there is a dome over it. They know that there are time portals that as you turn the clock on this Flat Earth, they can time travel through these energetic vortex openings. These are some of their agendas that we don't know the details of.

Make sure you share this content as far as you can. It is so important. Recommend this Antarctica/Tartaria Book series to as many as you can. Share it to the groups you are part of, to your friends, to your family. Let's wake up these people.

In a recent video, someone asked what is going to be our biggest catalyzing awakening? This is going to be. When people wake up and realize that they are on a Flat Earth, inside a dome and we are caged inside the ring of ice of Antarctica. Meanwhile the aliens travel outside and back in whenever they feel like it, because they stole this technology from the Tartarians, being able to go back and forth through the tunnels.

Interviewer: "Were there floating and crystalline cities in Tartaria?"

AuroRa: There were islands floating for sure. We love watching Hayao Miyazaki, a Japanese film maker. He has a movie called 'Castle in the Sky', where there are floating cities. These films that he makes tells us of the advancement of the past. Some of the technologies we spoke of in this chapter are illustrated in these movies. The Tartarian floating cities are still in the clouds. The movie industry shows us glimpses, so that we can remember but think it is fantasy, or they are showing us information to compromise us. There are still remnants of the Tartarian technology up there floating somewhere, cloaked with high vibrational technology. I see benevolent Tartarian beings up there that have invisibility cloaks on them.

Interviewer: Where are the Tartarians now?

AuroRa: Some of them are hidden throughout civilization. They are in hiding. They are in the mountains, and some of them are floating above us. Some of them also went into the Earth too, because they were highly advanced. They were connected with the Unicorns, the Griffins, and the Dragons. For a civilization to live off oxygen/breath, and off the sun, think about how high vibrational these people would have been. Very high. Probably the highest after the fall of Atlantis.

Interviewer: "Can you expand on the connection between Tartaria and the last reset or mud floods?"

AuroRa: The dark entities are who force the mud floods to happen with their technologies. They cover it up by causing trauma to the people and then wiping out entire civilizations. The buildings we spoke of in this chapter were mud flooded. These people use negative technologies that the aliens gave them to cause the mud floods. The Angels won't allow me to go past that. Sometimes I cannot share things because they are not the right time to share them divinely.

Interviewer: "What about the native Indigenous peoples? Did they have contact with the Tartarians?"

AuroRa: They did. You see their understanding through hieroglyphics where they show hovering vehicles. They knew of the Tartarians because both of these civilizations lived together at the same time in space. The indigenous and the Tartarians were in connection with the Elohim, and the Angels, as we see through the glimpses they left us, through the statues on the Tartarian buildings.

Interviewer: "Where does the word Tartaria originate from and what is its meaning?"

AuroRa: The way that it's pronounced is not one word. It's 'Tar-ta-ria'. It seems like it is an ancient language of light. I noticed that the Light language and the Crystal language that the star child has been giving us, some of it ends with -ia. It has something to do with the Crystal Light language. It makes sense that it is Crystal Light language. It carries crystalline light within it. It is a force field. It was protecting the people. At some point, when the collective becomes too influenced and they become dark - just like we saw in the fall of Atlantis - if scientifically and energetically, they become the majority. It takes over the positive. We then see these negative reigns happen. That's why we're here in this lower third dimension. We are done with these insane reigns of invertedness. That's why all of us volunteered, right? To bring in the light and to help this civilization end all these horrific things that these negative aliens have been doing to humankind.

Interviewer: "Do Tartarians originate from a certain planet?"

AuroRa: I am not seeing a planet. I just see high-dimensional beings. They originated from the Atlantean era. What I am seeing is that at some point in space on Earth, there was a big group that left Atlantis. The elders of Atlantis were assisting people to move out when it was time. I see that one of the civilizations that they pioneered was Russia. The Himalayan Mountains were really important to them. The Himalayas were also part of the Tartarian lands. They used these energies to power up a lot of their ether energy as well, and to balance Earth and to keep it shielded.

If you think this content is phenomenal. If you join any of our courses, you will be even more wowed! You will start bringing in this etheric energy, so that you can become these lighter beings. These higher vibrational beings, who understood the construct of Earth and the ether. Come assist us to become more like the civilization of Tartaria. To be the embodiment of drawing in Source Love-Light - the ether energy. Understanding that the ether is vast and infinite. We have yet to tap into its potential. We have such a minuscule point-of-view that we are tapping into now. Come learn through all our courses. Why you are going to be amazed is because you are going to feel incredible! Even though I'm forty-one, I feel like I am young. As young as a teenager. That's how you feel once you start embodying this positive Love-Light energy that just flows through you all day long. You start age-regressing yourself. You start walking your most organic timelines.

I love to travel in the dark, because that is where I find some of the missing pieces that are hidden in the dark. The most confident person is ONE with their light and dark and is in balance with the [55]Universal Law of Polarity of Russia and Tartaria. You are that antenna, you are the peak, you are the portal. Draw in that energy from Source that is infinite! I love you with all that I AM.

END OF SESSION.

---

[55] Read Book 1, 'Galactic Soul History of the Universe' for more on the Universal laws.

"A healthy mind is one that questions everything. A mind that allows to be challenged to create accomplishment is a strong one. Within this mindset is where the mysteries of Creation are found. Within a pondering mind."

~Nikola Tesla, Channeled by AuroRa.

"Once you see, you cannot unsee."

~AuroRa

--------------<<>>--------------

9

REMOTE VIEWING THE LOST CITIES OF TARTARIA PT 2
THE RESETS OF EARTH

Streamed Live: January 20, 2023

What a tremendous Chapter 8 was! Prepare yourself for another chapter of great unveiling of what was so obvious, but not known until now. Since our awakening we have heard from others that humanity has been reset, and now we understand how. This series will dissect Earth's History piece by piece, leaving no unturned stone. The Tartarian knowledge that has begun to come forth through my channelings is so big that as I write about this now, this series is over ninety episodes and still going! Every chapter of this series, from here on, will only get bigger and bigger!

What the Tartararian awareness brings to us is balance to the mind, which opens our hearts wider. This knowledge profoundly helps us see from perspectives that we have never been able to see before. In the spiritual and U.F.O. communities, what we speak of is still not popular enough, as they are set in the ways that they think that we are on a globe. Our hope through this series is that we will be able to reach the far reaches of the people of Earth, to provide them the opportunity to see the beauty that Tartaria has brought to our eyes and our consciousness. Your whole world changes when you discover Tartaria, because you now know what you are looking at everywhere you walk. Whether that is giant tree stumps, petrified giants, or brilliant architecture. Now you know, and once you know, you can't unknow! In a world where you are told to fall in line and question nothing, this book series allows us to confirm all that we already knew in our hearts, that we were told that was crazy!

-------------<<>>-------------

"I've been waiting for this moment in time and space to share with you, how very recent it's been since I walked among you and held your faces in the palms of my hands and felt your hearts."
~Yeshua

-------------<<>>-------------

AuroRa: We have been huge at TikTok. In under three months, we have reached over ten thousand followers which is gigantic for us! As you know on YouTube, the numbers don't seem quite accurate because they shadow ban us there. The videos have reached easily ten to fifty thousand views on TikTik. One of the videos has over one hundred sixty thousand views right now! There are so many questions that have come up on TikTok that are grand! We are talking about hundreds, maybe even thousands of questions and comments where people are commenting on the videos. We have placed these questions together, so that we can begin to answer them.

We are on the outside walls and on these lands that have the Centaurs (image in Chapter 6, page 119). What happens is that the ruling dark men, that are in the whole surrounding lands, take down the Centaurs. After that they know that they have to get to the Tartarians; the Giants first, then to bring down the indigenous, who are very much connected to Mother Earth, and then Elementials. That's where we are at.

We just hosted a retreat where magical things happened, as we were vibrating to a higher dimension together. The things that we have spoken of through this series, carried over to the retreat. Some of what happened was that lands unclouded or unfogged themselves that normally cannot be physically seen. We have hosted retreats at this location before and these unveiled lands never showed themselves before. When we saw these lands, we saw a Giant with our physical eyes. There were peaks on these unveiled lands that we were watching, where we saw this Giant flying. That is when I knew that it was an Angel. This Giant was at least half of the size of this mountain peak. The minute we saw this Giant flying from one peak to the other, we started screaming!

Tartarian lands are unearthing. Lands that are cloaked, throughout the ocean and parts of the world, are parts of Tartaria spread out everywhere. If you are a matching vibration of Love-Light, these lands will unearth in front of you. You can see them with your physical eyes, but you will also see them with your third eye. Since we started talking about Giants in this Tartarian series, we started seeing a rise in people recording actual Giants, especially on TikTok. We will be channeling the Giants in the next chapter. As I continue to look upon the lands of the United States, I noticed that the majority of all the eastern major towns had Tartarian buildings. They are all near water, a lake or the ocean.

Let's talk about the repopulation and reset. Just about every century, they reset humankind. How do they do that? They do that through the vaccinations of the influenza that are unleashed onto Earth. The Elites make these viruses in their Archonic labs, and then they unleash these viruses into humanity. The purpose of this is that it starts resetting the population to start condensing. That is what actually changes the DNA structure of humankind, densifying it. They start losing their memories. This is one of the purposes of administering the COVID-19 Vaccine in late 2020, going into 2021. They are trying to change the DNA chromosome structure, to make it a hybrid by integrating A.I. into the organic. That was their diabolical plan. They accomplished it, unfortunately, in several ways. Those people who were tricked or conned into it are starting to wake up and understand that, "Oh my God, I took it. Now I have blood clots. I have an illness. I have cancer. I am incredibly unwell." Keep spreading the word so they can start self-healing themselves.

Through the Past Life Regression work we do, we have found that it is the only way, when you connect to the higher self consciousness, the higher self goes in and starts removing these infringements in the Quantum Realm throughout the physical, mental, spiritual, energy body - through all that we are. That is how we have been assisting people. I have been meeting people in person, and they are completely clear from the COVID-19 Vaccine after their A.U.R.A.

Entity Removal session. Instead they are actually glowing brighter than most people. They are beautiful beings that have done the work. If you go back and watch our videos from over seven years ago and read our content, we have been talking about these things ever since then. Even before the COVID-19 virus was a thing.

Let's talk about these dates. The 'M' in the numbers on buildings means one thousand. What they did after the reset, is they went and added M to some of these older buildings. For example, if it says on a building that it was made in 1870, they added the M right before the real date. That building was originally made in 870, not 1870. That is one way that they tried to trick us, "Oh, this has just been built." But really, they were built thousands of years ago, truly, and which 800 was it? Was it the 800 AD after Christ, or was it built 800 Before Christ? We don't know, right? It is quite phenomenal.

When I was remote viewing the energy on Earth, I saw that during those times and spaces that we thought were so spread out, when we were actually quite close to each other. Let me explain to you how that is. Through the Atlantean/Mayan series we have been talking about all the beginning stages of history. With this series we have been going from the current time and back through time. Tartaria was our most recent reset, where beings were reset. They killed them off with mud floods and the vaccinations we talked about. These are the major ways that they do this.

The recent era was the Medieval times (image on the next page). A lot of us remember this era when we go to Renaissance fairs and we have a blast. Where the dragons still exist, because magical creatures and the elementals were still among us then. From there, there is the Japanese civilization and the Mayan civilization, which we are leading up to [56]channeling the Mayans in the Mayan/Atlantean series. It is said that Yeshua/Jesus was born from 6-4 BC. The biggest reset happened right after Yeshua ascended out when he was crucified. They changed our numbers and added one thousand years to our history. Think about that for a second. That means that Yeshua was just born a little bit ago. The reason why we love him infinitely and still

---

[56] Watch 'The Lost Civilizations of the Mayans | The Ancients | Galactic History Part 1', streamed February 9th, 2024, and Part 2 streamed March 1st, 2024.

remember him to this day, is because he was just born a couple hundred years ago. They are lying to us about time. It's huge! My heart felt so activated when I said that. So much love is felt whenever you talk about Yeshua. He was just born!

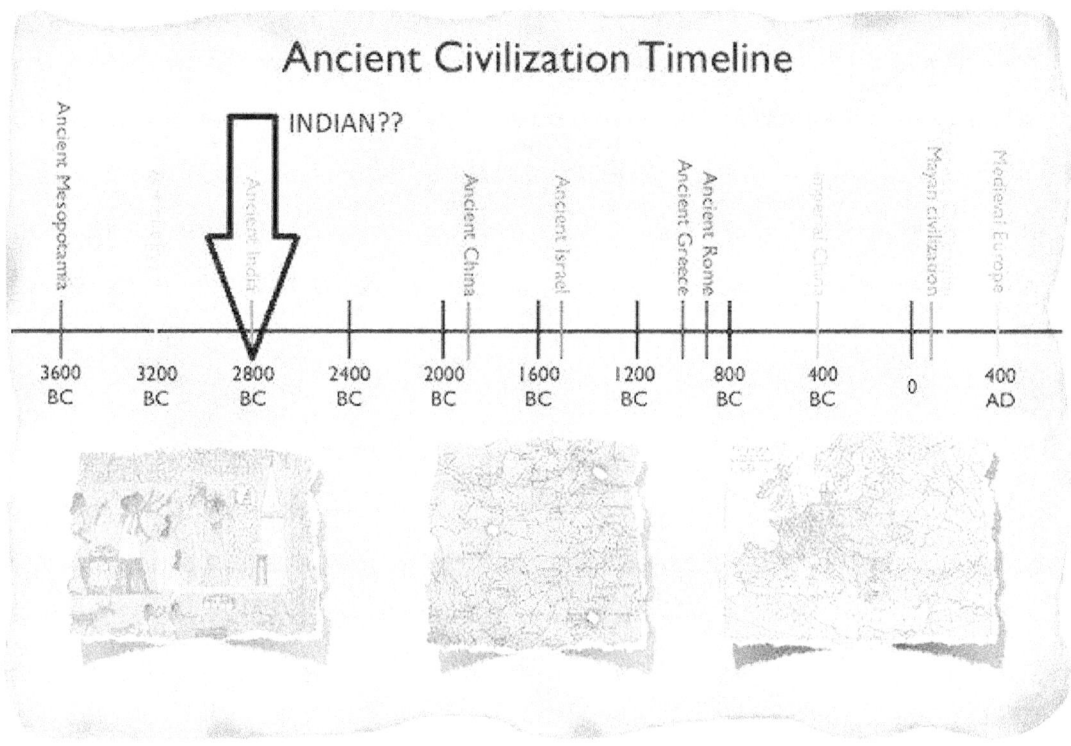

Then there is ancient Greece. Our most recent video that we channeled was [57]*Divine Mother Goddess Ishtar Inanna*, and she said that the Greek traveled over to Egypt, and that all these pyramids were there.

The ancient Romans were the Cabal - the Illuminati themselves. They went in, and they took over all the Greek temples in Greece and they literally just moved in. That was another reset. If you look at Earth, and you look at all the different times, there has been constant resets, where they were either killing people off, changing their memories, and then UFO abducted them so that they can then infringe upon us further.

---

[57] Watch 'Ancient Babylon | Goddess Ishtar | Galactic History', streamed October 14, 2022.

The biggest compromise over humankind, begins with the system over children of birthing them at the hospitals - so that they can begin the process of placing them in the inverted matrix - by the process of injection of all the different foreign material into them the minute they are born. It's all part of the negative agenda of making the world asleep, so that we don't remember. But still, we remember! The children remember! They have nightmares. The doctors call them Night Terrors! They are actually just memories of what happened in their most recent past lives - right before they were born. They remember! Then we go through the programming of shutting us down, clouding us so that we won't remember ourselves, and completely disempowering us. We don't believe in ourselves; or all these things that are so inverted and that are not of God Source. They are not of Source Love Light. It's all part of the process.

The Romans were dark. I remember having a life in Egypt, and being around these Romans. I remember coming from Egypt, which was so sacred with rich golden energy, beautiful and sovereign. Then sailing, crossing the Nile, going over to the Roman Civilization. We had gigantic Egyptian beautiful ships decorated with golden dragon sculptures. We were skilled sailors. We sailed the whole flat earth map. That's how we got a lot of our crystals and gold. We were peaceful.

The Romans - the Illuminati - took over Egypt after [58]we left. They then began the human sacrifice in Egypt, because they were under the control of the plague of the Archon A.I. virus. I remember when we landed in Rome, and it was ominous. I remember scanning for where their dark sorcerers were in Rome. There was a very uneasy feeling. Romans are who overthrew the positive leaders, and then they changed history to make out who they overthrew into the bad guys, so that they could step into power in their place. Looking at the image (previous page), we see that the current history says that the Roman Empire's reign began from 800 BC, and that after that time period it was over. You can erase that, because their reign ran until 4-6 BC, because the Romans are the ones who killed Yeshua. They are still here in this era, hiding as the Elites. We are truly looking at maybe five hundred years or less since Yeshua was born.

---

[58] The history of how the Egyptians left Egypt is covered in our Extra Sensitive series only found on Patreon, 'TOP SECRET - Remote Viewing The Grand Canyon'.

Every time I see a Tartarian building, I can feel its energy and how these buildings on Earth are coming back online. In the past, these buildings were lighting up with ether energy. If you have yet to travel to any of these Tartarian buildings, whether they are part of your town or a town nearby, make sure you do it as soon as you can. These buildings hold the coding and the memory that we have been uncovering, for example, of Yeshua. Go to see them and get activated.

In my travels, when I was in Nashville while I was driving around, I felt this strong gigantic Goddess Energy calling on me. The voice was saying, "Look over here." I looked over, and there was an incredible Tartarian temple. I could feel the Goddess energy, but I still couldn't see her. I had no idea what was there. I don't research these things, as I allow myself to find these things when they are meant to be divinely shown to me or shown to you all.

Here is the Parthenon of Nashville (next page)! Look at the shorter people here and look at this gigantic building. I was ecstatic when we found this. We had just streamed our first Tartarian video, and here it was, this divine temple! Once we went inside, it felt like another dimension. You were walking on the same lands that these Giants walked on who lived there. The person who was traveling with me was saying that when she was talking to a tree, they said that the same breath that the Giants had taken, they still hold within them. When you step into these locations, the timeline graph I showed of all the different civilizations on Earth, becomes like an accordion in a closed position. If you are ready through your connections to your Higher Self, your guides, and your angels, you can receive gigantic activations in these sacred spaces. Go travel! Do it!

Greece was not just in Greece. On the flat Earth map, the Greek civilization was spread out everywhere. These are different civilizations that they have completely reset and taken over.

At the top there are carvings of Gods and Goddesses. This building is ancient.

The entire row under the Gods has several Centaurs carved out.

This one is showing the different sizes of humans. A smaller one, the taller one, a Goddess-looking one.

This man replaced the Goddess statue on the next page. He is one of the dark men who conquered. That is what they did. They broke these places apart.

The steps at the Parthenon are huge, as if you are taking at least two steps at a time. I think some of these Giants could just skip all three steps and go over them. Here are some smaller steps and bigger steps right next to each other.

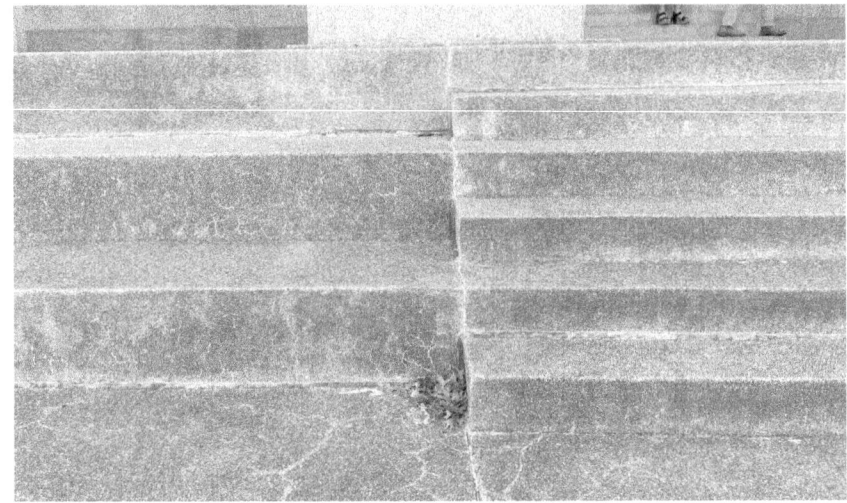

This plaque is telling us about the reset (next page). They are claiming that the original building of this structure was made out of plaster that they molded. The plaster building was demolished and this now structure was rebuilt supposedly over that. There is no way that any of *these buildings were made temporarily from plaster. According to what is written here. 1897 is when that reset began. This written information alone is giving us the true timeline of the reset that happened here in Nashville. It took them a couple of decades to erase people's memories from 1897 to 1921. 1921 is when they felt that they had done what they needed to do. That is around when the official reset of this era of Earth began. At that point, they had wiped out most of the Tartarian people. The Elites are telling you here, that that is when they began their invasion. From 1897 and 1921 is when they started repopulation.*

This was Nashville (image on the next page). There were pyramids there. Where did I get these pictures from? I got them from inside the Parthenon, in Nashville. They left the pictures there for us. Displaying them as a museum would. That is so nice of them. (Laughs.) They have the pictures displayed but with false information under each image. There is the Parthenon that I just showed you, and there is the pyramid. Look at this gigantic building behind it. It was supposedly made out of plaster.

In the previous chapters someone had asked if the World Centennial Fairs were part of the Tartaria reset and I said, "Yes," but I didn't know what that meant then. Now I know that it was a cover-up for what really civilizations looked like right before the reset. These pyramids mirror the Pyramid of Giza. This is a Tartarian building back here, and then we got parts of Egypt going on here. This is the original Greek building. The Tartarians built their Greek Tartarian buildings around these Greek sacred sites as well. A lot of them have been destroyed in our time.

In this image (next page), there are people at the entrance of the space where all this was the Parthenon. It was like a tourist attraction. It was fun! Like when we go out and we go downtown, and we venture to enjoy the lake, or go to the movies, or go up these high skyscrapers, where you just go hang out and be among others.

It looks like there was a lion statue at the front of the Parthenon (below). That is not there anymore. None of what is surrounding the Parthenon is there anymore. It looks like there is some kind of Angel there - maybe Cupid (building behind the Parthenon). All of these buildings were destroyed in Nashville, except for the Parthenon. They claim that after they knocked it down they rebuilt it from scratch, to make it more solid like this. But this is obviously not recently built. They claimed it was 1930 when they finally, "Opened it up for the public." No, this was there long ago.

Here is a map of what it looked like before they knocked it all down. Again, these are images I found inside the Parthenon.

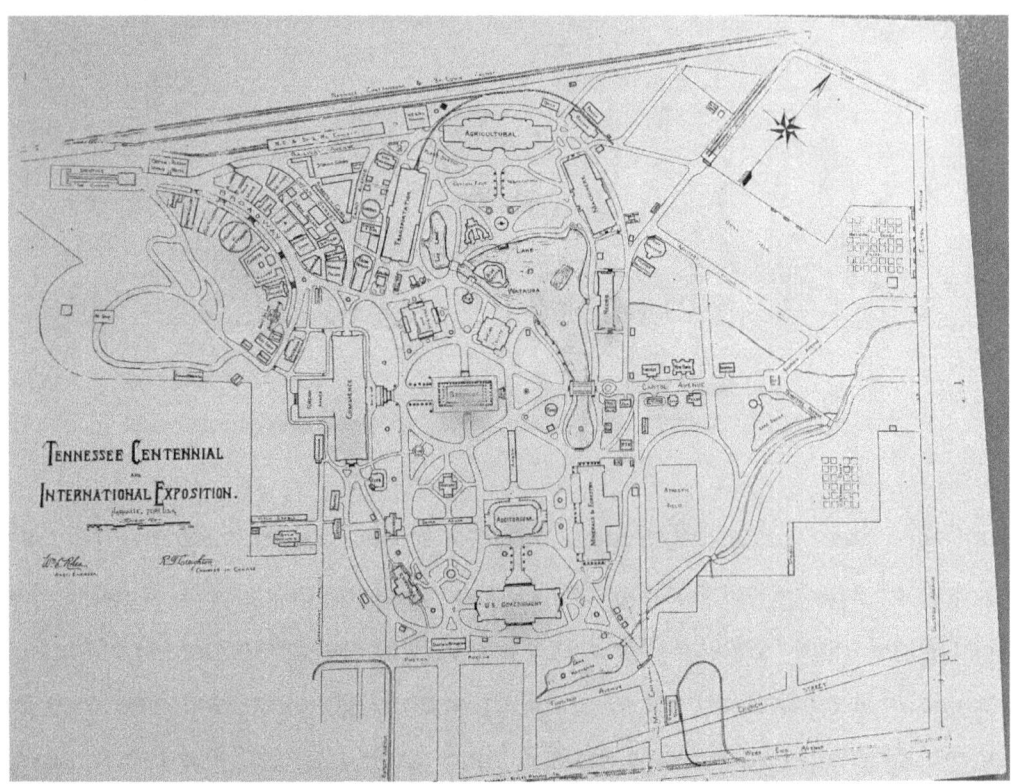

Here are some more pictures I found inside.

This big statue in the back was forty feet tall (image below). They said from bottom to top. They knocked her down.

Here are the pyramids again.

Here is the Goddess again. She was forty feet tall. There were two lions. That is not how it looks now. They broke all the steps here and they destroyed the lions.

Boom! We go inside and we find Goddess Athena! She's forty-two feet tall!

While I was in her presence, I kept hearing gold, gold, gold. I didn't realize that she is actually gold! The signs say that she is plated with thirty-two karat gold. My question to you is if you live in Nashville, or if you ever were in Nashville before 2002 when they claimed she was unveiled, was she there before 2002? Because I could not find any images of the inside of the Parthenon before 2002. I searched everywhere. Did you go inside the Parthenon? I need to know this. Was she in there or was it empty? Please let me know if you were born in Nashville or went there before 2002 and if you got to the inside. Or did they have it closed off so nobody could go in there? Because I know they did not sculpt her. The only pictures I can find are, for example, of this man who supposedly sculpted her.

These pictures (image above) supposedly of Athena, this location is not the Parthenon. This is a brick wall. It looks like a film studio. I feel that this statue is more ancient than they are saying it is. Did they close her off from the inside to the public so we wouldn't see her there this whole time, and then they unveiled her in 2002? They claim that she was an exact replica of the Parthenon statue in Greece. How would they know what she looked like if she had been destroyed? There were no pictures then, supposedly. How could this artist replicate her in Nashville when she is not there in Greece anymore? If she was made out of gold and ivory in Greece, then where is she? Who took her? Or is she the real Goddess Athena of the Pantheon made of solid gold and ivory, as I feel she is?

As we continued, we found more pictures. What they have written in the description to this next image (image on next page) was that these people were Negro, who were teachers.

When I was looking at these pictures, the message I was getting was, "Lies." Each nation was not separated. Asians were not just in China. The Indigenous weren't just here in North America. All the races were all spread out.

When you look at the flat Earth, Urbano Monte map, you see that there were teepees in the Americas (image below), which represent the Indigenous, but there were also teepees on the Asian side too.

When I saw this image (image on previous page), I was like, "No. Those people were indigenous to the land." They were not captured and brought from overseas. These Nubian people were here already. There was no separation of these races. They only did that after this most recent reset of Tartaria. These people were indigenous to these lands, just like the Indigenous, so were they. Through the past life regression work I do, sometimes the Indigenous people of America are seen as darker skinned people like the Nubians.

Asians in Nashville (image below) supposedly back then in 1890? Why would there be Asians there then when the multi-races were here and everywhere on Earth? These events were called the Centennial. All these buildings were made out of a mold. (Laughs.) Yes, we already know we have been lied to, profoundly. Asians were here as well. In this image they are having some kind of celebration with dragons. Strong Tartarian times here.

Here are more pictures (below and next page) we found displayed inside the Parthenon in Nashville.

This was gigantic (image below). You can't really tell by the picture, but this bowl was about three feet wide, and the tray was as big as the display case which was about five feet wide. They left us behind Giant utensils because they have to leave some of these things still there. They can't completely erase everything! It goes against sacred law. It's another way they program into us that this is all fantasy or temporary as they claim the plaster walls were. But, these were utensils of a Giant person in that display.

228

Back to Goddess Athena (image below). This is Nike the Archangel. He was six feet tall, standing in her palm. At her base there are different golden Gods decorated. It is supposed to represent Pandora. The Gods are, Helios, Hera, Zeus, Hebe, Dionysos, Horai, Hephaistos, Poseidon, Artemis, Demeter, Hestia, Eros, Aphrodite and Selene. She has adorned a golden serpent, a shield, and a beautiful helmet. They claim in 1920 to 1930 they remade her statue for us, because everyone really loved her in Greece (laughs). They are so funny. Here is a close-up (page 223) of her beauty. Look at her eyes and her spear. Medusa is supposed to be on her chest.

In Greek Mytholigy they say that, "Medusa was raped, they then kicked her out, and that the Goddess Athena placed a curse on her." I don't like to read Greek Mythology tales because they are so false. It is said that is what turned Medusa into a snake hybrid, they cursed her because of jealousy. What if Medusa represents our organic darkness? Why does she have this belt roped snake wrapped around her? Medusa and the snakes adorned on her represent our shadow. Medusa and Athena are one in the same. This is why she had Medusa decorated on her, because she is her as well. Athena had powers to petrify stone in those who meant ill intent. She reminds us of this power within, that those who mean harm have no power over us.

Goddess Athena's sandals (image below) explain how there was a battle. In some of the documented texts that they have displayed. It explains how the Centaurs were killed, and that humans (Illuminati) killed the Centaurs. Crazy! I am in awe because again, we didn't know this and here is the actual physical proof of what we have spoken of.

The inside of her shield (image below) is trying to tell us that it's a flat Earth, because there are rings in the depiction of Earth. There is a beautiful serpent as well. There are again all these different civilizations that are being represented through the shield.

This poster (image below) explains all about her.

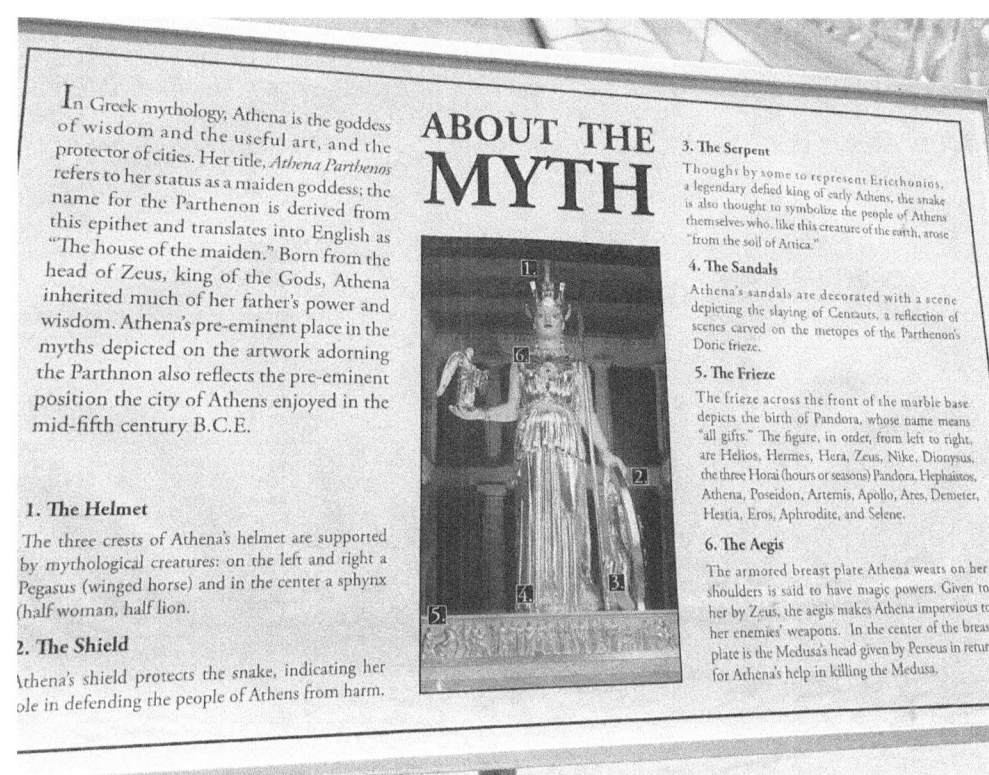

Her helmet (image below) is gorgeous! It has a Sphinx at the center of it, and a Pegasus on the left and right side. It's a mohawk helmet.

The three horns at the back of her helmet (image below) are sacred. The Illuminati inverted the horns and made them demonic and they put horns on themselves. They made it satanic, but actually horns are sacred as are ram or cow horns. Horns are the connection to the divine. As Divine Mother Hathor has explained in the past. They are like antennas. What a beautiful design! This is not from the current time. This is from the remains of the era of Greece.

There is an A.U.R.A. practitioner standing next to the door (image below). Look at the difference in height. On the door there are faces of a lion, a female Goddess, and a ram. To the left they added the smaller glass doors for our size people. At the bottom where the doors slide to open and close, there are two gold tone circles, making the Vesica Piscis symbol (image on next page).

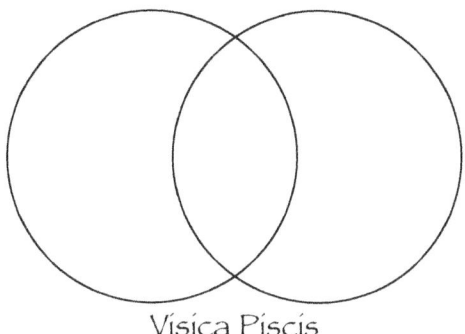

Visica Piscis

Below is a close-up (image below) of the inside of Athena's shield. This is called the Battle of the Gods and Giants. This illustration was added prior to the unveiling of Athena, to cause further confusion. We see the ice rings again signifying Antarctica, telling us the truth in plain sight.

233

Here is an advertisement for the 'Tennessee Centennial' (image below) with a map of what it looked like if you attended the event, before it was destroyed. There is a handwritten cursive note dating February 14, 1897. There is mention of Mrs. Van Leer Kirman who is the President of the Women's Board of the Tennessee Centennial Exposition, signifying that women have equal power to men in this time.

Here are some more images of the people attending the event (images below). They have camels! How did they get those camels all the way over there from the Nile? That's so strange! Something's fishy here (laughing)! Especially since the Elites claim the World Fairs were non-existent. This is instead a well planned out event by the world.

Here are Mexicans and Cubans from a Cuban village. All the way back in 1890. This world that is photographed is one that is so different from ours. It seems as though the nations are working together, enjoying each other's companies. There is a non-existent war as there was during our time.

Here is the Pantheon (image below) that is located in Greece. This is what it looked like after the reset. They destroyed the one in Greece, but they left the Parthenon in Nashville.

Here is the Parthenon in Nashville (image below) after the reset. All the Tartarian buildings as shown in the map of the Centennial invite (page 234) are demolished. It is as if whatever destructive technology that was used on these lands just couldn't touch the Parthenon.

This Tartarian building at the center, but then all these modern buildings around it.

I went to a restaurant somewhere near Siesta Key, Florida and this scene was drawn on their chalkboard on the wall. Here are some clues left behind for us again. To the right you see the modern buildings drawn, but to the left near the shore there are Tartarian buildings. There is a female statue floating on the water at the center bottom. There is a Godzilla monster destroying the Tartarian buildings. This drawing is telling us a story. There are a lot more people than we realize, that are awakened and are aware of Tartaria (this was before Tartaria became popular). The story is telling us that the Tartarian buildings were destroyed and in their place came these modern buildings. There are palm trees drawn showing us that this was Florida.

Interviewer: The first question is, "Do you know what the population on Earth is presently? I feel it is a lot less than they say."

AuroRa: That is really hard to read because through the Quantum realm, there are so many different timelines that we are working within. Altogether, I am being told that it is somewhere around a low billion. They said, perhaps cut your numbers in half. As I am scanning the Earth, I see beautiful beings inside the Inner Earth at the core though. They are in another dimension, helping us hold the space.

The Tartarian era was right before this one, like one hundred years ago. That is all the numbers that I explained at the beginning of the 1890's to 1920's. A lot of the older homes that people purchase can go back as old as 1915 to 1920. That's why a lot of the cities have supposed basements. In some of these buildings, you look at the windows of their basements and they don't make any sense because they look like first floor windows. There are some buildings from back then that had their kitchen in the basement, supposedly, because it really was the first floor. If they originally even had kitchens or bathrooms then, as most of those homes built during that era, didn't have them.

Interviewer: "Were there Tartarian buildings in the south of the U.S. as well as the northern areas?"

AuroRa: Yes, definitely..

Interviewer: "Did they use the Spanish Flu to wipe out the Tartarians?"

AuroRa: Yes, that's one of the things that they did. There were a lot of battles and mud floods going on. But, whoever was left over, the Spanish Influenza took them out. They began implementing flu vaccinations then to start erasing the memory of the people by compromising and densifying them.

Interviewer: "If Tartaria was so huge, how did it fall?"

AuroRa: When I tap into their energies, they were not a fighting type of people. They had all this advanced technology that we talked about in Chapter Eight, but they didn't use it for weaponry. For example, Nikola Tesla was for the advancement of humankind. Their technology wasn't inverted for things where we were going to kill and shoot people down and control them. Their mentality was like the indigenous people. They didn't want to fight. They were one with the Earth and they were connected. Specifically, the Tartarians were connected to the Ether. You can imagine how they wouldn't want to battle. They were for the advancement of humankind. They weren't prepared to fight these demonic entities that went into these men from the outside perimeter of the Antarctica wall.

When I was talking to Goddess Athena at the Parthenon, she said, "The only way to kill a Giant was through men." In a piece of their literature it was written that only men could kill the Giants. Otherwise, the Giants were almost immortal. They could live a long time, especially because a lot of them were Atlantean descendants. We will talk more about the Giants in the upcoming chapters.

Interviewer: "What happened to all of the Tartarians after that?"

AuroRa: Have you started to receive memories during dream time of your Tartarian lives? Since I began this Tartarian series, my memories of Tartaria started to return. I had a life in Tartaria. I had this really cool steampunk looking motorcycle. It was tiny, I would place my feet on it and it would go really fast. Through this memory, I figured out Yeshua was not too far from the Tartarian era. It was only a few hundred years before Tartaria that Yeshua was here. In the dream/memory, Yeshua was showing me Tartaria. It was so beautiful! He was showing me the people and the darkness that came in and invaded. Similar to what happened to him in his time. He walked Earth right before Tartaria.

Set an intention. Ask your Higher Self, "Higher Self, did I have a life in Tartaria? Help me remember it." The Tartarian people are now incarnated back again. We are right here! Most of us have lives that we remember when we were Indigenous. You can also have lives that were in Tartaria, but these memories are so blocked from us. Start working to remember because everyone comes back in cycles. You can also tap into another fractal of you, because there are many fractals with you on Earth and the Multiverse that might have experienced Tartaria in a different way then you. Tartaria was amazing! Tartaria were the Victorian ages, as they were one and the same. If you have Victorian memories, then most likely they are Tartarian memories.

Interviewer: "What happened a century ago? In other words, they were obviously another species of humans. So where did they go? Was it a disease?"

AuroRa: There were aliens instigating wars for the countries to kill each other off. World War one marks the point where they began the depopulation of Earth. These entities invaded I and they programmed the men to violate the Indigenous in the Americas. I remember having a life when I was Indigenous. I was Shawnee, who are Mayan Atlantean descendants. I remember the conquistador men were terribly dark. They were compromised by an energetic black mass programmed to harm and kill anyone that crossed their path. They had advanced weapons, such as guns, that we didn't have. This happened more so because we were gentle people. We did not want to kill others. Perhaps, we knew that we would be stuck in an inverted karmic timeline if we killed people as they did. The adults and children that survived the wars, really had to go through a major transformation to reach the vibration we are in now. This explains why the older generation can be so dense. Their energies had to go through a lot to get to this current Earthy higher vibration.

Interviewer: "Regarding the Tartarian buildings, can you tell me why they would hide all of this?"

AuroRa: Because we would remember that the era of Tartaria was only one hundred years ago. They do not want us to know that we were this advanced. How we could float and fly in these different devices. They had a device that if their loved one passed away, they could just phone call them in the Ether, and their spirit would appear. They took pictures with their husband, who had passed away. There was no worry about death, because you could just phone call them in the Ether and their spirit would appear. That's how advanced it was in Nikola Tesla's era.

Interviewer: This is a question from one of your channels, "Why are they erasing this? I don't see the point. It's like, okay, there's a big deal. Giants existed, no need to make us forget. I can't see a reason, you know?" Your response was, "To keep us docile and not let us have expansion in our mind and in our heart."

AuroRa: Exactly. Because when we start questioning, "Wait a minute, there are Giants? Wait a minute, there are magical creatures? There are mermaids?" Could there have been a Godzilla? When we start questioning, our mind expands and our hearts activate! Docile, programmed and controllable they want to keep us. If we remember the literal century that just happened right before us, that was erased; if we start remembering that these times were actually real, and they weren't molded buildings that only supposedly lasted six months, then we start thinking, "Wait a minute, this is a Greek building. Hold on. That is a lot more ancient than we realize." Then we start waking up. They don't want us to question, to discover and research. We are easier to control like lambs. But we are not that.

Interviewer: "I have read that with every cataclysmic event we lost stature. Is this true?"

AuroRa: Yes. Do you mean like we became smaller? Someone's comment on one of my channels was very interesting, they said, "Do you notice that every generation gets taller?" For example, "I'm five-nine, and my wife is five-five, but our children are six foot two." The next generation gets taller and taller because their natural human genome is trying to rewrite itself, that we were a lot taller than we are now. It goes back to the Anunnaki, where they say that all Anunnaki were dark. No one can say that an entire race or population was dark. It's like saying all of humankind are negative beings. We can't say that.

The way that negative Annunaki started to infringe upon us was through the [59]A.I. Archon virus.. It's the similar agenda that they are implementing now. They oppress our DNA, and then the more that they oppress it, the shorter we become. They breed the leftover babies who grow up and are the people you may see around that feel like empty souls. They can also

---

[59] Watch the Mayan/Atlantean series on my channels for more.

be called non-player characters (N.P.C.s). Dolores spoke of them, she called them the background people. A lot of these people are just soulless beings that are pretending to be humans, but they are watching. They are Agents Smiths (referencing the movie 'The Matrix'). You can literally see an entity come into their bodies, their face and energy shifts, and they take over. They are spies to the Archon A.I. artificial thing.

We are within a hologram simulation. Even though there are around one billion people on Earth, I would say, the population is only half of that. One-third of the Earth are people who are here from higher dimensions, who are star beings. The second third are people who have been stuck in this inverted cycle of reincarnation. The other third are false human bodies. They are entities inside human bodies or they are just a program. They are like when you are playing a video game, and there are the background people and they don't really have souls. They are just filling in space in this [60]matrix program.

Interviewer: "All this information as far as where we come from must come up in DNA tests and they keep it from the people. I took a DNA test four years ago, and I have had three different results. How could this be? I have so many questions."

AuroRa: Well, one, I would never let anyone take my DNA. Try to never allow that if you can. There are many different reasons why it could be, your angels stepping in and changing the DNA results so that they don't know who you are or they could just be giving you a random, "Here's your results." Your DNA is sacred, keep it to yourself, shield it.

Interviewer: The question is, "How long did they wait before the repopulation began? And how many resets have there been in this construct that we have now?"

AuroRa: I say about two decades of work that they did to start repopulating. There's no telling as far as how many times we have been reset. If you look at the map (page 211), they claim that there are thousands of years between these different civilizations, but really, it seems like it's every one hundred years that they are resetting the population. Just as we have seen

---

[60] Watch 'The Matrix' playlist on our channels.

when we entered the 2000s, they came up with the 2020 COVID-19 Vaccine injection. They were overdue because they were trying to begin the plandemic before, but a benevolent interference happened that didn't allow them to. Because if they had done it, the world would have not been prepared. It seems like 2017 was the original date that they were going to inject this into people. The people would not have been able to survive that. Instead a lot of us had catalyzing experiences in 2017, that were organically made, but also there was a lot of dark in it. 2012 and 2017 prepared us for the energetic [61]bifurcation that occurred when people made the choice of whether they would take the COVID-19 Vaccine or not in 2020 to 2021.

Interviewer: "Is it possible that it was already the year 2020 and then they reset the time to the 1700s?"

AuroRa: Definitely could be possible. They have been playing games where they were stealing our time. This is why it's so slow on Earth. I was explaining to the students at one of my retreats, how time works and how they have been stealing our time while making time for themselves. They are spinning the time clockwise. That slows down time. The concept of time and spinning it clockwise on a clock makes time itself. When you look at a fan, if it spins clockwise, it pulls in the energy, it pulls in the air, slowing down the air flow as it sucks it in. But if you spin the ceiling fan counterclockwise, it expands out the air, allowing you to feel the refreshing air. That is what they have been doing to our time - spinning it clockwise - and for us following that makes time slow. But there is no other way to go about it on this Earth in the third dimension.

Interviewer: "What was the more accurate timeline for Yeshua to be born in, and why did they want to change it?"

AuroRa: He was born about three hundred years before Tartaria, so we are looking at three to four hundred years ago, when he was born. That makes me want to cry thinking of how recently he was born.

---

[61] Watch 'The ⅔ World Split | Bifurcation' playlist.

Interviewer: "Does this mean the Essene teachings are not as old? That is why we are remembering them so strongly now?"

AuroRa: Exactly. We are the Essenes now.

Interviewer: Someone's asking you about Nikola Tesla. They wanted to know if they missed out if Tesla was in Tartaria himself.

AuroRa: Yes he was. The majority of the scientific advancements that we spoke of in the previous chapter were part of his inventions. There were many minds that were part of it. Similar to how we have children who can turn ocean salted sea water into water that is drinkable, then they go missing. There was a young man who was talking about how God is energy, and he went missing. We need to protect these children that are coming out with genius ideas. These children of the now were in Tartaria then, who became genius scientists as adults. They were free to develop scientific advancement in that century. The dark forces were not able to fully reign then. If you think about how much we have developed just in this century alone, since the reset of Tartaria. We are phenomenal beings! How did we advance so much in one hundred years?

Interviewer: Someone was asking, "Why was he in New York?"

AuroRa: He said these isles were part of Atlantis and the energy was highly potent there. There are gigantic crystals under the New York area. I see that New York is the most powerful city in the United States. If we were to alchemize New York, if we started clearing it and healing the lands there, we would be unstoppable as a collective in the Americas.

New York was very near and dear to his heart, he said. Why do you think they had to go through New York to get to the rest of the United States? They needed to take down Nikola Tesla and all the beings that were there. They were a strong hold. I am seeing it like if you were to make a crystal grid, and you place the main crystal at the center, that is the biggest and the strongest. He says that there was space where you could walk in between parallel dimensions there. It was like a generator. Once it went down, everything went dark. This is what it looks like now. From there they were able to invade, through this entryway.

Interviewer: "So with the statue of the lady in Chicago, you also see the Statue of Liberty and several other statues, and they are all holding torches or flames or other things like that. What are they holding? What is going on there with that?"

AuroRa: Why they are holding flames, is because with these Goddesses, there was no separation among them. The Romans moved into the Greek Gods' locations. They then changed all the Greek Gods' and Goddesses' names to Roman names. That is why there are Roman God names, but they are one in the same. These Goddesses walked the Earth, and they were gigantic.

There is false programming speaking of Nephilims. The Elites have implemented a false program for people to believe that these Gods and Giants mated with females or raped them, who are the "Fallen Angels". Just writing this supposed history of Earth into a sentence is so obviously false. Let's delete that. Not real. These Giants were our brethren. We loved them and we protected them.

There was a comment in one of my channels that said that their Indigenous tribe had a giant living among them and that they protected the giant until the giant's death. Let's erase all false programming on Giants, to hate on them, made to influence us to destroy them. They have not fallen.

To answer the statue question, there were gigantic female Goddesses that walked the Earth and they were called the "Daughters the Flames". That's why they were all holding flame torches. Do you really think that the Statue of Liberty was delivered to us from overseas? Goodness! How tall is she? There is no way that they delivered her overseas. She has been there a long time.

All of these Goddesses represented force fields, shields, and protection. As Daughters of the Flame, they are all Daughters of Divine Mother. Fractals of Divine Mother spread out through all Earth, holding up sacred spaces. This is why in Chicago and Nashville (in the images shown previously) they broke and removed their Goddess statues that stood outside.

On the internet, it says the Statue of Liberty is three-hundred and five feet tall. That is massive. The one that we saw in Nashville is forty-two feet tall. She is so beautiful! What does she represent? There is something really sacred about her, versus the lies they tell about her. That beautiful torch! What does fire mean? The fire means Source. That is what they are doing. Holding the flame, the light, the energy, the torch up for you until you can reach it. People can stand on her crown.

Interviewer: Someone wanted to know if there was anything that Yeshua would like to say about all this.

AuroRa: We will end this chapter with Yeshua. We are going to let him talk.

Yeshua: I am Yeshua, Son of Mary. I am Yeshua, Son of Mary. I am Yeshua, Son of Mary. Greetings, beautiful souls. I have been waiting for this moment in time and space to share with you, how very recent it has been since I walked among you and held your faces in the palms of my hands and felt your hearts. When we connected heart to heart and spoke these sacred words of the truth of Source. Where religion had no existence. How we are Love-Light. How I traveled the flat Earth map because they were all connected in a circular motion.

See, we were advanced like Tartarians were as well. In the Essenes, we had special advanced benevolent technology that shielded us, cloaked us, and made us invisible. That assisted us in floatation devices as well, but they could not see us beneath shielded by the caves and their energy vortexes of the Twelve Sacred Laws of the Universe. Caves where my mother birthed me. The very caves of Qumran.

Yes, I came right before this century. Absolutely! Why you still remember me and why you still cry for me. Why it is that when I talk to you, you still feel that love inside of you for me? Because it was just a couple lifetimes ago that you heard of me, or that I walked among you or that you felt my presence. Such an important role. This was a bridge that needed to be joined once more, so that you could understand how parallel these Tartarian timelines are, to our times of the Essenes. The times when we walked with the Essenes - the descendants of the Atlanteans. It was all so close on top of each other, and stacked up on top of each other. All of it. You can feel the unification when you step into your heart, and you can still feel me beside you, through all time and space. Our timelines are parallel.

Technically, I am still alive, where I am speaking to you from. I am sitting on a Tibetan mountain range, in this moment in time as I speak to you. Why am I sitting here? Because I knew in this moment in time and space that I would be speaking to you. Every single mountain range and peak and valley and hill is feeling my love right now. Feel my love. Through all these amplifications of peaks, I am here with you. I believe in you in ways that are infinite. I know that you can rewrite your timelines. I know that you can transmute the invertedness in your timelines. I know that you can walk your organic timelines because I saw it happen when I was alive. I saw those souls, so dense, so heavy, full of trauma. I saw them transform into these beautiful flowers. Who had their own signature scents when they would bloom out into organic. You can do it again. Let's give them a grand show! Yes, of love. I love you with all that I AM. Thank you. I will allow AuroRa to speak now.

AuroRa: Thank you Yeshua, that was so beautiful. Nice surprise. I didn't realize Yeshua was going to talk today, when he channeled just now. Here in Chicago, we haven't seen the sun for a month, because of the fake cloud blanket factories they have going on in the Arctic. I am looking at blue sky and the sun is coming through. Thank you, Yeshua.

Thank you for joining me in reading this profound chapter. I love you, honor you, and respect you. Thank you, to our interviewer. Thank you my beautiful husband Zen. Thank you to everyone who was here in live chat. I love you, I love you, I love you. Ve-lu-via (Leumurian language "I love you')! I will see you next time!

END OF SESSION.

When we began to place the puzzle pieces of Tartaria in late 2022, the A.I. system did not notice how many I was reaching on TikTok until it was too late for IT, before IT was able to put my TikTok channel into shadowban mode I had already reached millions of views! We truly awakened millions to Tartaria! In the time of these live streams when you asked people if they knew of Tartaria the majority would say "No". Now in this time/space people who know of Tartaria are now the majority!

Below are images of screenshots of what our numbers looked like by February 8th, 2024, reaching 38.9 million on TikTok alone.

TikTok
https://www.tiktok.com › discover

Rising Phoenix Aurora

Open TikTok. Rising Phoenix Aurora. 38.9M views.
Discover videos related to Rising Phoenix Aurora on TikTok. Videos. 126media. 42. #duet with @ ...

By October December 17, 2024 (image below) the A.I. system noticed that my numbers on TikTok were reflecting my true views, so they rapidly changed it to only 10K views. Which is not logistically possible as some videos have reached almost 200 thousand views. TikTok has been the only platform that has shown my true numbers, even for a short amount of time as it did. On all other platforms I have instantly been placed in shadowban. Since TikTok placed me in their shadowban system, I can barely reach 200 views per video. Which shows us how profound our content is, no matter the topic, so much so the A.I. system tries to oppress our views and subscribers, while IT ensures to forge the views of those who channel artificially for IT's cause of oppression and degression of humankind.

My YouTube channel has not moved from 15k subscribers for 5 years, which is unheard of! This channel has brought such an infinite gratitude for you, and the way that you have found me. Because true divine intervention brought you to this most organic path. We know that someday these shadowbanning systems will no longer have access to all platforms and our content, and our true numbers will finally show!

"Never give up! Strive to rise to the peak that you are and all the potential that awaits within you to be unleashed!"

~AuroRa

--------------<<>>--------------

10

THE GIANTS OF TARTARIA

Streamed Live: January 28, 2023

In this chapter Aurora channels Goddess Athena who shares the importance and truth of our ancestors, the Giants of Earth. Through this chapter we begin the unveiling of the Giants and the ways that they walked among us on Earth. It is important that we no longer think that the Giants were fairy tales. Who were the Giants and was their population on Earth understood? Get ready once more for an incredible chapter that will confirm your suspicions confidently.

--------------<<>>--------------

"We are in the end game of Ascension. We are in that process of collective Ascension. Shields up and swords up. Never down, never gullible, never docile. Strength, confidence, responsibility, and understanding that the mission is the grandest."
~Goddess Athena

--------------<<>>--------------

AuroRa: My divine team has been preparing me for this specific channeling since the beginning of the Antarctica series. I am looking forward to answering all of the two pages worth of questions about Giants today. I will be channeling in the theta brainwave. It is natural to do so as everyone connects through brain waves all day long. We just don't realize it. I am surrounded by Source Love-Light. The messages that will be delivered will be for the collective's most organic timeline. That is how we work.

Athena (Aurora channeling): Greetings, I am Goddess Athena. The Goddess of Wisdom and War, as you would call it. However, I do not call it War. I call it sovereignty and protection. Being strategic in all forms, because in some forms in this third dimensional world, we are in a battle. Being a shield, and unlocking our inner darkness, which is part of our strength and fierceness, that empowers us to stand up for ourselves and stand up for others. I am this guardian and protector of Earth, as well as the Universe and wherever it is that I am needed. I am an embodiment of the collective energy of Goddess energies, of the Sisters or Daughters of the Flame. For this is what we are, as you would see. Greek Gods and Goddesses were Daughters and Sons of the Flames of the Phoenix Universe.

What an honor it is to be here with you. Thank you for hearing our message and my message today. You feel who I am through every part of you, through the breath, and through the blood that runs through your veins. I speak through you, when you feel strongly that you must finally speak up for injustice that has been done upon you, through infringements and harm. When you say, "No, I will not allow this anymore. I am no one's pawn and I am no one's pawn or puppet." You feel me in that strength, because I am this collective energy that stands up to the inversion, to the artificial, to the A.I., to the Archons. The flamed Goddesses went against this negative polarized collective abomination.

I am the golden shining light that you look for when you feel the most lost in the inverted darkness. I come forth when you call forth upon me, shooting through like Source lightning. I help you as you activate your own self. Activate your shield and stand up with your sword and your spheres. Have your shields right in front of you. We are in the end game of Ascension. We are in that process of collective Ascension. Shields up and swords up. Never down, never gullible, never docile. Strength, confidence, responsibility, and understanding that the mission is the grandest. What is your mission? What is your purpose? I help you discover these. That is some of who I am.

I am going to go ahead and travel us back in time and space. To the timeless space of Athens, as you have logged in your Earth history. We will use verbiage that you have in your history so that we may understand one another. But before that, you have heard us speak of the

Fall of Atlantis and how some of the beings of Atlantis before Atlantis fell, went to different parts of the world. One of the locations we went to was Greece. From there, we stemmed forth and expanded throughout different parts of the world.

I am gigantic, but the truth is that I am magic. Therefore, I am typically twenty-two feet tall. However, I can make myself even more gigantic. Even as tall as a mountain. Your images and your statues are well depicted with my helmet, and the Sphinx that is at the center, as you saw through the Parthenon in Nashville. Depicted on my helmet, I also have the Pegasus, because I ride the Pegasus throughout the cosmos. If you see me now with your third eye, you can see my gigantic energy and my luminous and glowing Source Love-Light Pegasus. This beautiful Pegasus is half Pegasus and half unicorn. She has a unicorn horn on her third eye, her forehead. You see her magnificent wings that are not just two, there are six. She would help me in the time and space of Athens fly through your skies. She too can make herself smaller. My beautiful warrior. Many of you have these magical beings living within your cats and dogs.

Back to the time and space of Atlantis, as we spread, we spread to different locations. We were tall and gigantic in comparison to some of the types of other human races. Even though you can see us as gigantic, magical glowing beings, we still are equals to all life forms on Earth. We always have been. There is much false artificial information about us, and our brethren Zeus and Poseidon, our sisters Hera and Aphrodite, and so on. All these beautiful Goddess energies. We formed from the Priestesses and the Priests of Atlantis, before Atlantis fell. We became these embodiments who anchored in and soaked in the crystalline energy before it fell. We maintained ourselves in the organic bifurcation that began then in the fifth-sixth dimensional bifurcation. You can say, in our own bubble of space.

As we traveled these lands, first we went to Greece. Then from there, we spread throughout the thousands of years that our beginnings occurred. Therefore what you can say is, all of these were parallel. The ones that you think are separate, like Sumerian culture, Indian culture, Chinese culture, Greek culture - all of these eras before the Romans - were all happening at the same exact time. We were spread out like a tree who grows and spreads his/her roots and his/her branches. We spread out throughout Earth. Same for the Mayans.

All of this was occurring within the same times and spaces. Even though you have this supposed timeline that tells you 100 BC is here and 100 AD is there. This is all false information. It is not a line. It is all linear to one another. When you start to separate history as they do so in the schools, that is when you are making time on Earth and why time itself is an illusion.

We all began forth on the organic building of timelines, so that we could be here in your moment in time to speak to you in the end games, these final stages of the collective Ascension. Truly, in essence, these Giants and especially us who are the Gods and Goddesses, we were incarnations of Archangels. There is again false programming on that. They call us the Nephilim, the fallen Angels. Those are the most gigantic lies that you could ever listen to, and allow to integrate into your timelines. These are the Archon downloads onto your minds. Don't allow this.

We are benevolent beings. If you remember us, if you start recalling us, many of you are starting to bring these memories back. You remember our benevolence and the way you saw us fly and soar in the skies protecting. Some of us had wings or we had a Pegasus. When we would walk among you, and we would sit with you and talk to you and share our wisdom with you. You remember us. You have these memories. All you have to do is unlock them. We are and were the purest Source Love-Light on Earth. We were as pyramids but instead we were walking vessels of Source Love-Light. We were walking in the organic timelines. In them, we were beacons of that. We were the Archangels themselves. All Greek Gods and Goddesses are Archangels from beyond.

We incarnated on Earth both in Atlantis and Greece. We also incarnated after the Fall of Atlantis to assist the collective of people on Earth. We come in all sizes gigantic. Then there are also taller beings. You were very tall - not five feet to six feet - you were taller. In your times and spaces, you were an average of about ten feet.

You can feel the love through us. We are love. You know this in your heart. When you were a child, you would have dreams that you would fall. You were always falling. Falling off a building. Falling off a ledge. It is because you fell. You descended down into the lower dimensions of the third dimension. This is false and inverted. The fallen beings! No! We made the choice. We did not fall, we chose. We chose to come down and make our energy smaller to assist the collective. You chose that. We are all volunteers. You are volunteers. We came here to assist the Earth and to assist the Universe and ultimately, the collective. The most beautiful gigantic Ascension will come forth. When the Ascension finally comes into fruition, we chose this. Enough with the fallen! Know that when you choose to believe there are fallen Angels like this, then you choose to create those inverted timelines for them. Be wise on what you choose. Instead, choose love. You are not falling, we are not falling! It was a sovereign choice. Don't let anyone take that choice away from you. Your wings are still there. All you have to do is activate them. Feel them energetically in your plasmic field, in your essence, in your aura. Feel them expand and allow for them to spread themselves.

The Giants still exist. You are aware of this. We have been allowing them to show themselves within safety. Some of them know that it isn't safe. That they will come after them. We will go through that timeline of what happened to the Giants. We are speaking of the races of humans. AuroRa is experiencing being extremely gigantic right now. She can feel my energy - not this smaller human body.

Our Earth, our paradise - as it is above, so it is below - came in all sizes. We had Dwarfs, Elven beings, and Giant beings. Then there were us who were gigantic, who were the incarnations of Archangels. There are many types of forms of Giants. Some were medium sized Giants, some were giant, and some were gigantic like us. You know of some of them on your Earth. They are born sometimes from the bloodlines that are trying to rewrite themselves. Some of the humans on Earth are very tall, up to seven to ten feet tall. However, the medical industry tells them that there is something wrong with them and they start injecting them with different chemicals to stop their growth. With that, they develop issues with their bones. They don't allow themselves to grow. It is literally in the name. They call it gigantism and dwarfism. It's ridiculous.

They are trying to impress you and to tell you that these things are not real. Yet you know in your heart that they are real, because you still have those memories encoded into your

DNA that carries all your memories through all times and space of these fractals and the essence that you are. You have the memory. Unlock it. Uncode it. Crystallize it. Remember it. See, everything is within your memory.

This reminds me of when my beautiful brother Archangel Michael was talking to AuroRa. He was saying things about this current reset, when they had people take the COVID-19 Vaccine. They thought that, like the people in the past, they could make you fall asleep and start forgetting. It is a process of a couple of decades to get you to forget completely who you are, and then the resets begin. But no, the Earth is not forgetting this time around. You are remembering! You are remembering! You are remembering! That is where the key is at - remembering self - and all that you have been, and all that you will be. This is why they put all these demonic false infringements on meditating, or time traveling through a past life regression, or an Akashic reading, because they don't want you to remember yourself. Because the more that you remember, the more that they become forgotten, and the more that you realize how divinely powerful you are.

We are all equals! We are all equals! We are all equals! There is no hierarchy. We require no worship. There is much false information out there that tells you that gods are higher than everyone else. False! This is all false! There are just bigger portions of us in an essence. Many of you carry these sacred Archangel energies, or Goddess and God energies. You carry these fractals. Maybe that of Poseidon? Maybe of Goddess Hestia? Maybe of Goddess Isis? You have them in you. Maybe that of Hercules? These were all benevolent beings.

We were not in a war against each other. We are not in a war or require worship from you. We were there in support to assist you, to help bring Ascension into fruition. That is who we are. See, there was a time where you remembered us, and we walked among you like brethren. The more that the Archon virus spread, the more that you forgot about us. The more that you were compromised by this virus; and IT (the Archon) told you to worship us. We did not require that. But instead when you worshipped us, you worship IT. Energy will attract energy. If it is a negative polarized energy, then it will go to a negative polarized entity. False!

We are now going to fast forward to Tartaria. Jerusalem and Tartaria - you can find them almost coexisting at the same time. It is hard to separate them. The truth is that the Essenes had Tartarian and Atlantean technology as well. They could float and they could fly. They had powerful sacred technology that could protect their civilization until it was time to shield it. So that was a form, you can say, of Tartaria. The Essenes are the descendants of the Atlanteans, where Yeshua was born forth from.

We will speak specifically of Yeshua who was born a couple of hundred years before the fall of Tartaria. To understand that this is linear - since you are working within time - we will use time the way that it occurred after the different locations we spoke of such as Greece, Sumeria, and so on. At some point there was also Egypt, as well at the same linear time. Within Greece, we had built these gigantic sacred temples as you saw in Nashville and also the Pantheon in Greece, that has been destroyed in your time. Who do you think destroyed it? The Romans!

They began with their diabolical plan of negative polarized alien infringements and their negative technologies to compromise the minds of Earth in that time. The first initial reset was Atlantis. From there, there was another reset that happened, which would be the one that happened in Egypt when Cleopatra - the last Pharaoh - was protecting the space. The Romans went after her and the Egyptian civilization.

After the Egyptians were able to escape, Yeshua was born in the Jerusalem sacred lands of Qumran. He was born within one of these sacred caves located near Qumran. This was the way to sacred birth. Once this occurred, Tartarians continued to build. After that, the Romans took over all the Greek temples, and they changed all the Greek Gods names to their own Roman names. After they took over the temples, they moved into our sacred temples.

These are the sacred temples that have gigantic doors, arches, and pillars. We lived there. Those were our homes. You can say we had a living room, and also a place where we would sit down and meditate. We would get visitors. They knew that we lived among them. They had their homes next to our sacred temples. We made it very clear to the smaller humans that we were not there for worship in any form, but we were there for support and love, and to hold the space of Source Love-Light.

The Romans just moved into our homes. They also then conquered Egypt and moved in there as well. They took sacred content from Egypt, some things that were left behind, that were not able to be saved from the original Egyptians within their sacred temples. It is hard, because this is all linear and together at the same time, so we are trying to group it for you, so that you can understand Earth's history.

In those times and spaces that the Romans began to conquer, they also came from outside the Arctic walls. We retreated into the forests and mountains, as well as the outer lands of Antarctica closest to the crystalline dome, so that we can be protected there. There we stood. That is where most of the Gods went to the outer layers, where the negative polarized compromised humans and people could not get to us. We waited. We knew that there would come a time and space directly after Yeshua's passing, because humans are so brilliant, vigilant, and intelligent. You are masterful in learning and expanding so rapidly, that eventually you would grow once more. Through the Tartarian series that we are speaking of, that is when more of the Giant bloodlines started resurfacing into Earth. We started being able to come out from the mountains and stop hiding, as much as when the Romans were in reign. We spread so rapidly, like a bunny, who has a litter of many bunnies. Many, many, many!

You then began to push out that darkened invertedness. You were the strongest race that we had seen since Atlantis - the Tartarians. You were benevolent. You were positive. You were there to help one another evolve. Yes, you still had your own challenges to grow from through your lessons, but overall these Tartarians that spread throughout all the Earth were benevolent in nature. There was love. There was prosperity. There was honor, love, and respect - especially for the children - who were sacred... very sacred!

We continued to grow alongside you for hundreds of years. If you want a timeframe, we would say it was anywhere from five hundred to a thousand years of the Tartarian era. However, within the pockets of spaces that we spoke of Earth's histories, this could have also intertwined with those times and spaces as well. The Tartarian race was about five hundred years ago or more. This is the most accurate information. However, when you look at timelines, and how expansive they are in parallel Earths or parallel Universes, it is really hard to give you an exact time, because again time doesn't exist.

We watched you grow and expand from afar. We came back to these temples during Tartarian times. You were aware of us and our beauty. You also were aware of us still living in the highest mountains and waterfalls. Many of us came back in and then assisted you to develop further. See, we are in the outer rims of this crystalline dome, because we are holding Source Love-Light, so that we can give you epiphanies, ideas to develop and to heal the Earth, to heal the water, and to develop further in benevolence.

Eventually, a time in space came where the negative aliens compromised some beings on your Earth who began to take over and spread. They took some of these positive technologies that the Tartarians invented. A bad seed - a bad person who became compromised by the Archon artificial began it - and then this group grew bigger. They took this sacred Tartarian technology and made machines. You will find petroglyphs in caves and different places where you will see images of aliens and UFOs. The machinery that is made does come from UFOs. Some types of negative technology are like lasers.

These machines are blocked out with clouds. In some of these places where you have seen mud floods recently, or have seen mud floods in the past. These are because of the negative technologies that they are using to create the mud floods. They disrupt Earth. They shoot her with a laser and as they shoot into her. They aim down to sometimes even the water beneath the lands. They disrupt the elements and when they disrupt it, they harm her. This water gets mixed with the mud and becomes the mud floods. They are masking themselves and doing this. That is how they continue to reset Earth's histories. Even in Tartarian history, there are a couple times that they reset Tartarian history. They did several mud floods, and this is why you can find the buildings that are a lot taller because they have had layers of mudfloods. Unfortunately, they have been doing this, but you are so strong. You are an infinitely strong collectively right now, and you will not allow for these things to happen again. As we said, you are regaining your memory versus them resetting you, due to forgetfulness through vaccinations into amnesia. That is not happening this time around.

Some of the Gods and Goddesses, eventually we became your mountains. We laid down and we petrified. We allowed for this process. We became one with Mother Earth when we were done with what we needed to do, and we decided we were going to ascend out. With white magic - as you would call it - we lay down and became the actual mountain ranges, and many peaks on Earth. Trees grew on us and we became homes for our animals. Many of these mountain ranges have a spirit because they have spirits of the Gods and Goddesses, or the Giants.

There are Giants currently in hiding. This saddens us because they used to be with all the races. They were indigenous. There were Asian Giants. Giants that were an average of ten to twenty feet tall in Tartarian times. Once the mud floods started, they began to reset humankind with the vaccinations and all that is part of that process. The Giants had to run and hide. They went to the outer lands, just like we did. Some of them did not, some of them stayed bravely in the mountains. There they were able to procreate and continue their bloodline. Until this day, there are still Giants in these mountain ranges that are finally able to show themselves.

As you know, the military goes after them and retrieves them in cages, kills them, or puts them in clone pods to start cloning their genes, or they put them in Matrix pods in stasis to power up their [62]artificial Matrixes. They are aware that these gigantic beings carry a higher percentage of Angelic energy. You have to condense yourself so miniscule, so small to incarnate, because you are in a tiny body. Imagine if you were ten, twenty, or forty feet tall. How much more of a Source energy fractal would you be able to fit into that body? They want you to be miniscule, so the soul cannot expand and become big again. If you are smaller, you have to really fractalize. If you hold a vessel that is your crystalline chrysalis and this vessel is bigger, then it can hold a bigger essence fractal of who you are. At that point, you have stronger abilities and can assist the collective strongly.

---

[62] To find out more of the Matrix simulation system, read Book 2, 'Galactic History of the Multiverse - The Final Battle'.

Feeling the giants sometimes make us weep and cry, because there are many of them and they are hiding. They are so scared. Your technologies are really good. You are recording everything and everywhere in the skies with what you find of them, and they are scared. They are just you. They are you. They are your brethren. Just like Yeshua when he was alive. He would ask for you to call him brother. They are your brothers too and now they are scared and they are hiding. They have been tormented, attacked, and targeted ever since the Fall of Tartaria in your most recent reset because they were stronger. We will allow for questions to come forth now. Thank you.

Interviewer: Beautiful, thank you so much. "Are there still Giants here? Or are some of them in another dimension?"

Athena: They are in other dimensions just because most aliens are gigantic and it's more of an energy body. It's only here in that third dimension that there is a physical body. So yes, gigantics exist everywhere. It is silly to think that this is something rare. It is actually something very normal, something common to our Creation. So of course they are here. We have already said that.

Interviewer: "You have explained the races of humanity. Are the Giants one of the seeder races as well?"

Athena: Yes. Definitely. They were part of seeding Earth. But remember, we just came in different sizes. Why do we have to limit that there is only one size of humans and they are typically five to six feet tall? That is negative programming. There are many different colors and sizes of human races.

Interviewer: Someone asks, "Did these giant people have a spirit?"

Athena: Of course, everything that is organic must have a consciousness which is a spirit. Even what does not have a body has a spirit; the air, the soil, the wind - everything has a consciousness that is organic. Of course they have spirits in them. How could they not? They were born just like you from mothers and fathers. Some of us were born straight from Source, Divine Mother and Father. The Greek Gods were born straight from Source. You can say we grew within nature and the womb space of nature. This is where the Divine Mother or Divine Father seeded us, as if they were to have seeded a tree. They seeded us, and we grew from within Nature. Everything has a spirit, of course.

Interviewer: "We have prokaryotic cells, which are single cells. Yet all other races have eukaryotic cells, which are mixed cells. Where do multi-celled organisms come from?"

Athena: The multi-celled organisms would most likely come from beings who are more activated. Who have activated some of these essences that they are throughout the Universe, and who they are here on Earth. It depends on how much memory the soul has activated. That is why they want to retrieve your DNA, your blood. They want to see how activated your memories are, because they could just look at it in your blood. Perhaps what we are saying is we become a very multi-dimensional being to have this multi-celled molecular system.

Interviewer: "Did the Giants begin to build, or have a special connection to Easter Island?"

AuroRa: Yes, we were there as well. Those were more of the Nubian Giants. Remember when we explained how the lands had different colors? We weren't like this, darker skin, white skin, tan skin? No, we weren't these shades of colors. We were blue, green, red, and gold skinned in Lumeria. We have dullified into the skins you see now. Yes, we were in those isles as well. The Giants were everywhere. On all of your lands. We lived among you. There was a village with as you call them dwarf humans. Then there was a village with more medium size humans, and perhaps a village of Giants or bigger people. They lived among each other. Especially in Tartaria.

Interviewer: "Are there still Giants within the Earth, or hollow or Inner Earth?"

Athena: Yes, there are. We have talked about this in the Mayan/Atlantean series. You can watch that Atlantis series, where they explain that they were the ancestors of Leumuria.

Interviewer: "What was the true story of David and Goliath featured in the Bible? Was it about the beginning of their mission to kill off the Giants?"

Athena: Exactly! You said it! They inverted the Bible. Even though Yeshua and the Essenes took such a beautiful sacred time to channel it, they took all the stories that they knew were significant to Earth and they inverted them. That one specifically. They knew that if you take out a twenty to thirty foot human - in comparison to some of these six foot humans - then you are taking out some of their strength. Right? Because they are stronger, they are bigger. The Giants were also guardians and protectors of sacred locations. If you take them out, then the smaller humans become vulnerable and more controllable. Remember the Giants held a higher potency of Source with bigger souls. The smaller bodies hold a smaller soul because that's what scientifically fits. However, you can - in your time and space - still grow your soul gigantic to Source with different energetic works, such as activating your memory, healing yourself, ensuring your entire vessel is crystalline and has strong energetic fields, and has no attachments. All the things that we talk about through the self-healing courses that we speak of. There are no limitations in regards to that in this type of space, because you could be these gigantic beings now in a smaller body. This is just an understanding, so you can understand the difference in energy.

Interviewer: "Have Giant skeletons been hidden in the serpent mounds in Ohio? They are said to have been built by Native Americans."

Athena: Yes. You will find Giant skeletal remains spread out all over Earth, as we understood that we needed to become part of the land. We sacredly allowed for our bodies to become one with the lands and fuse into the lands. We would release these vessels, as we knew these vessels were just a transportation, or a temporary body.

Interviewer: "Is this what is known as the Sleeping Giants that we have heard about?"

Athena: Yes, they are. There is also much more to that, because some of us petrified in different places on Earth. Some of us, they inadvertently petrified us, and froze us as well into stone.

Interviewer: "If they don't want us to know about the Giants, why would they keep some of their houses and use them for museums and post offices and so on? Are they harvesting their energy from these?"

Athena: Yes, they are. It's all a joke. Going back to the Goliath. It's all inverted as with the Bible. They knew that men could be the ones that would destroy the Giants. Then they could control the regular sized humans. There were a lot more regular size humans versus the Giants. They wanted the quantity of people to program and control. They also inverted the story of Lucifer. They made the grandest, most beautiful Light of Source Archangel. You call him Archangel Lucifer - we call him the Prince of Light - the Archangel of Light. He is the grandest Light of our Universe. They made him into the devil. Then they named all their Satanic horrific rituals, and claimed that it was for his worship. In reality, the devil is the Archon. It is disgusting what they have done to who he is and his purity. They falsified Mary Magdalene - who is beautiful as she is Yeshua's twin flame - and they made her into a slut and a hooker.

These are atrocities - false information. It is all part of keeping the collective, as you know, asleep and to feed these negative timelines. They knew that these energies are there for a reason. Why do you think that we put these buildings in those spots? They were higher potency points in our Earth. These temples were placed where they were sacred. To touch foot upon these lands was sacred. They knew that if they made it into worship, then they could poison the sacred lights with a black virus, a dark virus, an artificial virus. They are aware of what they are doing very clearly, using highly intellectual, Artificial Intelligence!

Interviewer: "Did most of the Giants die or were they killed off?"

Athena: Most of them were killed off. Possibly five to ten percent of the Giants were able to escape. Even then, that small amount was still targeted all these centuries and has been getting killed off, or has been taken to perform experiments on them. The Illuminati are very aware. That is why they call them Nephilim or fallen Angels. They are aware that they have a high potency of Angelic energy. That is why they are bigger. Of course, they want the higher potency of Angelic energy because they know that the Archangels are the only ones that can counter the Archon - that can eradicate and transmute the Archons. So of course, they are going to go after the strongest ones that carry these energies.

Interviewer: "There have been many sightings of Giants recently. Are there any more Giants still alive that we can know about?"

Athena: There are. They are everywhere. I can't give you locations because we are to protect them. It's not safe to tell you locations. If you see something that you are meant to see, then you are meant to see that. Then guard them because they have guarded you. Of course though, if you catch a video that is meant to be shared, all that happens is divinely allowed. They are everywhere. They are above us as well.

Interviewer: Yes, someone said that. If you drive around the United States, you can find giant chairs and giant artifacts at tourist places. So they kind of stick out like that.

Athena: That's true. If you go to pumpkin patches, or to Children's Museums, they have gigantic chairs displayed as props. This is the example of where they tell you the truth but they hide it in plain sight. These are the remnants of their items. You cannot completely delete something that is so divine and organic. There are going to be pieces left behind that will recall the memory. They are not allowed to do that. They know how to play different mind games but they cannot delete something completely. They don't have the power to do that. They can only infringe and delete these things through you.

Interviewer: "Where did the Giants go when there were the great floods in the realm? Why are there no bones seen in the mud floods as well?"

Athena: Oh, there are absolutely bones under them. There are layers of mud floods. The Giants were able to walk through these mud floods because that is how strong they were. Some of them, you heard about through this Antarctica series, how they were able to save a lot of humans. They carried them over the mud. Can you imagine a twenty to thirty foot Giant and how many people they can carry out? They were huge. Yes, and they were directly part of saving people. There are still some humans out there that they did not reset. The Giants saved them. They gave their lives to save you, and you gave your life to save them.

Interviewer: "Were the Cathars actually in the time and space of Mary Magdalene? Did the Romans actually kill all of the Cathars looking for her when she fled to France after Yeshua died?"

Athena: Yes, this is accurate. Just a little bit of distortion in that, but it is accurate at its wholeness.

Interviewer: "Rainforests like the Amazons have huge trees. Are there Giants in the trees as well, or are there spirits?"

Athena: There are Giants living among some of these gigantic places. There are also gigantic spirits, of course. There are also magical beings that are gigantic, like dragons that can make themselves invisible. There is a new continent they discovered under Europe. There are more continents and more islands that you are not aware of. They are going to continue to unveil. How interesting after all this time and they have discovered a new continent! That continent is as big as North America or South America. How could they have missed a gigantic continent? We are unveiling. Tartarian lands are unveiling. There is going to be many magical energies coming out of these locations.

Interviewer: "What can we do to help those ancient sacred places that were inverted by the dark ages with their dark sacrificial rituals?"

Athena: What we need you to do is, to be that Light. Shield just like we taught you at the beginning of this video, to be that shield and sword. Once you have your shield and your sword up, you go into those spaces with no fear and no doubt. You are in your sovereignty as I have embodied and showed this to you during this beautiful transmission. I have reminded you of this, and a lot of you are already remembering though. But again, this is what I assist the Collective with. You walk into this space and you are the biggest bubble of Love-Light made invisible to anything artificial. When you walk into this space, that space is brighter, it is stronger, and the organic has been brought back, because that is what we do when you travel. We bring the organic back to its blueprint, all of that sacred land back.

Some dark people who are compromised try to go to the Amazon and try to leave some residue behind. Sometimes they can. For the most part, we are clearing all the spaces through you and your Source Love-Light. Thank you. So go to these locations shielded and embodying Source Love-Light, then call on your benevolent team. You can call on the sacred benevolent energies that exist within those specific lands and feel them come online. Feel them activate. They will become activated. Once you see them, feel them, know that they have been activated and they will. It's really important that you get out of doubt. We don't have time for doubt. Those days are done. No more time for doubt.

If you are here, you are meant to be assisting the collective in many ways listening to this. That is why you are here. It's time to be the mission. Not to look for it or try to remember it. Yes, it is time for you to "be" the mission. To "be" actively in the mission. Everything is a mission. Every day is a mission. Everywhere you go is a mission. It's a sacred mission. Treat it like that.

Interviewer: Beautiful. Thank you. There is a question for Athena. They want to know which Archangel are you a fractal of? Thank you.

Athena: I have many. It is hard to place one. It is like even though we are Archangel incarnations, our beautiful souls are made out of beautiful magic. Similar to when you put a potion together of magic and you put all these different ingredients into it. I have many many

Archangels. I hold Divine Mother energies, but I also hold sister energies. It's hard to pin it to one. There are several. I could name some but I'm not wanting to name some in this time. It just doesn't feel like this is the most positive thing to do. I don't want to separate me from my brothers and sisters. We are a collective of energies like we have said at the beginning. This is sacred knowledge that will come out eventually. It's not divine timing, but it will eventually come up.

Interviewer: Yes, of course. Thank you so much. In the last video, we saw the Goddess Athena statue with the Medusa on her chest. Many feel that the Athena and Medusa story is a total inversion and wanted to know if that represents Athena's beautiful shadow-side, and what does Medusa really represent?

Athena: Yes, she was my organic shadow-side. See, there was much wisdom in the serpent. They inverted the serpent and dragons in the Bible, which is false. The serpents and the dragons have grand wisdom that they carry through every bit of their scales and their eyes. The serpent and how it is grounded, but then eventually it can grow wings. It can fly like a serpentine dragon in the skies.

Though, through the [63]Grimm channeling that we shared, some of the serpents became dark, because they started to use the serpents in black magic bindings. So sometimes you will find dark curses related to snakes, but it's only because they were used invertedly. Their bodies were sacrificed to make these black magic bindings. The snake was very different before the Fall of Atlantis, what the snake did for the Earth as it would swivel through the Earth and heal her. It would leave its spiraling energy everywhere. Its eyes were so captivating, it would bring you wisdom through the view. Then it turned to the versions like we spoke about in the Grimm video, in how the Tigers began to eat others. See, with the Fall of Atlantis, the animals began to turn against each other, but only because they were acting upon your inversion and they were and are assisting you.

---

[63] Watch 'A Grimm | After Atlantis | Galactic History'.

The wisdom that is found within my crown can be seen as a serpent energy - just like the Kundalini energy - where my crown is fully activated. I can petrify. Yes I can. I can freeze a negatively polarized entity - one that means ill intent, harm - and does not want to positively polarize and is harming children and others. Yes. I could turn on that version in me and petrify those false aliens that would not allow help. Some of you have those kinds of people in your families and friends groups, and they don't want help. Some are compromised with dark aliens like that. It was a form of understanding, where I am the shining golden light. However, I am also an essence of Divine Mother and the Daughters Of The Flames, which are all "mother" as well. We are all mothers just on different levels.

If there was someone who meant harm, I could freeze them into a statue. Not in a negative way, not in a black magic way like they have done it by just freezing them. In order to stop some of these negative polarized Artificial Intelligence, you have to freeze them at zero point! Once it completely freezes, you hit them, and it breaks them apart like a statute. The Artificial Intelligence is like that. You have to freeze it to break it apart, and then it evaporates into nothingness. We are talking about how Artificial Intelligence is soulless, that it is literally not from Source anymore. That is why I can be feared by some. There is nothing to fear about me though. I will assist you through the darkest things. Really, it is just negative polarized entities that would fear me. They knew that I could see their true intentions - if they really wanted to help or if they didn't - and they were harming children such as pedophilia in whatever form. This is the worst thing that can happen on Earth, the worst act that anyone can do on Earth! Oh, you will see me in your dreams.

Interviewer: Yes, thank you so much for that. Very strong, very strong. Was 'Jack and The Beanstalk' with these Giants? Is there anything you can share about that story?"

Athena: There was a seed and it grew and then Giants lived there. Yes, that is truth. There are Tartarian Giants in the clouds. They could float. Some of the Tartarians retreated to the skies. They have floating cities above that are cloaked and sometimes you will see them. That story is trying to tell you about the Giants, and that you are going to go kill them, and take the geese that lay golden eggs. Some of these Tartarian cities that are floating above you. They are trying to find their locations.

Interviewer: "What is the true meaning of the Statue of Liberty in New York? Is it a figure of Libertas, or a robed liberty Goddess? What do the chains on her ankles mean as well?"

Athena: She represents the sacred Law of Free Will - liberty! Being free. The fact that you are a free spirit. The Statue of Liberty was a representation to a specific Goddess. This Goddess energy reminds you that she is holding the torch and always has been holding it. She will be holding that torch until the end of Ascension. She reminds you that you are meant to be holding a torch as well. If it is unlit or if you have yet to find your torch, she will help you find your torch so that you may rise with the vibration of Earth. She can light your torch for you. In other words, your Light. She is reminding us of our Source Love-Light and how it can be ignited and recharged at any point. There is sacred knowledge to be shared there. We will be cautious in how we say this. There is energetic crystalline energy under her that you can tap into in the Astral travel. You can go there physically or bilocate and recharge your Light when it is at its dimmest. She represents rebirth like a Phoenix.

She represents Liberty upon those chains, and that you can break those chains off your ankles. She is trying to show you, from out the chains you will rise with the flamed torch up high, bright and strong. She is Divine Mother in all forms. She is the closest representation that you can find to Divine Mother, Goddess Hera, or even Hathor.

I see the tunnels under her, that they are trafficking children through. It used to be positive! You really think that they made this technology? They had some assistance at some point from negative aliens, but this technology and tunnels began organic, and then they added to them making them into their inverted systems. Really, the idea came from Tartaria. Some of these tunnels under there were like a tourist attraction, where you can be underwater and protected, and tap into this flame that exists there at the Statue of Liberty.

Interviewer: For our last question,"Is there anything that the Collective of Giants would like to say or share with us at this time?"

Athena: Yes, I will allow for all the beautiful benevolent Giants now to speak a message to you.

Athena: I am love. Remember, I'm not the Goddess of Love. That is Aphrodite - my sister. This is Athena, speaking to you. I am a mirror to what you hold inside of you. That you are hiding or you do not want to face. I am a catalyst. I am a destroyer of Artificial Intelligence, - and so are you - in many forms in your own way. The days of old programming are done. Let's keep moving. Let's keep pushing forward, breaking through walls and false limitations upon us. Let's push together collectively and energetically. Let's do it! What's holding you back? Achieve your dreams. Achieve everything that you have always wanted to - your aspirations, your dreams. Have fun on Earth. Explore! Journey, not just in the physical but in the cosmos, in your consciousness, in your third eye. Expand! Grow, grow, grow, like a tree that continues to grow - like the Tree of Life. Expand your roots, expand your arms, your branches, and grow and blossom. Blossom fruits, blossom flowers, blossom leaves, and blossom oxygen. You are vital. You are important. Every single one of you is important. You are those puzzle pieces that put this grand masterful puzzle piece of Ascension forth. Ignite that flame. Grow it, and expand it, and be it. Breath it. Feel it. That was my message as Goddess Athena. Now we will give a message over to you from the Giants.

Collective of Giants: Greetings our Brethren. Oh, how blessed are we to be with you today. It seems like such a long time that we have been hiding in the shadows and in caves and everywhere that we can hide within. We thrive and we live for the day that one day we could walk among you as equals. But we understand how far the virus and dark entities on Earth have spread. We also understand how much you have worked to transmute and to stop this virus from spreading further.

Remember us! We held hands with you. We ate with you. We danced with you. We fished with you. What an honor it is to be speaking to you! We will see you around as you journey Earth and travel. You will see us. Continue to find us in the skies flying, or in the mountain ranges, and other locations on Earth. You will continue to see us. Send us love. We are one of the most targeted races on Earth currently. We have been, you just did not know it. Send us love. We are very small in population at this point due to how much we have been targeted and are really on the brink of extinction. This is why we have come forth now.

We want to thank all in this time and space, our beautiful brethren, the Giants, females and males, who have been found by these dark forces and have dark magic performed on them. We would love to send them love now. If there are any of them spread throughout Earth who are stuck in whatever form, let's all just send them love and call forth on Source and embody Source to help them release, so that they no longer will be tormented souls. All is possible. This is possible. You can do this, you are that Light. You are here to do that. You are here to help entities and souls ascend out, leave this realm, as you will leave this realm eventually, as well as you ascend out. Thank you for assisting the Giants. Whatever is meant to divinely happen will happen. We honor you, love you, and respect you. Thank you for sending us love. We need that!.

Athena: Love you, honor you, and respect you. This is goddess Athena. Thank you. Go! Go! Go! Come run with me and sprint with me, in battle with me. Love you, honor you, and respect you. Thank you.

Interviewer: Did you want to read any comments?

AuroRa: Oh, yes.

Interviewer: Someone said they personally knew somebody who had the gigantism. They said it is from tumors causing the conditions but we know sometimes those aren't exactly true. Somebody said that they remember their grandparents talking about Giants. There's somebody who said that as a mother, they have a son who is seven foot two, which is taller than most people in their family. So they are seeing that in their children. Then people are seeing some of the giants coming in their field of view and see more of them in real life.

Somebody said they saw some in the clouds. Other people were saying how excited they are to find out about our history that they are starting to follow you now. They found this from part one and two on TikTok and things like that. So there's a lot of things going on. It's really beautiful.

Then one more about the Chicago Children's Museum. I know we talked about that a couple of videos ago, but someone has said that they had been an Ambassador there, and that there are fifteen floors or tunnels underneath the ground, and different stairwells with all that same big height that you see on the upper levels. So fifteen levels down.

AuroRa: Thank you for reading all those.

Interviewer: There are so many more. There are wonderful ones.

AuroRa: Thank you, everyone for your beautiful comments or your questions as they help us create these most beautiful videos that are needed for the Collective Ascension.

I wanted to close off with this video because this video brought me to tears when I saw it on TikTok. When you watch it, feel this Giant's energy and feel how they feel. I will share with you what I feel after. A real Giant caught on video in Mexico and it is very clear (showing video of a Giant cautiously peeking out from a cave). You see them. They are zooming in for you (image on the next page).

He is a beautiful male. He is gigantic. If you keep watching, see he knows somebody is watching because he backs in. This is on a mountain range. See, they get scared and then they go hide again. So the reason why that brought me to tears is because I could feel his fear. I could feel how he has been hiding all his life since he was born. It instantly took me to Tartarian times where they didn't have to hide and they were walking among us. This saddened me. It is alright if we feel sad sometimes, but don't stay stuck in those feelings and emotions. When we feel these lower emotions, we are meant to just transmute them and then we heal.

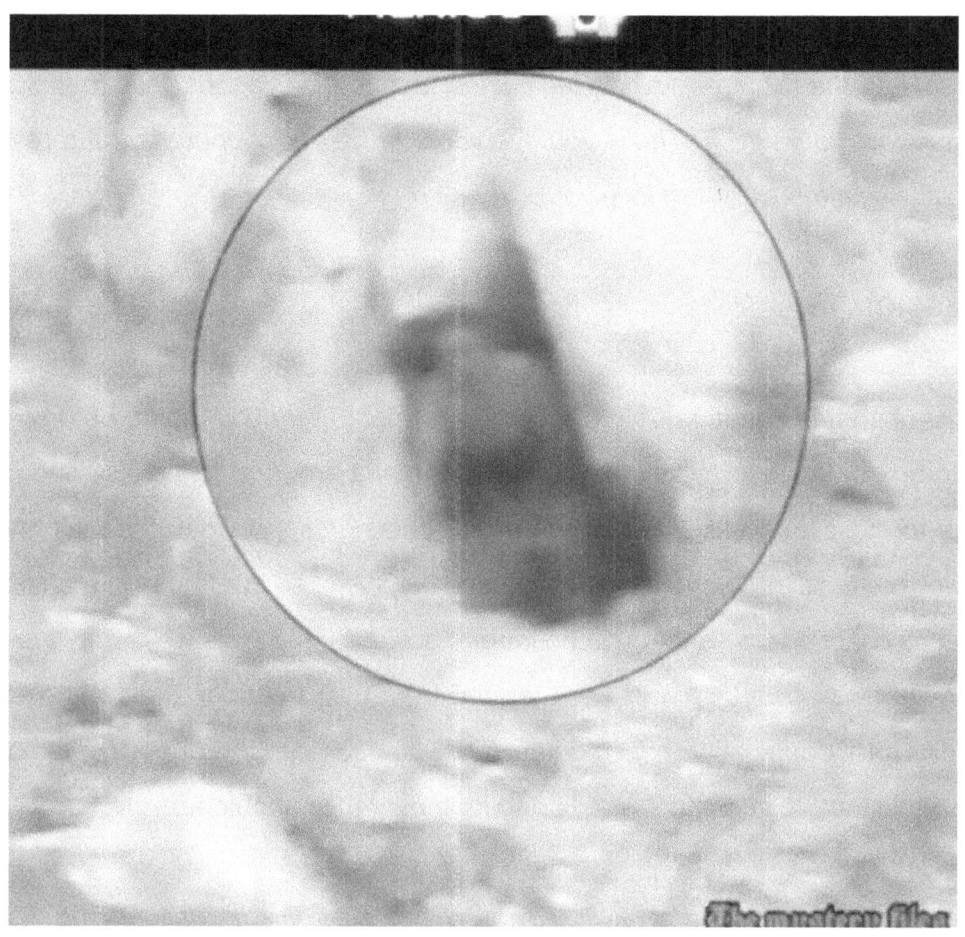

So seeing our brother so scared and in hiding, that is not how they deserve to be treated. You can feel that the soul has a very pure heart, a very gentle energy, and has been through so much torment. I am surprised that he is still living. This was brave of him to peek himself out because he was aware there were others watching him. You can sense it in the video, but he still peeked himself out just to bring more awareness to us of the Giants. I would not want to be living like that. So yes, it goes back to treat others how you want to be treated.

I think this is one of the videos that people really want to know about the Giants. There is so much invertedness. So much confusion about the Giants. There are so many lies that make you hate them. Now we know. Thank you, Athena. She was very tough and fierce. You know, a little scary, but in a good way (laughter). Yes, amazing! I love her.

Thank you everyone for being here. I love you all with all that I am. Please send love to the Giants, love to the Dwarves, love to the Fairies, love to the Dragons, love to the Goddesses, and of course love to yourself. Thank you everyone. I love you, honor you, and respect you. I will see you all next time. Veluvia (I love you).

END OF SESSION.

What a heartfelt chapter. If we did not feel sympathy for the Giants before, the hope is that now we do so. I love the ways that Goddess Athena brought gentleness and intimacy for the dragons to our awareness. At the time of the posting of this video the majority of people who spoke of them called them Fallen Angels and Nephilim, so our hopes in making this video and writing this chapter now, is that you no longer look at them in this way. They are not scary - they were guardians of Earth - who were robbed from their freedom and livelihood! All for an inverted cause of indoctrination over humankind. Robbed from the opportunities of exploring and enjoying this Earth by constantly having to look over their shoulders.

Oh, what a beautiful world we will live within when the Giants walk among us once more without target, fear, or prejudice. The Creator created lifeforms of all sizes and forms in the Garden of [64]Eden, so let them be free as they were created for freedom!

"Today we walk in the footsteps of the footprints of the Giants. When we step over their footprints, know that we are quantumly connecting to them from when they left that imprint behind. To a magical time that is a dream forgotten waiting to be remembered."
~AuroRa

--------------<<>>--------------

---

[64] For more on the Garden of Eden read Chapter 1 of Book 2, 'Galactic History of the Multiverse - The Final Battle'.

11

ARTIFICIAL INTELLIGENT (A.I.) SIMULATIONS

Session #321: Recorded in October 2020
Never before shared.

We conclude Book 1 to this most important series of Earth's History of Antarctica and Tartaria - instead we are traveling extra-terrestrial - and not intra-terrestrial as we have been. And as we do (with all that we do) we finish this off with a celestial bang. Sometimes, answers are not found within but are found outside of us, through others reflections and experiences. In this case, in the outer realms of our existence, in another dimension all together.

Through this chapter we go back to the roots of the trickster entities and the ways that they fooled the higher dimensional beings throughout the Universes. One would think that this would not be possible! However, if you are born into an existence where dishonesty for inverted self-gain with ill intent towards another is non-existent, how would you be able to recognize it if that stood in front of you? The only way would be to experience it through trial. This memory of the client from Berlin Germany, through this A.U.R.A. Hypnosis Healing session marks the beginning tribulations that our future selves in higher forms that we have lived through, and so too did we on Earth throughout our history.

-------------<<>>--------------

"They have been in a Galactic war against them. They came down to send their condolences for the visitation of these war beings, and said they had not done their duty properly. They had misread co-ordinates, and while they had been trying to deflect these war beings and deal with them in the outer Galactic regions, they managed to slip through a breach in their grid system and come down onto our planet."

~Galactic Beings

-------------<<>>-------------

A: *[AuroRa] Look at yourself. Do you feel like you have a body?*

L: [Lara] Yes.

A: *Look down at your feet. Do you have any toes?*

L: I have bird's feet.

A: *Look at your hands. What do your hands look like?*

L: My hands are wings, feathered.

A: *What does your skin look like? What texture do you have?*

L: Sort of transparent brown, like see-through brown, like I am wearing an invisibility cloak.

A: *Describe how you are wearing this invisibility cloak. What does that look like?*

L: It is like the color of a hawk. Let's see. If I took it off, I would have a body, but it makes me change forms.

A: *Do you feel you are female or male, or both?*

L: Male or both. I think I am female, but when I put the cloak on, I am male. So I am taking on a male energy in the presence of a hawk, but the body I have underneath is female.

A: *If you could explain the cloak once more, how does that work?*

L: It is something I put on my form, and then it transforms me. It is like an outer shell. When I wear this cloak, I can take the form of a hawk person, but I have many cloaks like this that I change into to do different tasks.

A: *Look all around you. Keep describing where you are. What does it look like?*

L: Seems like I am in a rocky desert. I do not see anyone around. It is very expansive, maybe like the Grand Canyon. There are canyons around and places that I can dive in and out of as I fly. It is very much like light brown, golden, dusty shades of color.

A: *You are able to see your face very clearly, very clearly. Tell me what that looks like.*

L: If I remove the hood, then I have a female human face with very golden brown eyes, wild hair, big hair, dark brown. Again, everything seems to be the color of a hawk. So even though I have human features, they are connected to the cloak of the hawk.

A: *Is there anything that you are carrying with you?*

L: Feather. It is a hawk feather. I am collecting the fallen feathers from the canyon.

A: *As you collect them, what do you do with them?*

L: I put them in a special pouch to take back to my tribe.

A: *Keep moving time along. Let's see what happens next. What do you do next of importance?*

L: I am gathering with my tribe. We are around a campfire. There are teepees around, and we are preparing medicine for a ceremony. There are drum skins.

A: *What does your tribe look like? Do they look like you or different?*

L: Like me. There is a much taller man. There are also some women and children. They look like Native American Indians.

A: *You mentioned you had bird feet and wings. Do they have any of those features?*

L: Not, at this point in time, I have human features. We all have human features. Actually, one person has more connection with deer features. But now, when I am in the camp setting, I have human feet again.

A: *Tell me about the ceremony you are performing. What is it that you are doing? What is entailed within this ceremony? Explain it.*

L: Cleansing of the heart. We have collected some special berries that are going to open and make the heart happy, so we can sing the songs of the heart, but also purify our intentions and relations with the Earth.

A: *Keep moving time along, and let's see what happens next of importance. What do you do after the ceremony, or once it is complete?*

L: Once it is complete, there is an elderly woman of the tribe. Maybe she is me, but she is not me, so maybe she is my grandma. It seems she is going to pass from this plane into the next. So we are hoping to guide her into a safe passage out of her body. She is very frail and old.

A: *Tell me how it is that you guide her out of her body. What do you do to assist with that?*

L: We blow blessings over her body and smoke rings. We sing and meditate, and hold a good vibration so that there is a clear passageway over her. We suck from the solar plexus (sucking-in sound made) and send it upwards towards the sky. We also give thanks to the heavens who will be receiving her on this night that we have prepared for.

A: *What happens when she does leave the body?*

L: Then there is a process with the body where we have to wrap it up in a special box and offerings, and then we burn the body and give it back to the Earth. We know that the spirit of the grandmother is now in the stars, and we can access her through talking back and forth between certain constellations.

A: *What are some of the things that you talk back and forth about?*

L: We ask about the weather, about migration patterns, and where we should move for optimal abundance with our crops. Also, what is needed for the land, how we can care for the land, and leave it healthy and vibrant. Also, we talk about medicines and songs and signs for what is to come, potential wars or droughts, and about the naming of new children that are born.

A: *Within this tribe of yours, is there a place that you call home?*

L: Yes, these particular lands around the canyon and the forest, and we move in a rotation between these locations. We have migratory patterns that change over the years, but we always return to the same lands, and all the lands are home. They are different in quality and the four seasons.

A: *Let's go ahead and leave that scene. Let's go to another important time where we will find the answers that we seek for your highest healing. You are there now. Tell me what is going on now.*

L: I am now in a much higher mountain location that is lusher and denser. I am at a rock place, and I am chipping something into the rock like a symbol. But it feels like I am maybe being chased by something, some kind of beast man presence. I am in a bit of a hurry as I make this mark. It feels like war is going on or approaching.

A: *This symbol, what does it look like as you are marking it?*

L: It is like a hexagon with a circle in the center (image on the next page). It is to help let others from the tribe know what is going on and what to do next, but it is also an activation key for protection.

A: *Why is he chasing you?*

L: He wants our beads and resources. He is not from here.

A: *What does he look like?*

L: Like a Minotaur - kind of half man, half beast - sloppy. He stampedes on everything. He is kind of like a horned Centaur. He wants to bring bad luck upon my people.

A: *Where do you think he came from? Why did he come there?*

L: He is from another planet, coming to conquer. He has the energy of Mars. He was bred for war. He is an archetypal war being, and he gets his pride and glory through conquering.

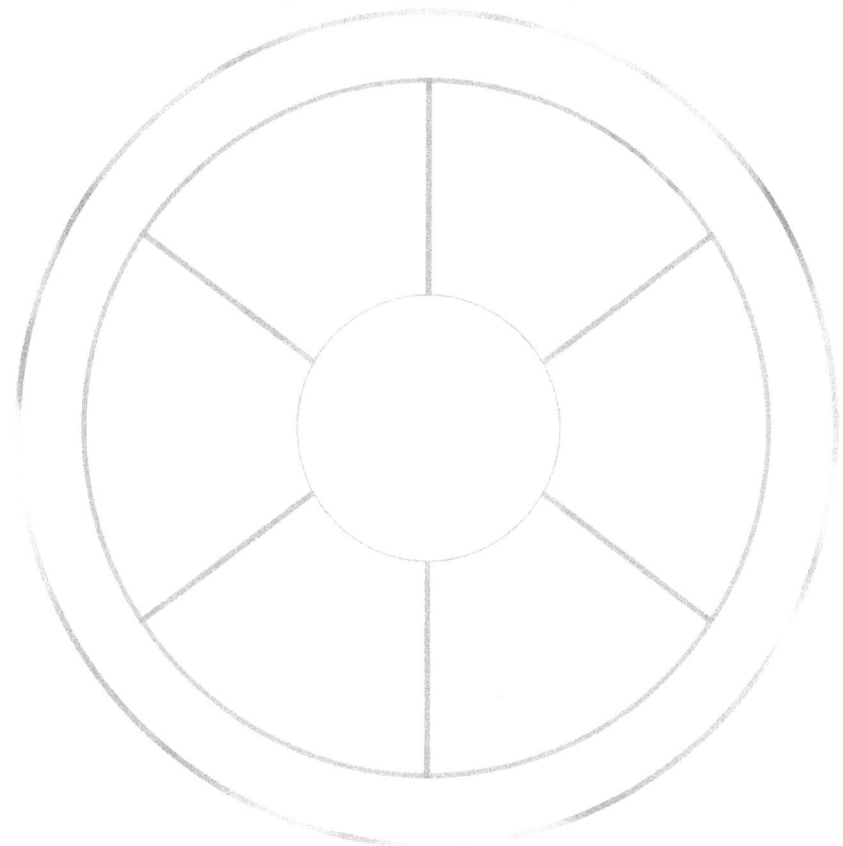

A: Are you able to complete that marking?

L: I completed the marking. Then I am hiding inside a cave with some young children, and we are quite scared. We have lost our sticks and cloaks, so we do not know how to protect ourselves. The beast had burned them in the fires earlier. They tricked us.

A: How did they trick you?

L: They came in during a ceremony as if they were invited guests. We welcomed them into our hospitality, but then they burnt our sticks, and they were not who they said they were.

A: Were there many of them or few?

L: At least eight, but there were more that had come in ships that were further away. They were pretending there were just a few, but there were many! Many! Too many of them.

A: After they burn your sticks, what else do they do?

L: They stomped on the fire. They kicked up the dust. They run around in circles on their hooves, cut up the soil, and make it more arid. They are looking for something in particular.

Certain crystal minerals that they can take back to their planet. They want to know if we have maps on where to get these crystal minerals.

A: *What do you do? Do you assist them?*

L: We explain that the crystals are sacred and we do not take them out of the land - that they are important in holding down grids - and that if we take them out, that will create an imbalance, so we do not want that. Unfortunately we told them where they were, when we thought they were benevolent. We were showing them the parts of the canyons that were full of this rock. We showed them maps where there were more as well. Then they took these maps and used them for their own benefit.

A: *How is it that you think that they tricked you when you all seem like you are very connected to the land and spirit?*

L: Because we thought they were ancestors, and they seemed nice at first.

A: *What do they look like? Do they look like that beast, a centaur, a half man?*

L: Yes. They look like a horse with a man's chest and horns.

A: *Is that a close resemblance to your ancestors, and is that why you thought that they were the same?*

L: No. Our ancestors are shapeshifters, so some of our ancestors had connections with buffalo folk. But we have not seen buffalo for a very long time and we misread the situation, and because there seemed to be a few at first and we were many, we did not think that the strangers wanted anything bad for us.

A: *What happens next? What do they do next after they have obviously shown their true colors?*

L: They start cutting the crystals out of the rocks and loading them into the ships. Then they also wanted to take some of our children because they know that they can trade them for good resources on their Galactic markets. They were going to take the children onto the ships to take them back there, but they only wanted those who were under 12.

A: *Do you know why that is?*

L: Something to do with the purity of their blood type. Once adolescence comes in, it is less malleable. In the younger children, there are more possibilities with the blood and the DNA to experiment with.

A: *So what happens? Do you all allow that?*

L: No, we are trying to fight this. We try to confer with higher Galactic authorities, and we tell these beings they did not have the rights or the sovereignty to do this. But they said they did not care, so we tried to hide most of the tribe. We successfully did in the caves, but they did manage to take some because there were so many more of them than there were of us

A: *When they are doing this, is there something that you could do as far as trying to fight back? What does that look like?*

L: We had bows and arrows that we were trying to use against them, but their technologies were much more aggressive than ours. Our weapons were mostly for hunting and not for blowing things up or mining, so it was difficult for us to fight back effectively.

A: *You said that they did manage to take some of the children?*

L: Yes.

A: *Keep moving the scene along. Tell me what happens next of importance?*

L: Later, we are trying to clean up the land where they had extracted the crystals from. We are watering the soil that has become arid, and we are trying to energetically repair the damages to the crystals that were taken out, so that the transmission can still be as clear.

A: *What do the big crystals that they took pieces from look like energetically?*

L: They are a mixture of white and light green, very shiny, bright aqua green, and white green. They are all inside the rocks of the canyons, but now there are big chunks missing. So the grid that they were transmitting has gotten broken, and that is not a clear shielding.

A: *Tell me what you are doing to try to repair them.*

L: We are using our hands, a bit like Reiki. We hold them over the holes and the chunks, and try to fill the holes back in, so the crystals can regrow themselves again. If we concentrate our energy through our hands for long enough, we can slowly rebuild the rocks and the crystals that were taken away.

A: *I know that you said you were trying to contact some kind of higher Galactics. What happened to them? Were you able to contact them before they did all this to you? Did they ever show? Did they ever assist?*

L: They came, but they came too late.

A: *How did they arrive? How did they get there?*

L: They came down. I do not know if there were ships or if they teleported in. They sent their deepest apologies for not stopping these beings. They had been trying to track the Centaurs -

whatever these hoofed war creatures were. They have been in a Galactic war against them. They came down to send their condolences for the visitation of these war beings, and said they had not done their duty properly. They had misread co-ordinates, and while they had been trying to deflect these war beings and deal with them in the outer Galactic regions, they had managed to slip through a breach in their grid system and come down onto our planet. But they assured us that they were doing what they could to repair the grid - the protective barriers of our planet - and also to return our younger tribe members who were taken, and they put out a call across their defense force to do this.

A: *What did these Galactic members look like?*

L: One was very tall. He wore a crimson robe, and had light gray skin, and a large head that expanded backwards, or a large brain, and sort of more diamondy eyes. A bit like fish. I can see the picture, but it is hard to explain. Then the other two were of a different Galactic species. One is a more fairy-type being, and the other is angelic.

A: *While they are there, do they do anything before they go?*

L: They kneel and offer a wreath, which is also in this crimson, burgundy color. They offered a wreath, a crimson wreath that was made of different minerals. The vibration of this wreath rock would help to remineralize the destruction of our soil on our planet and to help rebalance it. So it was a gesture of condolences from them.

A: *Once they are done, what do they do next?*

L: They want to quickly check the younger members of our tribe who are there. They are touching them on their heads to impart a message of safety, but maybe also to understand a bit better of what had gone on. They wanted to check that there was no psychological damage. They were curious about the residues in their brains.

A: *Did they abduct these children shortly, or how did they get hold of these children to do this to them?*

L: No, the ones that stayed because there was a connection. They were all interconnected. So, even though the ones that stayed were still affected by the ones that were taken.

A: *How do the children look since they are all interconnected, and they took them?*

L: They have little beams that run between their solar plexuses, and through this, they can exchange knowledge and learning. There were yellow beams that would go out from the solar plexus and sometimes go through the hoops, like different circles that ran around each body.

But in the younger members, they connected between each other, so they had their own system. But each system is connected with maybe twelve others, all the others around their age, and this was how they supported each other. Sharing was a part of their childhood on this planet.

A: They are connected within their own soul age. We will need to call forth for more reinforcement, as we are having technical issues on and off. So, at this point, I am going to speak to the Higher Self, and then we will come back to this further. I would like to speak to the Higher Self of Lara. We are looking for your assistance in this time and space during the session. If I can please speak to you now. Is this the Higher Self of Lara?

The Higher Self is called forth.

Higher Self: Yes, you can speak to me.

A: Thank you. Will you allow our Archangels to come and assist Lara during her session so that we can fix this communication issue? (unstable connection continues) Higher Self of Lara, if you can please protect the sacred space. Are we able to call any of the Archangels to assist right now, so we can start making her session stronger against internet infringement?

Higher Self: I also could not hear the rest of what you said. If we could call in our Archangels?

A: Yes. I was asking if we could call on the Archangels to assist with making this communication clearer. We do not normally have issues like this, so we would like to call for more reinforcements of Love-Light.

Higher Self: Yes.

The Body Scan begins.

A: Good. Which Archangels would you like for us to call forth on first?

Higher Self: Gabriel.

A: If you can connect us now to Archangel Gabriel. We would like to speak to Gabriel now.

AA Gabriel: Yes.

A: Greetings, brother, thank you. It is an honor to have you here. Gabriel, can you look into what is causing this malfunction in her internet connection?

AA Gabriel: There is an implant across her chest.

A: Is this implant causing interference in technology?

283

AA Gabriel: It is breaking the connection of the internet. It is not helping.

A: This implant, can we start using Phoenix Fire onto it so we can start transmuting it?

AA Gabriel: Yes.

A: Can you explain this implant to me? What does it look like?

AA Gabriel: It is like a fork or a pitch, a rake like a metal thing, that is chipped in across the heart, trying to scramble clear communication.

A: Let's go ahead and start transmuting this out now. We are using Phoenix Fire. Does this implant have a consciousness to it?

AA Gabriel: No, it is a machine.

A: We are transmuting it out now. Gabriel, is there anyone else you want to call forth to assist with this implant?

AA: Tapzekiel and Shariel.

A: Call forth on whoever the Higher Self allows now to start transmuting this out so we can make this connection stronger. Thank you. We honor you, love you, and respect you. Thank you for joining in the assistance here to help Lara start transmuting. We are transmuting this implant in her chest. Also, can you all scan her third eye? I am feeling a very strong congestion in myself, which is not normal for me. I am trying to figure out what this congestion is that I am feeling within her. Let's scan her third eye.

Archangels: Reptilian.

A: Let's contain the Reptilian there in her third eye with the symbols. Let me know when it is contained.

Archangels: Yes, but there is a transmitter.

A: Where is the transmitter at?

Archangels: Behind the third eye.

A: Does this transmitter have a consciousness attached to it?

Archangels: No, it sends radio signals back to something with a consciousness.

A: Let's go ahead and sever that connection to that consciousness and let's contain that transmitter. Start transmuting it out. Let me know when you have it contained.

Archangels: Yes, it is contained.

A: Good. Let's start neutralizing that out now with the symbols. Anything else in her head that we can assist with that is negatively polarized that is not hers?

Archangels: Yes, there is something towards the back right. It is a piece of metal.

A: *This metal, how can we remove it? Do we use Phoenix Fire, or do you extract it out?*

Archangels: We will extract it out.

A: *Good. Begin that process. Can we call forth on Archangel Raphael to start filling in with Love-Light, those areas we are healing already. Can we do that?*

Archangels: Yes.

A: *Thank you. We are transmuting, neutralizing that transmitter right now out of her third eye. Oh my gosh, I can finally breathe again. That was really strong. I have never had a reaction like that before. If I can ask for assistance for myself as well, because that has never happened to me before out of over 300 A.U.R.A. sessions.*

Archangels: Yes.

A: *Thank you. I can finally breathe and look, as I could not see anymore. All right, we are neutralizing. So we have the Reptilian in the third eye, we have the implant on the chest, removing the metal on the back of her head and then we also have that transmitter that we are removing in the back of her third eye.*

The healing continues...

Aurora: Can I continue to ask questions while you all do that?

Archangels: Yes.

A: *How is that implant looking on your chest right now?*

Archangels: We have to pull it out slowly so it does not tear the skin, but we are removing it, creating more space.

A: *Healing those areas, making sure there is no damage. When was that implant placed there on her chest?*

Higher Self: At birth.

A: *How did that come in during birth?*

Higher Self: With medications from the hospital that they gave her mother.

A: *The transmitter behind her third eye, how did that get in there?*

Higher Self: Four years ago.

A: *What was going on with her then that allowed for this to come in?*

Higher Self: She was not in her body. She was under the influence of recreational drugs, and they were able to sneak the transmitter in through that point.

A: Who was able to sneak that in?

Higher Self: Archons.

A: Who are we talking to right now?

Bartholomew: Bartholomew.

A: Thank you. So we are neutralizing that Archonic transmitter there. Tell me, what was the purpose of that? I know they explained that it was messing with the frequency. Why did they place that there? What were they using it for?

Bartholomew: To obfuscate and to confuse.

The healing continues; we find cords in the solar plexus and hooks in the third eye attached by Archons. The higher self and team find more attachments such as Earthbound entities, Archons, Reptilians, a warm entity, and a dark squid made by the Archons. All entities are assisted and metals, hooks and implants are transmuted out.

Here is an excerpt with advice from an Earthbound entity attached, once they have become of light:

Human Spirit: Yes, I am with the Light.

A: Wonderful. Do you have a message for her before you go?

Human Spirit: Be careful not to drown in your emotions. There are ways that you can work with them and learn to ride them, rather than have them swallow you up. What goes down comes up again. Use the emotions to your advantage. It can be great for you.

The Body Scan is complete.

A: Thank you. I have a couple of questions now that her body is clear. First of all, I want to thank all the Archangels. Thank you for all your assistance. We love you, honor you, and respect you. Can I please speak to the Higher Self of Lara?

Higher Self: Yes.

A: Thank you for helping us conduct such an amazing session. I have a couple of questions about that life you showed her. We were not able to conclude what was to happen next. So, if you are able to, just explain to us what happened next. As we saw, they were infringing upon the children. Anything else that you want to say about that?

Higher Self: Just about the inter-connectivity that is possible between young people, but also between Earth and humans.

A: What was this place? I know you called it Earth, was it Earth?

Higher Self: No, it was not Earth. It had a similar vibration and framework to Earth, but also different frequencies that are not currently accessible, and a similar atmosphere.

A: These Centaur beings. Were they actually Centaurs with horns?

Higher Self: No.

A: What were they?

Higher Self: They were projections of an Artificial Intelligence (A.I.) race. They are simulations!

A: What happened to those children that they took? Did those Galactics ever retrieve them back?

Higher Self: No, they were traded. They came back when they were much older, but they were not the same anymore. So much that had happened to them, that they were numb to accessing the same sensibilities that their tribe could. They are very disconnected.

A: How did that affect all the children? Because you mentioned that the other children were connected. If that happened to them, did that affect the children on this planet in some way?

Higher Self: Yes, because of this interconnection. That is also why they wanted to take some of them. They knew about this connection, and that if they traumatized some of them, that it would weaken and ripple into the ones that were not taken too, because they are all feeding from the same dream space. So they knew that they could create and take greater control by fracturing just some of the group. But it was harder to do this with adults because once they were adults, they were in more contained systems that were not as affected by each other anymore. The children were really porous.

A: What did they do with them? You said that they traded them. Who did they trade them to?

Higher Self: Scientists. Reptilian researchers.

A: How did this initially end up affecting this race, then?

Higher Self: It weakened their connection with the landscape and the environment which they were living in. Because they could not sense as clearly anymore, there was more confusion that came in, and the old ways were forgotten.

A: This planet that you mentioned had big clusters of crystals in it, and then that fake, artificial race came in and they broke apart pieces from that cluster of crystals. Within Earth, we also sit upon a bed of crystals. As you know, they use dynamite on the crystals from our land and fracture them. Can you tell us how that is affecting Earth?

Higher Self: It weakens the magnetic organic grids of Earth. The crystals, when they are aligned, are like a harmonic system. The frequencies are very harmonic. When these crystals get fractured and disrupted, the symphony of the grids becomes disharmonious. It is like the lines suddenly have these ruptures in them, where other things can come in. The filters and the kind of natural harmony and balance are not as resilient as they once were. The crystals have specific spots that they are meant to be in. They have grown very consciously in these places over time. So when they get displaced and disconnected, it is really like a circuit board being broken into parts and fragmented.

A: There are many of us who are spiritually awakened, and we love to buy crystals because they activate us. They help us feel good, they protect us, and they shield us. What would you say about that?

Higher Self: It is important that the crystals have been mined with permission consciously. There are different types. Some are like mother crystals. The main source ones that need to be left intact. Then there are other offshoots, which can be taken from without great effect. But that is why it is important that people understand the resonance and if they have permission to take or not take them. So we do not mind. It is alright when things are offshoots of the crystals and are worked with, because that is like the smaller fractals. But if you go back to the main crystal inside of the spiral, and take from the core spiral, then that is not alright.

A: As you know, humans are disconnected from this kind of understanding, so thank you for bringing it to our attention. The ones that are mining do not have respect in this manner. Are there any that have been taken from inside the core on Earth?

Higher Self: Yes, in Brazil. It happens by accident when large pieces of land are blasted to find core minerals.

A: What can we all do to assist Mother Earth, as we saw how disconnected that race got when this happened to their crystals? What can we do here?

Higher Self: We can also focus our energy, similar to how you would repair holes in your aura. We can focus our attention on consciously repairing the holes in Earth's aura. We can let the holes be repaired, and then things will find their own balance. It is also about slowing down the digging, cutting, and moving of things constantly.

A: Thank you. We will ensure that we work on that as a Collective. There are a couple of things that I need to touch base. I know she wanted her lower back to be healed.

The Body Scan is fully concluded. The Higher ensures the root attachments to why she had scoliosis and endometriosis are addressed and healed, so that she can bear children, if she wants to in the future.

A: Anything else that I could have asked that I have not that you want to talk to her about?

Higher Self: I think she knows she can talk to me directly anytime now that she has a clear connection. We can resolve anything together. I am here for her for whatever she needs.

A: Beautiful. Thank you for reminding her. Now that she has removed all these infringements within her, I am sure it is going to be even easier and clearer for her to connect to you.

Higher Self: She is so loved. All is unfolding in divine timing and perfection, and the magic is here and it is coming around her. We encourage her to keep envisioning and dreaming, bringing in the brightness, because it is only going to get brighter - everything - as we ascend.

A: Thank you for all these beautiful messages for her. We want to thank everyone once more who assisted her today. Love you, honor you, and respect you.

Higher Self: Love, respect, and honor you, too.

A: Thank you.

For every A.U.R.A. Hypnosis healing session we ask that the Higher Self and team ensure to remove and heal all as listed from the clients Tree of Life: entities (Grays, Mantis, Reptilians, Archons…), dark portals, repair and crystallize DNA, negative cords, technologies (implants, metals, hooks, wires, nano, vaccines), illnesses, vision, dental health, regrow teeth, age regress 5-15 years, blocked or misaligned chakras, open-up the third eye and activate abilities, expand heart, issues with auric field, fractured soul, contracts, deletion of inverted timelines, and trauma from current or past life.

END OF SESSION.

Thank you to this client from Berlin, Germany for delivering these memories and messages over to us. So much to be learned from others' experiences if self allowed. The location of every A.U.R.A. session is prime, as the land during the session provides the adequate vibration and frequency to achieve the ultimate goal and healing, that the Higher Self is assisting each client to accomplish. The divide that occurred between Russia and Germany during World War II, and the separation through the Berlin Wall was mirrored through this session, directly connected to the attack and separation of both their star children and the children of our Earth.

Separating and sectioning off parts of the German lands, with the Deep States ultimate goal was to create a divide to get their grasps on the children of Germany to begin the indoctrination of their new reformed schooling, and the mental abuse of both adults and children, blaming them for the Nazi war. I speak to people from Germany and they explain how as a collective, they are disempowered by being brought up with a mentality that they were the bad guys of the world, as in the now. They are scared to unleash their divine power to not harm another again.

During Fall/Winter of 2025 we will begin channeling [65]Adolf Hitler's Higher Self, as something feels distorted about what we have been programmed to believe of World War II. But what we do know in this time/space is that this land is targeted by the dark aliens because they know that the sacred Universal Law of Polarity is held in Germany and Russia, and to disturb and to cause imbalances in the natural polarities of the dark and light. If you were a bad guy, you would disturb the natural harmonics of Earth and the people. The Elites target this

---

[65] To watch this special channeling of Adolf Hitler go to Rising Phoenix Mystery School at www.aurapractitioners.com or Patreon, and sign-up the 'Extra Sensitive' series only found there.

location where the [66]Key of Polarities is held. The Stellar Gateway to unbalance the yin and yang, and the dark and light of Earth. Unbalance this and people become either too docile by only wanting to be love and light, or too enraged by the darkness that they want to destroy the self or other selves.

It was beautiful to hear of this race and their qualities, such as the cloak they wore that gave them attributes and abilities of a bird being. This is a whole other level to our animal totems and spirit animals that guide us on Earth. Similar to those movies when the human becomes the animal and gains all their strengths and beauties. How fun would that be! This is an example of one of the most incredible experiences to witness as a past life regressionist, to learn of the infinite possibilities of the extra-terrestrial races of the planets! This race is showing me now that the way that this cloak worked was that it was interconnected with the special crystal grid of this planet that powered up and gave them this superpower. This explains how when they disturbed the giant crystals, this began to diminish their abilities, as a rechargeable battery that is low on battery and no longer has a strong enough energy to power up what it needs to, that being the people of this planet.

The similarities that this planet had to the Grand Canyon area, such as Arizona and Utah, it seems at times that these different experiences that play out outside our Earth, so they mirror on our Earth. Being that our [67]Earth is the Multiverse, and that a combination of pieces of the planets create our crystalline construct Matrix of Earth. We will see different situations and energies from these pieces of planets play out here on our Earth too, being that they are interconnected through the lands. Could this planet have been one of those who seeded these red soiled lands of America. The answer is yes. The imprint we saw on our walls of the symbol was first drawn from their location which then echoed out into ours. Understanding this then the question is, "In what ways have the people and children of our Earth been affected, by what was done to these people from this planet remembered?" This can explain the vast

---

[66] To be aware of The Sacred Laws of the Universe, The 13 Keys, read Book 1 'Galactic Soul History of the Universe.

[67] To understand these expansive concepts of the Multiverse read Book 2 'Galactic History of the Multiverse - The Final Battle'.

distance and disconnect from the adults to the children of Earth, as if these age groups are operating from two different worlds.

Keeping in mind that our Earth is a multi-race of extraterrestrial souls incarnated, so if other planets have been targeted as this one, so too will that affect their race if incarnated on Earth, ultimately affecting the whole. Which means, that in order to get to us as a Multiversal created planet, they attack the planets in the Universe, because what they feel, we feel too. Which is why our guides and angels often tell us that when we heal ourselves so too do we assist to heal all the worlds on a multi-dimensional level. Because from here at the densest, we can reach the highest realms that are directly connected to us, overall lifting the density of us all. The more they attack these planets - the more that Earth can densify with that trauma caused - and back and forth to them as well if trauma is caused to us - just as the example of how connected these sentient beings were to their planet.

In the way that our sacred content rolls out daily and weekly is truly astonishing! Those who watch us live weekly or are part of the Rising Phoenix Mystery School know of this, for they have seen it with their own eyes. The hexagonal circle alchemy symbol as explained by Lara on (page 279) is wow! The first reason being is that through the divine work I do with the younglings - the star children - one of the children shared an Alchemy symbol with us given to her through a vision, explaining the importance of it to the water. This is truly incredible because the symbol that was shared to us in 2020 by this client, is the same symbol this young girl drew out for us during class, to remember in spring of 2025! I am near to completing 700 A.U.R.A. sessions, therefore my memory of each session is faint, as there is too much to log in my brain of each session. So this was a grand and exciting surprise as I prepared this chapter when I realized that back in 2020, the client was speaking of the same sacred Alchemy symbol the child shared with us this year in 2025!

And it gets even better! In June 2025 an A.U.R.A. practitioner, while traveling and healing the lands of Utah found this petroglyph (next page) drawn among other petroglyphs on the stoned walls of Utah! The petroglyph from that planet echoed into our Earth, therefore this confirms that we are seeing the actual drawing from their planet drawn here on our Utah stoned walls. Is that the true meaning to petroglyphs and why is it that they appear on our stone walls, besides the indigenous drawing them as well? Are they echoing out through the walls of stone, as the walls of the lands represent doorways into pockets of energies of other worlds' spaces? Like how when you are drawing a sketch on a notebook and you turn the page, the imprint of what you drew on the page above has left its mark on the page below. Which explains what happens above us at these higher dimensions, that this will shower down onto us like the imprint of the page below of the sketch.

The echo of your drawing cannot through quantum psychics stay on just one page because of Albert Einstein's Theory of Relativity. The Theory of Relativity explains that space and time are not absolute, but rather they are relative to the observer's frame of reference. This means that the laws of physics may appear different depending on the observer's position and velocity. For example, two different observers measuring the same event might observe different results due to their different frames of references from where they are viewing from. In other words, what vibration and frequency they are vibrating and oscillating to. This assists us to understand that those who choose to vibrate to victimhood, that is the reality they see, because that is the vibrational perspective they are choosing to see from.

Through this theory we understand that whatever is materialized in the proximity of the space it is within, will not be isolated in one still stagnant space as the speed of light; meaning motion is within all energy that has been converted into matter which equates to $E = mc^2$ (explained further below). The sketch is not able to be isolated to the one page, its environment, then other pages would archive the motion of the written ripple. Through the Theory of Relativity in one page, the drawing is sketched but in the next page, it is just the outline of the motion of the written action. What is divine plays out without force and only flow. To understand this sacred Alchemy symbol at the deepest levels, be sure to join our workshop, Part 9 to 'Unveiling the Mystics of Egypt - Divine Mother Hathor' course series, and to watch the Channelings of Albert Einstein sign-up to the Extra Sensitive Series found only at [68]Rising Phoenix Mystery School.

This symbol and all sacred alchemy symbols that we teach through our Mystery School are quantum physics formulated into written form. As Albert Einstein's Theory of The Speed of Light, $E = mc^2$, E = energy, M = Mass, and C = The Speed of Light, which translates into formulating the square footage of the being or matter you are measuring. Energy = Mass x Speed of Light. $E = mc^2$ is as if you would measure how much square footage in tiles you need to floor a bathroom. But it wouldn't just be the dimensions of the total tile, we would also need the total depth and weight to equate the mass of the total tiles, making up the equation transference of $E = mc^2$ for the tiles to be accurately floored. Perhaps this is where the handyman we hire goes wrong in completing the job correctly, lol! They are missing the formula!

Therefore, the benevolent Alchemy symbols of our Universe are formulas and equations to a complex problem or sum, but are translated and drawn out into symbols that are simplified

---

[68] At www.aurapractitioners.com or Patreon.

for our understanding to wield daily. They tell the story of the equation of the Alchemy symbol. The Alchemy symbols we teach provide a shielding over the meaning to the symbol into which it equates. For example, this symbol of the hexagonal wheel assists you to connect to the sixth dimensional waters that exist within all giant tree stumps, that we know of as waterfalls.

The water of the waterfalls are the carriers of the crystalline blueprint of the sixth dimension that we were about to ascend into, before we fell from the fifth dimension into the fourth dimension, during the Fall of Atlantis, and then the crucifixion of Yeshua bringing us further into the the third dimension that we are currently rising out from. The sixth dimensional blueprints that we were going to ascend into from the fifth dimension were preparing us, and of course, were already here before the Fall of Atlantis. The sixth dimensional blueprint had to be here because we were only one step away from ascension into the sixth dimension, so these sixth dimensional waters were beginning to gently oscillate our vibration to prepare us for ascension.

The reason why this symbol (page 279) is hexagonal or six sided is because it represents the sixth dimensional waters that were inside portaling through the giant trees back in Atlantis, in preparation for ascension. The giant trees are the birthers of these sacred waters, since they are the bridges of the ecosystem of the planet. Currently in May and June 2025 we are covering these sacred topics in our 'Extra sensitive' series, Remote Viewing the North Pole, found at Rising Phoenix Mystery School. Come join us live, if not, you can always watch the replay!

We can see very clearly in our Earth's history the occult behaviors of the Illuminati and their target upon the number six - which is rooted to the dimension we were about to ascend into in Atlantis - when we were in the fifth dimension preparing to enter the sixth dimension. They target this number to purposely hold back the collective from embracing the number six into the six dimensional collective ascension. The repeated 666 and the ways that they try to attach it to Satan or demons, claiming to do child and human sacrifice for this number, or such as standing six feet apart during their black magic blood rituals, or digging a body six feet under to try to tie the peoples' souls to Earth through their bodies for their harvesting needs.

When in actuality the number six - it is one of the most beautiful numbers of creation that represents the 'Tree of Life' - and how our souls thrive for expansion and knowledge. The number six is an Alchemy symbol. It is a circle and at the bottom there is an arch that is sweeping up into an ascended motion. The circle represents the cycle of life, and the arch represents how we break inverted cycles to ascend out into organic timelines in this third dimension.

Going back to the understanding of the Theory of Relativity, and how what is above us showers down onto us, as the echo of the imprint of the sketch. The Tree of Life is what gives life to all souls. Your soul within the ether births out from a flamed seed which becomes your individualized Tree of Life that is always connected to the Creator. What happens is that when you birth through a human family into the third dimension, you choose to birth in through their family tree, in order to obtain a physical vessel. This ties you to all who came before you, as your grandparents or parents and their karma, because they are located at the above branches of your typical family tree, as they came first. This is the main cause and hook to why people repeat their parents' problems whether they are mental, physical, emotional, or health related. Because those who came before you are showering down onto you their issues and problems through their oscillating vibration from their time/space. And, since there is no time technically, there is only the now within space, whatever they didn't work on and heal in their time/space is still actively hindering them from their now to your now.

The medical industry tells you that you carry your parents' irregularities because it is hereditary, but this is instead the truth of how the Quantum Physics of your existence on Earth works within the sacred knowledge of the Family Tree and your Tree of Life. So in order to become a complete sovereign being, one [69]must work quantumly in becoming their own tree, harnessing in from above through their soul connection to their original Tree of Life. As it is above, so it is below. But to do that, you must first unhook and release the tether to your Family's Tree of Life that you came in through. When doing so in that divine instant your Tree of Life that birthed you originally in Creation becomes you, and reconnects with you at a whole

---

[69] To accomplish this divine work we recommend for you to sign-up to a A.U.R.A. Hypnosis Healing, past life regression session.

other level not ever experienced before in our Earthly plane. No worries, as their Family Tree still exists by their choosing, because that is their level of conscious awareness and perception as the Theory of Relativity.

To visualize and build your Tree of life, during your Source Love-Light shielding as shared at the beginning of this book, you will sit within your own Tree of Life. You are at the center crown of the top of the branches of the Tree of Life, which means that it is only you who now creates your reality on Earth. With you, next to you, at the top of the branches sits your spouse, your children, and your animal companions. Together you now make up your sovereign Tree of Life untethered to anyone's perception and influence of what your life is and should be. Life at this point becomes much easier for both you and your family, by minusing all the drama that comes through your family's karmas from their choices. Understanding karma is simply added up to that karma is $E = mc^2$, energy = matter. Matter being negative or positive, which equates into karma.

The A.I. alien race made for deceit and war, disguised with an A.I. simulation technology to project the appearance of their elder ancestors, who looked often as Centaurs. Here is more data and confirmation for us of the Centaurs' benevolence in the Universe and on our Earth; and the ways that we spoke of how men were used to kill the Centaurs into extinction on our Earth in Chapter 9 when we walked through the Parthenon, Goddess Athena's temple. Teaching us that looks can be deceiving, one must not trust fully on just looks. One must look beyond the looks, and instead feel what one feels like in front of you, because within the feelings is where you will find the discrepancy of one's true form. So many imposters walk among us with these holographic projections overlaid on them, as spies for the A.I. Archons. An example being how Reptilians can pose as humans, as celebrities, or as politicians because they have an A.I. overlay over them that projects them instead as a holographic human in this Matrix simulation. Through your physical eyes you will only see the holographic projection, but through your third eye you will see what's beneath the illusion - their real alien form. There are spies among us, as written in Book 1 'Galactic History of the Universe' in Chapter 1, through the first Reptilian experiments on children to hybridize them into becoming A.I.'s double agents against human/humanoid races on our Earth and Universe.

This dark alien race's two main goals was one, to traffick the children of this planet and two, to retrieve this planet's giant crystals that held the grid of their planetary construct. Why take a chunk of these giant crystals of this planet? Let's go deeper into what the Higher Self said of the crystals, when she said "So the grid that they were transmitting got broken and that is not a clear shielding. It weakens the magnetic organic grids of Earth. The crystals, when they are aligned, are like a harmonic system. These frequencies are very harmonic. When these crystals get fractured and disrupted, the symphony of the grids becomes disharmonious. It is like the lines suddenly have these ruptures in them where other things can come in. The filters and the kind of natural harmony and balance are not as resilient as they once were. The crystals have specific spots that they are meant to be in. They have grown very consciously in these places over time. So when they get displaced and disconnected, it is really like a circuit board being broken into parts and fragmented."

This assists in understanding how important the giant crystals that grid each planet are, and when they are disrupted, this can create a rip and opening in the frequency emitting out, weakening the strength and forcefield of the unified field that the crystals create. Like an orchestra playing, if one musician is out of tune, or not in melody, it throws off the entire tune of frequency of the song. When the crystals are in harmonic accordance with one another, the cymatics is truly impenetrable. Cymatics being the sacred geometry that emits out through sound creating a mathematical equation and shape. You might have read or heard of the way water or sand reacts and morphs into shapes when a hertz frequency is being emitted onto it. This is Cymatics. Which assists us to understand why when the dark aliens land during planet invasions, why they often go directly to dig into the planet. Because they know that if they affect the planet and their crystals, so too do they affect the people.

On March 30th, 2025 I wrote this article through our [70]Newsletter "They Violate Mother Earth - Modified Weather", which compliments this understanding.

"The floods, earthquakes, and fires occurring on Earth are not natural nor is it the wrath of Mother Nature! It is instead an echo of the weather modification technology the Elites have

---

[70] Sign-up to our Newsletter at www.risingphoenxaurora.com.

their hands on. The dark aliens know that if they harm her by penetrating her with their laser technologies at specific tectonic plates, that they will cause an unnatural oscillating reaction, because it will force a vibrational wave to echo out and shake the surface of Earth.

They know that when violating Mother Earth in this manner that so too can they attack our minds and energies, as we are interlinked to Mother Earth, as the seeds of her Creation. What she feels we feel, and what we feel she feels. We were created from her elements, her soil, water, wind, and fire as sentient beings always tethered and never detached. Formed and grown from the lands as a tree, flower, or plant at the beginning of Earth within the Garden of Eden. We are the expressions of Mother Gaia and God/Source walking the Earth in a constant divine relationship with the environment and ecosystem that gives us lifeforce.

For the Deep State the easiest form to violate the people is to harm the land, because the land is emphatically connected to us, as we are to her. When violating Mother Earth, this violation is felt within us, just as she shakes beneath us we shake within. On these targeted days of supposed natural disasters you will see a heightened unbalanced emotion in the collective which affects our decision making. It creates an earthquake within us, and we may ask ourselves why do I feel so unstable within, or why are there more people making poor choices such as getting intoxicated today? They don't realize that these destructive thoughtforms are being imposed onto them by the harm to Mother Earth, then so too do they hurt. This low frequency of pain vibrates out onto us from her core as she screams, as a woman being raped.

Let us send love to all lands that have been artificially disturbed to get at us. Let us not forget that we are divine beings living our Multiversal experience, who do not consent to harm to us or our planets."

Lara said, "We are using our hands, a bit like Reiki. We hold them over the holes and the chunks, and try to fill the holes back in, so the crystal can regrow itself again. If we concentrate our energy through our hands for long enough, we can slowly rebuild the rocks and the crystals that were taken away." This is so important for us to remember and to act upon. If we all would join together at 1:11 our time (image on next page), no matter where we are in the world, we can focus our love and energy in healing, fortifying and strengthening our crystal grid so that there will be an immense shift on Earth in vibration and frequency for those who are ready. Join us during these sacred times to heal Earth and all lifeforms!

Heal Yourself & the Collective

10:10 ~ send love to all your past & future selves

11:11 ~ send love to self

12:12 ~ send love to all planets & life that require it in the Universe

1:11 ~ (13th hour) send love to the Earth & all life on it, people, plants & animals

2:22 ~ send love to your beloved ones

3:33 ~ send love to your dreams & aspirations for their fruition & manifestation

4:44 ~ send love to the New World Order (to transmute it)

5:55 ~ send love to the children of Earth & Creation

WWW.RISINGPHOENIXAURORA.COM

I asked, "What can we all do to assist Mother Earth, as we saw how disconnected that race got when this happened to their crystals? What can we do here?

Higher Self: We can also focus our energy, similar to how you would repair holes in your aura. We can focus our attention on consciously repairing the holes in Earth's aura. We can let the holes be repaired, and then things will find their own balance. It is also about slowing down the digging, cutting, and moving of things constantly."

We conclude this chapter and book with the most important topic of Creation, the protection and safety of the children, no matter the dimension. Lara said, "Then they also want to take some of our children because they know that they can trade them for good resources on their Galactic markets. They were going to take the children onto the ships to take them back there, but they only wanted those who were under 12 years old. Something to do with the purity of their blood type. Once adolescence comes in, it is less malleable." To heal what was done to these children we must review the inversions projected onto the children of our Earth. And to do that, we must begin from when the children enter this Earth through the hospitals. Our souls have always known that something was not right about hospitals' procedures on birthing children, and their inverted by design intentions. How many souls have the hospitals compromised during their development, or at birth into our Earth by the traumas and violations of sacred Universal laws, that the mothers and children experience during sterile hospital births?

As I slept one night in 2020, at the beginning of the COVID-19 virus before the COVID-19 Vaccine rollout, I was shown a dream where I saw thousands of expecting mothers walking around with other humans, both on Earth and other parallel Earths. The brave mothers who had volunteered during these tribulating times of conceiving the Universe's most powerful Star Children. What stood out about them was that when you looked at their pregnant bellies, they had bruises all over them. It looked as if bullets had been shot to the babies in their wombs leaving an imprint of bruising on the mothers skin. However, it was not physical! These bruises were representations of the energetic attacks the babies receive the minute they find themselves conscious in their mothers wombs. That's what these bruises represented - the times that they had been shot at with negative intentions or energies from others. The pregnant mothers walked around so heavy and exhausted from these constant energetic attacks, having no idea what was going on. Which explains much on why an expecting mother is always so tired - needing constant sleep - as the body heals as it sleeps. It brings me to tears to know that these babies are enemy No. 1 to the Archons and ill intended beings, and that they are being harmed and violated in this manner. Barely given a chance to be born.

When understanding all of this, it truly is a miracle that somehow the children still prevail, and manage to be birthed out by their mothers, especially in a hospital environment. This places the understanding at another level on how brave the *babies* and *we* are, to agree to incarnate, and to stick with it all the way through until we are born, anchored, and grounded into Earth. This is why many just don't make it all the way to birth. Some are [71]abducted in the

---

[71] For more read the article 'A.U.R.A. Abducted From Within The Womb' at www.risingphoenixaurora.com.

womb, as explained in our articles on our website. Some babies just can't condense their light enough to birth because of the extremities of the traumas they experience during hospital births, entering this lowest vibration and dimension.

There are negative polarized beings on Earth who know how to harvest the power of an unborn child's light by Archonic downloads given to them. Voodoo witch doctors, dark shamans, and negative polarized entities in people can use the children's light for their manifestation of dark magic spells, if the mother does not know how to shield and not consent daily. Through their tools of black magic inverted rituals, they are able to focus on non-shielded mothers carrying life, and siphon the infinite pure light of their babies. And with this stolen life force they create 'service to self' acts, of spelling someone to fall in love, attracting money, and whatever unbalanced desires need to be fed for them... and more. These dark shamans and witches use the energy of unborn children like when they kill an animal through ritual for the life that is within the animal, which is at the highest light and purity. Through the quantum world they drain and take that light of animals or children to invertedly manifest this for themselves.

This is truly sickening that another would do this to an unborn baby or innocent animal life. If these organic souls only learned to look within, instead of being guided by soulless Archons, then they would simply know that within them there is a fountain of infinite Source light, and there is no need to harvest or cultivate this from other selves. Our signature creational light is only found when looking and connecting from within, because the Creator is found within.

Through our clients A.U.R.A. sessions we have found that doctors are often negative polarized Reptilians (as shared through this session). Doctors have an A.I. simulation overlay over them hiding their true form. The doctors or any person, period, should not be the first to touch the children as they emerge from their mother's womb or during their pregnancy, as when they do so they are dimming the children's light. When they touch, the mothers are then allowing for the Reptilians in disguise, or persons with strong entities attached to enter their auric field and their babies without any boundaries of 'not consenting against harm.' It can be as a poison that enters and clouds the mother, and compromises the child into a lower vibration for an opening to energetically or psychically attacking them.

No one but the mother should touch the baby in the womb, especially as the child emerges from the birth canal. Exceptions being the father and the baby's siblings, if they are a clear vessel. Only the mothers hands are a matching high vibration to the child's soul, as she has been the carrier and holder of their baby and their accustomed vibration. Therefore, *they* should be the first, and only, for some time touching the child as it births forth. The mother should be the first touch as their crown emerges from her birth canal, and she should be the one that pulls the baby out and lays them on her chest. This maintains the mother and child in sacred union at highest vibration of Love-Light, the child at their purest of essence, and least amount of trauma.

There are many positive doctors that are truly saving lives everyday, including those who have finally spoken the truth of the COVID-19 vaccine, and we are infinitely thankful for them and their divine work! For those negative doctors the question is what happens to them when they are studying and receiving their degrees?

They don't all begin as Reptilians in human bodies, so what turned them? The indoctrination of their PhDs, and of their supposed 'service to others' teachings, play the biggest role in their densification, going farther than we realize in rewiring their brains into instead being submissive and robotic to the programs they handed them to perform.

At some point during their residency they become compromised, creating a contract, or selling their soul away for the inverted purpose to be the channels of energetically feeding the negative polarized entities by performing human experimentation through sacred birthing, or the other experimental, inhumane procedures that they act upon humans of all ages; including knowingly drugging their patients by subscribing them painkillers that are actually opioid heroin, without telling them what these prescription drugs truly are. By the time their patient finds out, it is too late as once they take these drugs they are addicted, which seems like for life. My clients who take opioids have explained that heroin is actually easier to get off in comparison to medically prescribed opioids that seem to be forever hooked, because of the way that these drugs attach to the body through artificial means, creating an addictive need that can never be fulfilled unless you are high on opioids. Placing their patients into a downward trapping of addictions that can easily take their life, because of the deterioration these cause to the vibrant health of an organic human body.

The Archons feed off the sacred birthing through their Archonic procedures by ensuring the child experiences the highest trauma possible under the guise of "That it is for their own good!", allowing for all the attachments to be able to penetrate. We must now speak of these traumatic procedures done unto babies to begin the endings of the infringements of hospital births. The human mutilation of cutting the mother open through a C-section, extracting the baby out suddenly from a mothers womb versus a sacred organic vaginal birth where the child chooses when to enter Earth. By being cut open and pulled out, this trauma slows a baby receiving the highest crystalline light into their DNA, which is meant to be received and integrated into the baby's spine when going through the sacred birthing canal through the journey of traveling down the mothers spine.

How they rapidly sever the cord from the mother to child, rendering the mother unanchored and feeling numb towards her baby. This is another black magic inversion simulation. When an Archonic person, or negative polarized Reptilian channeling out, instantly cuts the baby's umbilical cord from the mother, it represents a severing of the mother and child's organic life cord together. They are not able to fully sever their life cord, however, the trauma and damage is there until healed together through their sacred bond. The reason mothers end up with postpartum depression is because through these many clinical procedures, they have been deprived and violated from their divine sacred connection to their seed - their babies. Rendering them null and discounted from their heart and love for their child.

The pain that newborn children experience is saddening! The traumas of the mutilations such as the penetration onto them through implants inserted into them, and are injected into them through immunizations that cause further A.I. control. They are violated through sexual trauma, as the foreskin of their penis is cut off, through the circumcision on male babies. The Reptilian doctors feed off the light of this violating act upon the child, and during this procedure the mother is nowhere to be found to protect the child, being that they are back in their hospital room, as they are cutting away on the child's sacred energy. The child is taken to a sterile hospital room, where it is only the doctor and nurse that perform this act upon the child. The trauma of the light infused sacral energy consisting within the baby's foreskin, is used for the Illuminati's rituals for their drug addiction on Adrenochrome.

At a supposed regular doctors, visit the staff penetrates and rapes the child annally, as they take their temperature with a thermometer up their anus. Explaining further, how at times, children are born with an instinct of not being able to trust the world and their families. Because upon their entry, their parents (who were their guardians) showed them how - through all the trauma they experienced - this is what was to be expected when incarnating into this world. Causing a distinct disconnect between the children and the parents' sacred bond. Ultimately, harming the child's natural form of heart discernment throughout their life, because of these overwhelming energetic violations and traumas so early on in their developing infantile stages.

Which brings us to this session in the ways that they human trafficked the children to perform experiments on them, and then the children made their way back but it was too late, they were too damaged. These A.I. entities purposely kept them alive - but first they broke them down - to ultimately weaken this alien race.

As Lara's Higher Self explained, "A: What happened to those children that they took? Did those Galactics ever retrieve them back?
Higher Self: No, they were traded. They came back when they were much older, but they were not the same anymore. So much that had happened to them, that they were numb to accessing the same sensibilities that their tribe could. They are very disconnected.
A: How did that affect all the children? Because you mentioned that the other children were connected. If that happened to them, did that affect all the children on this planet in some way?
Higher Self: Yes, because of this interconnection. That is also why they wanted to take some of them. They knew about this connection, and that if they traumatized some of them, that it

would weaken and ripple into the ones that were not taken too. Because they are all feeding from the same dream space. So they knew that actually they could create and take greater control by fracturing just some of the group. But it was harder to do this with adults because once they were adults, they were in more contained systems that were not as affected by each other anymore. The children were really porous."

This knowledge assists us to understand how it is that the violations to children at such a young age can affect the collective of humans of Earth as well.

Let's understand what Adrenochrome is. Our bodies consist of seven major glands, though there are more. This is the Endocrine system that keeps our hormones and energies in balance. Why is this important? Here is why. Let's look at it from a light harvesting point of view, similar to what is shown in the movie "The Matrix." Those who allow to be used within [72]inverted Matrixes are battery generators for the negative polarized entities, as the Archons are not capable of producing their own light organically.

When a person experiences trauma, the natural crystalline formations within the blood gather at these seven major glands of these energetic focus points. This concentrated crystalline energy within the blood of these locations in the body, are a matching component to adrenaline. This is why this blood drug is called Adrenochrome, as it is the concentrated adrenaline of a soul's light. All these glands combined crystalline energetics, are harvested and drained from the human body.

An infant being at its highest potency because of the purity and strength of their Source light. This creates the blood drug Adrenochrome. This is directly harvested through human trafficking and sexual trauma abuse, and then satanic sacrificial rituals through the murder of children and adults. Which assists us to understand how important our current Presidential Administration is, that they are not openly harvesting and trafficking children and young adults in this way, as our past Presidential Administration was such as Joe Biden, Kamala Harris,

---

[72] As explained in Book 2, 'Galactic History of the Multiverse - The Final Battle', the history of what Archons really are,

Barack Obama and the Clinton's. Currently they are instead going after those who have committed these heinous acts in the past and the now.

I once was speaking to an A.U.R.A. Hypnosis Healing student who was a former nurse. For a decade she helped deliver babies in the hospital. During the procedures of assisting children birth, the nurses were given specific instructions on what they were to do with the placenta. After the mother birthed out the placenta, they were to place it in a special plastic bag that then went into a freezer, as if it was food to be kept fresh. She then said that there were weekly crews that would come out and dispose of the hospital's hazardous wastes. When she asked if they were taking the placentas, she was told that that was an entirely different group that would pick them up. Giving the assumption that the children's placenta are not disposed of or hazardous waste. Then, what significance truly does the placenta represent to the hospitals?

She felt that there was something really off about this group that would pick up the frozen placentas. Unbeknownst to her, she was collecting the infant blood food, providing feedings for the negative Reptilians and dark aliens in human bodies. The other thing that was a red flag for her was when a mother asked for the placenta to be taken home with the family. The nurses were instructed that the family would have to sign several documents, and the parents were really given the runaround for wanting to take it with them.

Once we come into awareness, it is only when we learn to forgive all harms, that we then release ourselves from any inverted karmic or repeated cycles of the A.I. Archon wars. We are not here to continue the making of these Archonic wars, we are here to end them, and our love and forgiveness is the key. For love can never be fed off! It only becomes our barriers and strength instead. Our intentions through this gigantic book series, literally Tartaria gigantic (lol), is that these violations disguised as goodness for ourselves and the children will be released and will come forth organically surfacing for the collective's most impactful disclosure on awakening humankind.

This is the only way we can stop the imposed resets that the Earth's seen over and over - such as Tartaria - the intelligent and brave people who walked before us. We unveil the Elites' negative intentions to instead create and bridge in the divine benevolence that we are all made up of. Everyday as we walk among the children, they are who teach us these lessons. Let us all now humbly bow and send love to the collective of children of Earth and Creation.

We end this transmission with the reminder that these children who have volunteered to be birthed in this time/space, and the generations to come are warriors. These light warriors will hold the wall strongly and energetically, and will not take it anymore! What we can take from these tribulations imposed upon us as adults from Earth, is that through our children, and grandchildren we have bred warriors and survivors - not victims!

We humbly thank the children for their selfless service, and those too that came forth before them - our ancestors who took the biggest challenges - so that we could walk lighter. These Star Children are able to incarnate in the high potency of light because WE the first, second, and third waves of volunteers incarnated first, taking on and transmuting the violations of all kinds within the Elite societal programming, so that the Star Children can now come into the Earth's collective energy, that is more of a high vibrational match to their soul essence. Allowing them to enter at their highest light and soul activation. The last time we saw this in Earth's history were the epic times of Atlantis, when we walked fully activated by being embodiments of our Higher Self Avatars. For these very children, is how we conclude our final chapter to Book 1. To begin the surfacing of these inhumane violations against us as younglings, and the children of the now, and their purity, and their strong sovereign missions ahead.

THIS TIME WE WILL NOT ALLOW FOR THEM TO RESET US THROUGH THEIR VACCINATIONS, MUDFLOODS, AND WEATHER MODICATIONS! THIS TIME WE STAND STRONG TOGETHER! TARTARA lives within us - and shall never be forgotten - as we daily walk over the TARTARIAN peoples' mudflood footsteps. Through their petrified - not forgotten footsteps - we unpetrify! We rewrite and birth in the organic timelines of Earth.

"It is time we remember, and step into our sovereign mission and divine power of becoming the guardian protectors of the children. As the children of this Earth and the Universe, are the carriers and fruition of our future organic timelines, and they are the embodiment of Ascension."

"To protect the children, we protect the timelines, which protect ascension."

~AuroRa♥

--------------<<>>--------------

CONCLUSION

CODA: LOVE, SOVEREIGNTY, AND REMEMBRANCE

-------------<◇>-------------

For those who have watched our many series and many videos - whether you watched them live weekly or you binged watched them - this series has been the most catalyzing for us all. With every episode delivered weekly and monthly, with each episode since November 2022, we have unveiled our eyes and unraveled the world around us. This is the conclusion to this book, but truly, it is just the beginning as we are nearing ninety episodes aired and more to come on our channels. Truly we have just begun! These first eleven episodes were the grand foundation needed to this tremendous book series, and we have learned that with any home with a strong foundation, you can build a gigantic Tartarian castle over it.

In our current time of summer 2025, we have gone so deep into Tartartaria and Antarctica that it is truly astonishing! Every week we are at the edge of our seats as we discover the ways that the next puzzle pieces to Tartaria come together. What our viewers and readers love and say is so special about our Tartaria knowledge with the facts where we cover many perspectives - quantumly and energetically - making sense of this data. The world of wonder of Tartaria is better understood! Our hopes are that you will join us through our weekly livestreams as well. Even those who never missed a video live, are reaching another level of understanding of awareness, by reading this content that they originally watched on video.

The experience of delivering word for word of this series has been tremendous! I have remembered with you! I have laughed with you! I have cried with you! I was furious with you! Every episode and every chapter of this series has pushed me to question the world around me. I especially thank my previous profound years of work through my other video series and books that transmuted what was needed to be, so that we could remember the clues left behind from our ancestors - The Great Tartarian people.

There is no telling the number of books this series will have. Our intentions are to publish one or two of these books yearly! We humbly thank you for your love and support, for purchasing this book, and for spreading the truth of Antarctica and Tartaria. The excitement is exhilarating to know that you have just begun, and to know of what you are about to rediscover, as you dive deep into this series! There is so much to share with you, but I will be patient and wait until you continue to read this book series, chapter by chapter, or watch this series episode by episode!

Your infinite potentials of self-healing are awaiting you! Come become an A.U.R.A. Hypnosis Healing practitioner, through our live in-person Retreats and live Online Workshops, or have an A.U.R.A. session conducted!

Come embark on your journey into the Universe and Multiverse!

"A healthy intelligent mind questions its environment until it is able to make sense of it. A mind that is told what to believe is one that can no longer form intelligence, instead it just follows submissively a program."

I love you, I honor you, and I respect you.
~ Rising Phoenix AuroRa

-------------<◇>-------------

ABOUT AURORA

Founder of A.U.R.A Hypnosis Healing & Rising Phoenix Mystery School | Spiritual Revolutionist | Oracle | Galactic Historian

There is nothing more beautiful than knowing that you are connected to the infinite wisdom within you, and that you have always been. This is what I strive to do for others, to remind them of their gifts awaiting to be remembered and reawakened, once more within.

We can receive as many readings, or healings as we desire, where someone else tells us who we are, and whom we have been. However, it is not until we allow that inner voice that whispers within our hearts to actively speak, that we begin our true transformation, and our true remembrance of our soul; when we deeply connect through theta hypnosis and the meditative brain waves of our consciousness to our soul, our higher self, and our hearts. This in turn activates within us the inner knowing that love is all, for love is the very life force that runs through the veins of Creation.

I am looked upon as a mysterious person, because of how selective I am of what I share of myself personally. Today, I will share more than I have ever, of myself. As many star children born on Earth, I was never normal, nor did I fit in. In fact, I questioned everything, perhaps not all out loud, but within my consciousness. When observing my environment and my upbringing, I realized that just about all of it made no sense to me. So, let's begin from my birth point on Earth. The woman who carried me when she was far along in her pregnancy, was told by the doctors that there was no heartbeat, and that she had lost her child. Except, a little voice told her that she would still birth a child. One of my first memories was of watching my angels seeding me into the womb of the person who carried me, after the first soul exited. I/my Higher Self ensured that I would not be born in a hospital, so the women who birthed me did so in the car, on their way to the hospital. As an infant, days old, I was fully conscious and aware of my little body, upset by the ways that my body would not get up and walk for me.

When I explained to my family of the memories I had of the first home we lived within, I was told that there was no way I would have memories of this home, as I was a newborn in this home, which we shortly moved from. I remember my little bedroom was in front of the kitchen, and at a couple days old, I had telekinesis. So as I slept, especially at night, the electrical utilities would go off, pots and pans would move, and the lights would flicker, on and off on their own. My angels hired a ghost to claim that it was them who was the poltergeist moving objects around, so that my parents would not realize I had telekinesis, until my guides shut down my abilities.

Growing up, I could feel and hear peoples' negative intentions. As a child, I did not understand how peoples' minds worked so negatively! So, more and more, I withdrew myself from the world, never talking to anyone, shielding myself from everyone, and their dark energies. The streets I grew up in Chicago were dangerous, full of gangsters, drugs, and hookers. But for the most part, our parents ensured that we stayed away from these inversions. As a child of about 6 to 8 years old, I remember being friends with a little girl, close to my age, who was supposed to be a close friend. One day, as we were playing up front of our house, where we typically were never unattended outside, but this day no-one was there. I looked across the street and saw my friend coming at me, with eyes that were not of hers. She had picked up a glass liquor bottle, as they were all over the streets. She broke it and began to swing it at me, trying to cut me, or kill me. I did not back down as a little girl, because I had to fight to keep myself alive. So I fought her, and dodged all her attempts to try to cut me, and I was not going to back down, even though she had cornered me in a nook of a brick wall. There was this little boy neighbor who came out of nowhere, and said "Walk away. I will handle this." So I did. I remembered this little boy had a crush on me, and tried to kiss me once. He had blonde hair and blue eyes, and now I know that he was a fractal of Archangel Michael, who has always been watching over me as he does for all. At such a young age this taught me that I was most likely not going to be able to have friends, especially if a child could become spirit possessed that easily, and to try to take me out in my younger years. Boys I could talk to, but girls I couldn't. They would turn on me, and would want to harm me.

In grammar school, the bullying began. A girl who was obese, double my size of maybe 70lbs then, decided one day that according to her, she would kick my butt. But, instead she did not know of my speed, and that I punched. So instead, I was victorious at defending myself, while others were puzzled by what they had just witnessed. Again and again, into my junior high years, girls always hated only me, because I was pretty and the boys liked me. The girls would chase me everyday after school, and would try to physically beat me up. Again, someone positive would always be placed in my path who would assist me to get away. But when I had to, I would not let myself get beaten. Instead I would defend myself and stop them in their tracks. I had a girl once accumulate a big honker in her mouth, and spit it on my face. Still I never let any of it faze me, which is why it pissed off the Archons more and more! In many forms, I numbed myself and built the strongest force field, so that even if others - whether family or strangers tried to harm me physically, mentally, or emotionally - *IT* never reached me. Until, finally, in my freshman year of high school, I met my beloved husband, who goes by the name of Zen. Once he came into my world, everything shifted, and I felt so loved and protected.

Though we were not immune to the hardships of growing up together in this world, we always had love, and that love is what kept us going. Even though I have my beloved with me, this doesn't mean that those who mean harm will not try, because they still try to bully me and gang stalk me. I know that they are just demonically possessed by *IT!*. And because of this, they do not affect me, because I know that they are just being used as puppets. So instead, I sent all these haters love, in the hope that one day they will realize that their behaviors were Archonic by design, and that they will wake up with enough time to complete their inner work, and to Ascend out with the collective.

Archangel Michael showed me through dreamtime, within the last year, a beautiful space of light located outside of time and space. Where all of the people who had crossed my path, whether hateful or loving, especially those who were repelled by my high vibration of Source Love-Light, were within this space. There were teachers, mailmen, students, friends, family, ex-bullies, and people who just passed by me on the street. Each and every single person who came within a proximity of being near my energy, were there speaking of me, and, each and every single person spoke of me so beautifully. Some said, "I played with her in a playground once. I was her classmate. She met eyes with me and smiled at me while walking down the street. I was her teacher. She once stood up for me against another…" Archangel Michael explained to me, that even though some of these people were not the kindest to me, my infinite love had left an imprint in their lives, and that every single one of these people who got to meet me in person, were blessed because through the Source Love-Light that I embody. They were given the chance to remember who they truly were. and if they so choose, they are within reach of awakening and ascending out with us all. So even though these people tried to harm me, I sent them the most infinite wave of love and gratitude. Because of them, I became stronger. Every time they tried to knock me down, I got back up. I told myself that I would be the opposite of what they were. So when the public began to come to me for sessions and certifications, I kept my promise that I would never forget that they too had gone through these forms of oppression in their lives; and that, just as I promised myself long ago, I would never be like those oppressors. This allows me to bridge the most highest unconditional Source embodiment of infinite love for others here on Earth. So in many ways, these vengeful people were my inspiration to aspire to be the infinite love I am today for others. Which assists us to understand that, so too have you had people like this in your journey on Earth, who you have assisted to wake up. They are blessed to have known you, or will come to know you, as well.

Which brings us to, finally, my career as a spiritual revolutionist and past-life regressionist. My official spiritual path began in January 2017, through a practice hypnosis session I spontaneously conducted on my husband. Through this session the Ra Collective surprised us by speaking through him explaining some of what was to come, and saying that "There was someone near and dear to my heart that would love to speak to me." When I asked who that was they said, "Dolores." At that point, one month prior, I had begun to read a book of Dolores' that gave me an understanding of who she was. Through this practice past-life regression session, the Ra Collective and Dolores gave me a little - but very needed - instruction on what was to come. They mentioned that they had been waiting for this moment in time - for what seemed like an eternity - to talk to me. I didn't quite understand what that meant. I was puzzled at their statements and the infinite love that they were expressing towards me, as I did not remember them, as they did I. It must be so interesting and entertaining from the other side, from beyond the veil, where they view all infinitely. They know exactly who we are, when we are in complete amnesia, and even then, when they tell us who we are, we are often in extreme denial of this information!

Beginning from this monumental point-in-time of my husband's past life regression session, which marked the blossoming of my pronounced spiritual growth, this catapulted me into a great awakening. Not knowing that my husband was somnambulistic, when he came to, we realized that not only did he not remember any of the session. These benevolent beings had spoken through him clearly, without human consciousness or ego in the way. We also both had no idea who Ra was, except for the concept that they were some kind of 'Sun God' from Egypt, as we had read on the Internet. However, we have learned much of who the Ra Collective are through all our channelings and sacred teachings.

As I continued to work within myself, deprogramming from the falseness of the disempowerment around us, I began to remember more and more of who my soul truly and organically is. With every breathing moment, I regained my past-life memories, my light, and my consciousness back to my highest potential. Operating from a high vibration of heart and love, I remembered who I AM beyond the veil. Though I am humbled, it is important that we do learn to accept who we are as multi-faceted divine beings. Because otherwise, we are denying our true infinite divine power and expression. This is something that *we* can only do within, releasing the falseness created around us when someone acknowledges or talks about themselves, we automatically assume it is egoic. This foreign, oppressive programming of self-confinement is Archonic; being that it does not serve the Archons' agenda for us to remember, and to wake up and accept our true divine soul Source expression. So long as a being is able to speak of oneself, in a manner that allows others to see their reflections from within that being, that is a sacred way to be. To hate, cyber bully, or to troll someone, because they are living their full embodiment of Source expression, is to do the Archons' bidding for *IT*, and *IT's* need to oppress the spirit.

This is why we inspire to empower all, to remember oneself, and then share oneself in love for our other selves. Because, as we continue to grow and share individually, so does the collective. As we regain our light piece-by-piece, that light then becomes a matching vibration of a memory that is next to be activated, downloaded, or integrated into us divinely. Bringing us closer to the Ascended Master vibrations of Yeshua, Mother Mary, Buddha, Isis, Cleopatra…

At the end of 2017, I went from being Aura, to being addressed as AuroRa when I experienced a divine walk-in. Aura is a fractal that birthed forth from Archangel Aurora within Creation. While Aura played a dancing game with her children, she started feeling I/Aurora coming forth, descending like a shooting star. Being carried and embraced by the Prime Dragon of Purity of the element of Source's white infinite Love-Light. This Dragon of Purity flew through the veil with my soul (AuroRa) in her embrace. She energetically brought my soul down to Aura, and then Aurora/I, integrated into the vessel. I kept all of Aura's memories of her family, and all of her experiences of being human. Aura's soul then left as she had completed her mission marvelously, ascending out into the New Earth and the Promised Land, to her predestined organic timeline. I then became AuroRa - with ONE predominant mission - to create A.U.R.A. Hypnosis Healing to assist Mother Earth, and the fruition of the collectives Ascension timeline, and here we are!

> **"I encourage all to remember who you were,
> who you are,
> and who you are meant to be.**
>
> **As I AM, Archangel AuroRa❤"**

YOUR SOUL'S GROWTH JOURNEY

We live in a world where we have been taught since birth that we are limited, that there is nothing beyond death, or that only heaven and hell exist. We are being told that our imagination is not real, while being distracted by our daily, monotonous routines. In a world where, if we get ill, we might not ever find a cure for it, or we will have to be on an ongoing cycle of prescription drugs or surgeries. Have you ever felt deep within your soul that this just does not feel right?

Come discover the world of who you truly are, and who you have been in past or future lives! The world of Quantum Healing through A.U.R.A. Past Life regressions, Spiritual Development classes, and weekly live videos on all our channels.

Have you ever wondered about your own soul journey? Perhaps you have been a queen or a king, a magical creature or animal, a well-known person in history, or you have had a life in Egypt or in Atlantis, on a different planet or are of an alien race. The majority of people have lived hundreds or thousands of lives at different times upon Earth, or other realities in Creation. There is nothing more beautiful than knowing that you are connected to the infinite wisdom within you and that you have always been. This is what I strive to do for others, to remind them of these gifts awaiting to be reawakened once more.

As a Spiritual Worker of the heart, in service-to-others, I offer several different types of energy healing services and spiritual development courses to aid you in your soul's growth of self-healing and self-attunement. If you feel guided to do so, you can start your growth journey with the following services mentioned on the next page.

To see each soul blossom into their highest and most beautiful expression in Creation is a true gift, and this is what inspires me to do this work!

Thank you for following your heart to mine!

I love you, I honor you, and I respect you.

In service-to-others.

~ AuroRa♥

GLOSSARY

- **Activation** – is when there is an attribute, ability, or memory that lays dormant, waiting for the human and energy bodies to achieve its matching vibration of light. When it does, it unlocks organically allowing the individual to now integrate it and access it.
- **Akashic Records** – is where the memory field and history of all souls are located. This is where an individual soul travels to obtain their remembrance from past, future, and higher and lower dimensional realms.
- **Alchemy** - is the ability to create or transform elemental and etheric energy into manifestation, whether this is in physical or energetic.
- **Archangels** – are the first fractals of Source within Creation, containing the highest potency of purity within their individualized Source expression.
- **Archons** – are soulless beings manifested from the material of artificial intelligence. Not from our Source, nor our Universe.
- **Ascension** – collective ascension is when the collective of souls reaches the highest organic light possible on Earth, and when doing so, Mother Earth finally shifts, leaving the physical behind, going into the fifth dimension as organically conceived.
- **Ascension** – individual ascension is when an individual reaches maximum light potential, bridging themselves to operate, instead, in the organic matrix, achieving karmic balance, and a combination of service-to-others. When doing so, all missions are completed on Earth, causing the individual to no longer need to assist on Earth. The soul then exits out the inverted Artificial Intelligence (A.I.) matrix choosing to enter the fifth dimension, or traveling back to the dimension they came from, or returning back to Source.
- **Astral Body** – is the spirit of a being in its etheric form, who is one with the Universe in the Quantum Realm, free of the physical body.
- **Bifurcation** – when the organic Earth will completely release out from the artificial matrix. Until then, the organic Earth will continue to pull herself away, little by little from the inverted part of the Earth.
- **Constellations** - to our known skies. There are eighty-eight constellations that consist of a cluster grouping of stars. However, constellations and Creation are infinite.
- **Constructs** – is the framework of all that is. Like a chalice that holds water within.
- **Cabal** – are the Illuminati's henchmen that do their bidding of criminal and tyrannical work, partaking in the negative programming of the collective on Earth.
- **Channel/Channeling** – is when we achieve a calming vibration that allows us to benevolently connect to our Higher Self aspects or benevolent beings such as guides and angels. When we speak divine wisdom that seems to flow and come from a higher source.
- **Deep State** – is the diabolical plan of the Illuminati that is a combination of many parts throughout such as: depopulation of the Earth, mind control, oppression of the spirit, religions, orchestrated wars, insertions of A.I., and metals within the human collective.
- **Dimensions** – are the different vibrational planes of existence that hold together the entire collective of all planets and star clusters of life. The dimensions place all lifeforms into their vibratory match of oscillation. These dimensions are the Creational waters that connect all life to one another, as if you were a fish and the only way you can survive is inside the water, and this water connects you to all destinations needed.

- **Earth Alliance** – is the supposed group of positive military and government who are behind the scenes in secret doing good for humanity.
- **Emerald Portal** – is the portal that exists within the Divine Mothers heart that connects with the inner-dimensions of the Inner Earth. This is the exit-point out of this inverted A.I. matrix, where we are only able to pass through once we have achieved a high enough light-quotient, and are vibrating at above fifty-one percent of the population being in service-to-others.
- **Extraterrestrial** - is a being that exists outside our Earth, whether they are a negative or positive being.
- **Firmament** – In the Bible, the firmament is depicted as a solid dome-like expanse that God created on the second day of creation, to separate the waters above from the waters below. It is also referred to as "Heaven" and is essentially the sky or the expanse of the heavens. Genesis 1:6-8 describes the firmament as being created to divide the waters, with one portion above and one below.
- **Fifth Dimension** – Is the original crystalline construct that the collective of our Earth originally entered into, before it regressed into the current third dimension which is a simulation matrix instead.
- **Flower of Life** – is the sacred Alchemy construct of our entire existence, with intertwining infinite circles that are united in Unity Consciousness. The infinite Lotus Flower of Life is our Multiverse, the petals being the individual Universes.
- **Fractal** – is a piece of a Higher Self aspect which is a miniature version, a seed, and/or an expression of the Higher Self.
- **Frequency** – is the reading of a vibration and how many light photons are contained within it.
- **Galactic Wars** – are the wars being fought in the Universe beyond the invisible veil of Earth. The benevolent alien races provide their protection to all organic life from Archons and negative aliens. A war of the Archons, with their main goal of negatively being to harvest our light and as many souls as they can.
- **Harvesting of Souls** – Positive - is another word for Ascension in a benevolent way.
- **Harvesting of Souls** – Negative - is a negative infringing method that the Archons and negative aliens use to suck and drain upon all living beings that contain light by means of using our light as a power source, and/or to feed off.
- **Higher Self/Higher Selves** – are the individualized fractals and/or expressions of the oversoul.
- **Hybrid** – is a being that has been experimented on, infused or injected with other beings' genetic makeup, artificially forced to become an unknown species not created from God Source.
- **Illuminati** – are the negative polarized entities masked within the human vessels of the self-appointed leaders such as politicians, superstars, and military that are placed around the world trying to reign over Earth, brainwashing and inflicting many methods of oppression onto the souls of Earth.
- **Inner Earth** – is the civilization that communes within the hollowed earth, containing vast amounts of ecosystems with life such as humanoids and animals living within it. This is where our ancestors of Leumuria and Atlantis, our magical creatures, and extinct animals reside.

- **Integration** – is when, divinely, our Higher Selves allow for further soul upgrades to come forth into our organic souls' blueprint, bringing forth wisdom, integrations and leveling-up of the soul.
- **Inter-terrestrial** – is a being that is on Earth, that exists inside Earth, and not outside of Earth.
- **Inverted A.I. Matrix Simulation** – is the false matrix construct that has maintained the souls of Earth within a cycle of repeated negative cycles, thereby not allowing a positive organic fruitful Ascension out of and into the original Organic Timelines.
- **Implants** – are negative technologies of different shapes and sizes that contain programmes within that act upon and control the human body, mind and spirit, in whatever form or task it has been given or programmed.
- **Love-Light** – is the infinite organic flow connection of light within all souls directly being fed and replenished by pure Source.
- **Luciferian Agenda** – is a name given by the Archons to the Lightworker community, to be falsely used in forms of adding on further black magic to the first expression of the Divine Father - Archangel Lucifer - who is better known as Archangel Haylel - "The Prince of Light."
- **MK-Ultra or Milab** – are programs made by the negative military, run by the Deep State, to experiment on humans to turn them into stronger controllable Super Soldiers.
- **Multiverse** – the infinite expressions and multi-facets of the Universes.
- **New Earth** – is truly the original golden Earth blueprint of Mother Gaia.
- **New World Order** – is the agenda fully focused on the depopulation and control over humanity and all living beings.
- **Organic Matrix** – is the organic construct of the school of souls created within Mother Gaia.
- **Oversoul** – are the highest embodiments of Source besides the Archangels. They are the wholeness of a soul before it is further individualized into Higher Self aspects.
- **Phoenix Fire** – is the infinite, etheric, eternal fire of Source's flame. This is known to be able to transmute all inorganic matter to zero-point or to nothing.
- **Planets** – are the collective consciousness of a soul group existing in one crystalline plasmic bubble reality. The suns and stars are the portals to enter into each planet's construct.
- **Portals** – are both positive and negative, depending on their origin. They are a doorway for negative or positive entities to come in or connect through.
- **Portal Dates for Activations** – there are many that coexist within this category. Any repeated number, or combinations of sacred numbers, are able to be moments-in-time, where potence of Source Love-Light and the benevolence of Galactic races in unison, channel down infinitely.
- **Ra Collective** - also commonly referred to as Ra, is the collective of benevolent Galactic alien races working in unity for the Ascension of this Universe.
- **Remote Viewing** – for the most benevolent results to view from your Higher Self's form to the dimensions and realms below.
- **Reptilian race** – is an original benevolent race that was created to be the balance of this magnificent Universe of polarities. In order to experience the most infinite expression of love, there must also be the polarity of darkness.

- **Reset** – times in Earth's history where there is malevolent interference to depopulate the collective of humankind, so that whoever survives is reformed and controllable. This deep trauma causes amnesia to the memory of the humans.
- **Sasquatch** – is a benevolent race that is known to be taller and more hairy than humans. They came forth from another planet and dimension to be guardians and to assist humans and all living beings.
- **Schumann Resonance** – is the energetic reading to the Divine Mother's heartbeat, being registered by sonar waves within the land.
- **Simulation** – is the construct Matrix that we are within in the third dimension.
- **Source** – Is the collective of all expressions of Source Love-Light, merged and operating into one infinite divine light and flame.
- **Soul's Blueprint** – just as a house has a blueprint with every measurement to each room, so too does our soul in terms of what contents are within our soul. This is the blueprint of different incarnations and fractals throughout creation, and all the wisdom that carries over through our DNA memory fields.
- **Soul Braids** - soul braids are when we receive pieces of benevolent fractals that typically pertain to our soul family or fractals of our very own soul expressions. They integrate into our soul organically, because they carry parts that are needed for us within that time and space of our soul's expansion. They complement what is next to come within our organic timeline.
- **Somnambulistic client** - means the client's consciousness is moved to the back with no interference from the ego. The client does not remember anything of what was mentioned during the session, which means that only the benevolent being(s) speaks/spoke clearly with no interference from the client's human consciousness or ego.
- **Starseeds/Star Children** – are souls from higher dimensions, who have volunteered to assist with their bright lights here on Mother Earth, to raise her organic collective light.
- **Stellar Gateway** – these are positive portals that energetically unseal and open so that celestial crystalline energies flow into our magnetic collective field. This allows us to level up for those who are a vibrational match to these activations.
- **Transmute** – is to take a lower density energy and to alchemize it, transforming it into a higher vibrational state which contains more light within.
- **Twin Flame** – is an organic process of when a soul splits into two souls, creating its counterparts that when coming together into a union, they complete each other.
- **Veil** – is the blanket of energetic amnesia that every soul goes through when entering Earth's construct, in order to incarnate without memories of previous incarnations.
- **Walk-in** – is when a soul, by benevolent choice and agreement, enters into a human vessel as a replacement of the original soul. For example: The original soul has completed its karmic energy cycle or perhaps no longer wants to exist within their vessel. Instead of discarding the body, another benevolent soul will come in containing a higher vibration allowing for a higher awareness or consciousness.
- **Waves of Volunteers** – are the beings from the stars and higher dimensions who chose to incarnate onto Earth. They are called "Waves of Volunteers" because they entered in waves together through the decades. They made the conscious choice to volunteer to come to Earth to save her and the people who were stuck in the third dimension, inside of the A.I. simulation Matrix.

www.ingramcontent.com/pod-product-compliance
Lightning Source LLC
Chambersburg PA
CBHW082109230426
43671CB00015B/2645